Dear Anne + Roland
  Have a great trip
     Regards
      Mohit + Iqbal
         Feb 2023
            India

To Mohit
with lots of love

Dushyant
12-03-2017

CORBETT
NATIONAL PARK

KONARK PUBLISHERS PVT LTD
206, First Floor,
Peacock Lane, Shahpur Jat,
New Delhi-110 049 (India)
Phone: +91-11-41055065, 65254972
email: india@konarkpublishers.com
Website: www.konarkpublishers.com

Konark Publishers International
8615, 13th Ave SW,
Seattle, WA 98106
Phone: (415) 409-9988
email: us@konarkpublishers.com

Copyright © 2017
Ashima Kumar and Dushyant Parasher

All rights reserved. No part of this may be reproduced or utilised in any form or by any means, electronic or mechanical, including photocopying, recording or by any information storage and retrieval system, without prior permission in writing from the publishers.

Cataloging in Publication Data--DK
   Courtesy: D.K. Agencies (P) Ltd. <docinfo@dkagencies.com>

Kumar, Ashima, author.
   Corbett National Park : domain of the wild / text, Ashima Kumar ; photographs, Dushyant Parasher.
   pages cm
   Includes bibliographical references.
   ISBN 9789322008772

   1. Animals--India--Corbett National Park. 2. Animals--India--Corbett National Park--Pictorial works. 3. Corbett National Park (India)--Pictorial works. 4. Wildlife conservation--India--Corbett National Park. I. Parasher, Dushyant, photographer. II. Title.

QL84.5.I4K86 2017   DDC 591.95451   23

Typeset and Design by: Dushyant Parasher

Printed and bound at Thomson Press (India) Ltd.

Cover: The elusive Sajgarhi male cooling off in the idyllic setting of Sajgarhi Nallah—a stream in the Dhikala zone.

End paper: Ramganga river shimmering like a stream of gold. An evening view from Dhikala complex.

Previous page: A young male tiger at a water-hole.

This double-spread: A young elephant enjoying an evening mud-spray by the river side.

CORBETT
NATIONAL PARK

DOMAIN OF THE WILD

Text: ASHIMA KUMAR
Photographs: DUSHYANT PARASHER

KONARK PUBLISHERS PVT LTD
New Delhi • Seattle

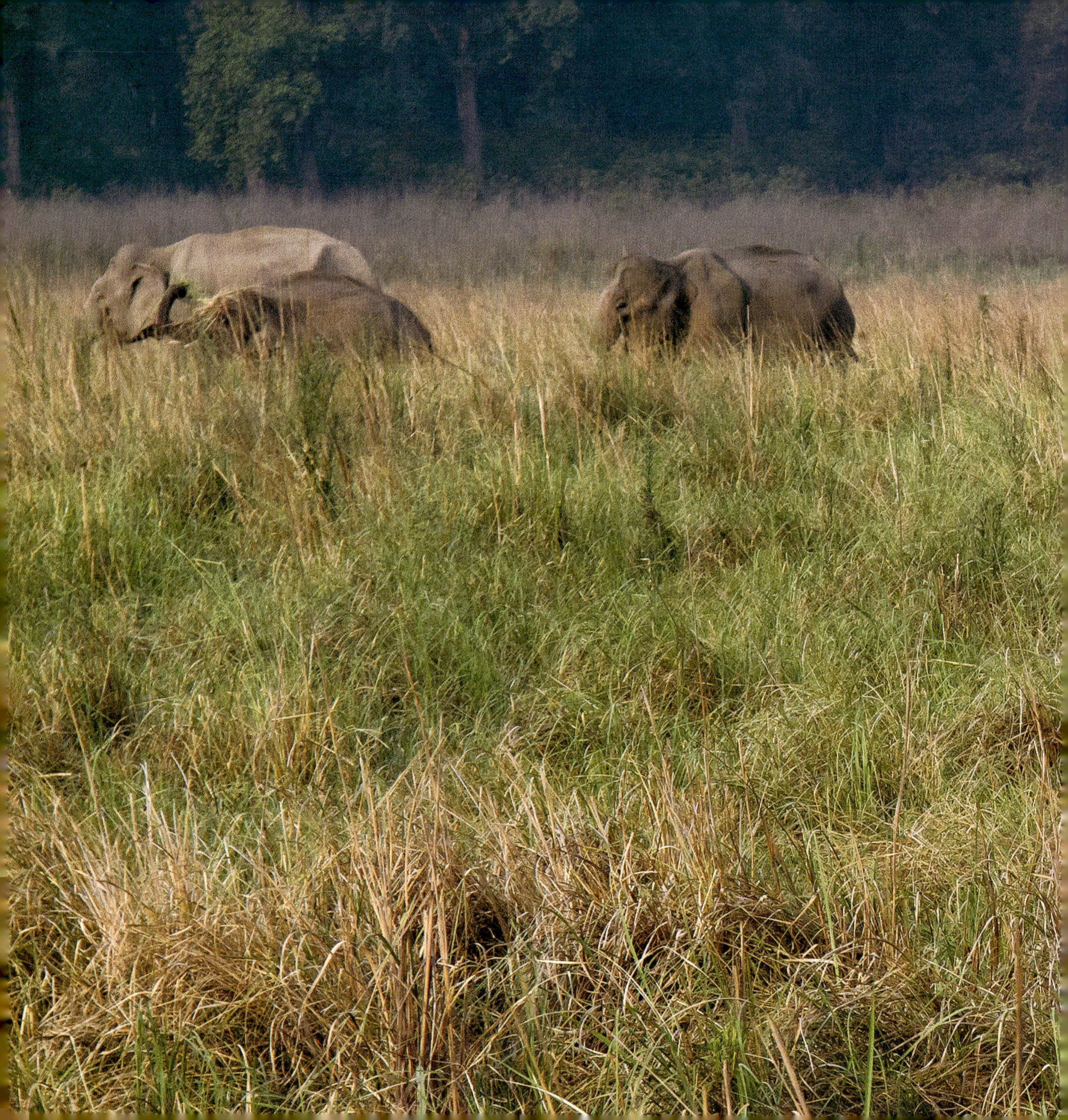

Dedicated to the protectors of our environment and wildlife

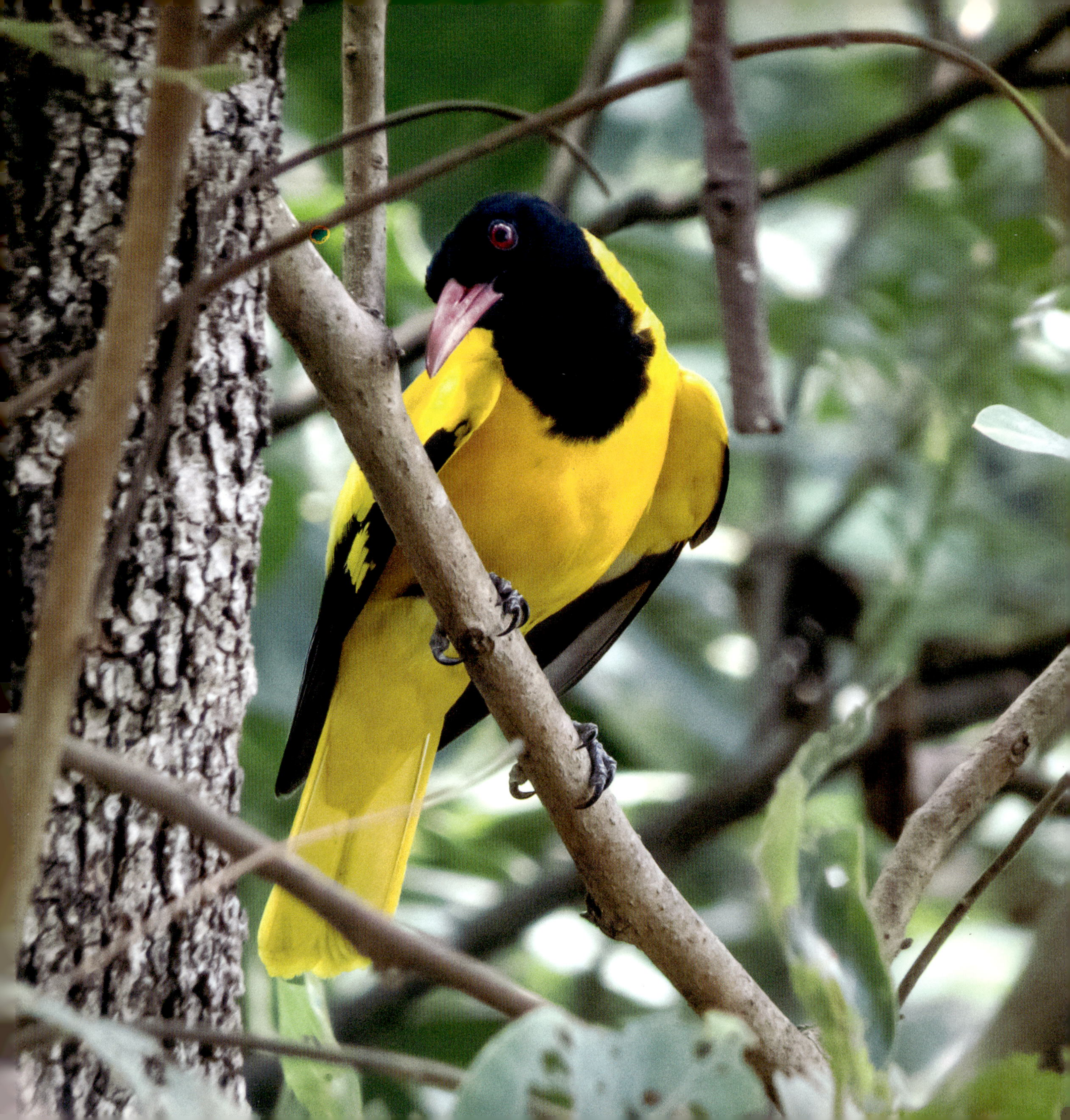

CONTENTS

FOREWORD
by *Bittu Sahgal*   11

THE CHARISMA OF
CORBETT NATIONAL PARK   15

DARK DAYS OF
DEFORESTATION
—*turning trees into wood*   23

JUNGLE RAJ
—*the race for trophies*   29

FIRST VOICES OF CONCERN   35

DAWN OF CONSERVATION
—*a ray of hope*   45

PROJECT TIGER
—*an effort to save the tiger
from extinction*   53

UNDERSTANDING
OUR LANDSCAPE
—*tracing the journey of
natural history*   59

CORBETT MATRIX
—*the green grid*   73

THE MEGA FAUNA
OF CORBETT
—*gems of the green vault*   97

OTHER FORMS OF WILDLIFE
—*small wonders of nature*   115

WAYS OF THE WILD
—*a civilized world*   131

BIRD LIFE OF CORBETT
—*wildlife on wings*   139

HIGH UP IN A MACHAN   153

FORESTS
—*lungs of our environment*   159

THREATS TO WILDLIFE
—*fighting for survival*   165

DEVELOPMENT VERSUS
CONSERVATION
—*in search of a balance*   171

*CHECKLISTS OF
CORBETT NATIONAL PARK*   174
BIBLIOGRAPHY   185
ACKNOWLEDGEMENTS   186

Previous double-spread: A tiger at the Dhikala grassland looks as if he is standing guard over a group of elephants.

Facing page: A Black-hooded Oriole strikes a graceful pose for the camera.

Following double-spread: (left) A Burmese Python and (right) a Crimson Marsh Glider.

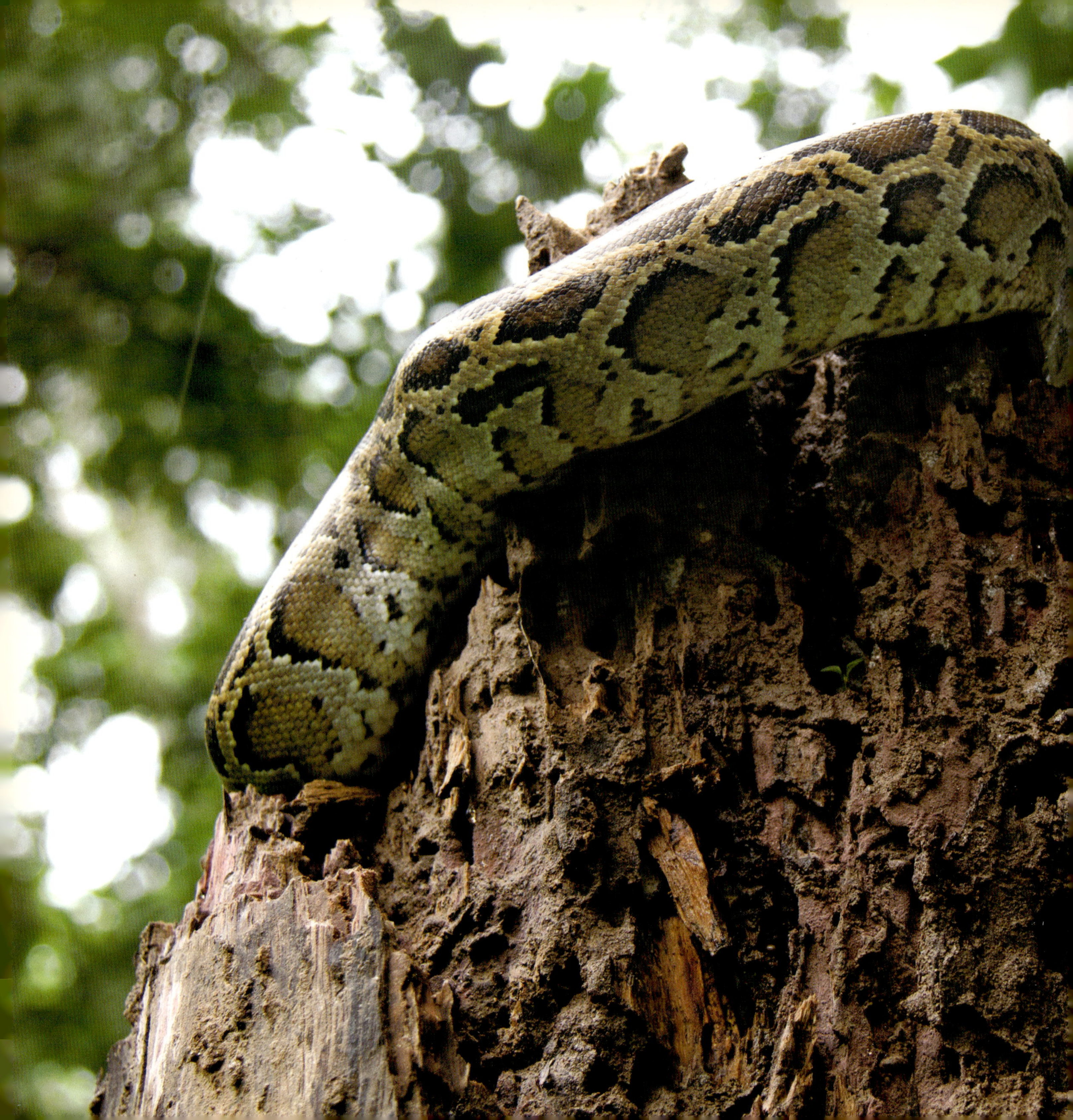

For the wise man looks into space and he knows there is no limited dimensions.

—Lao Tzu

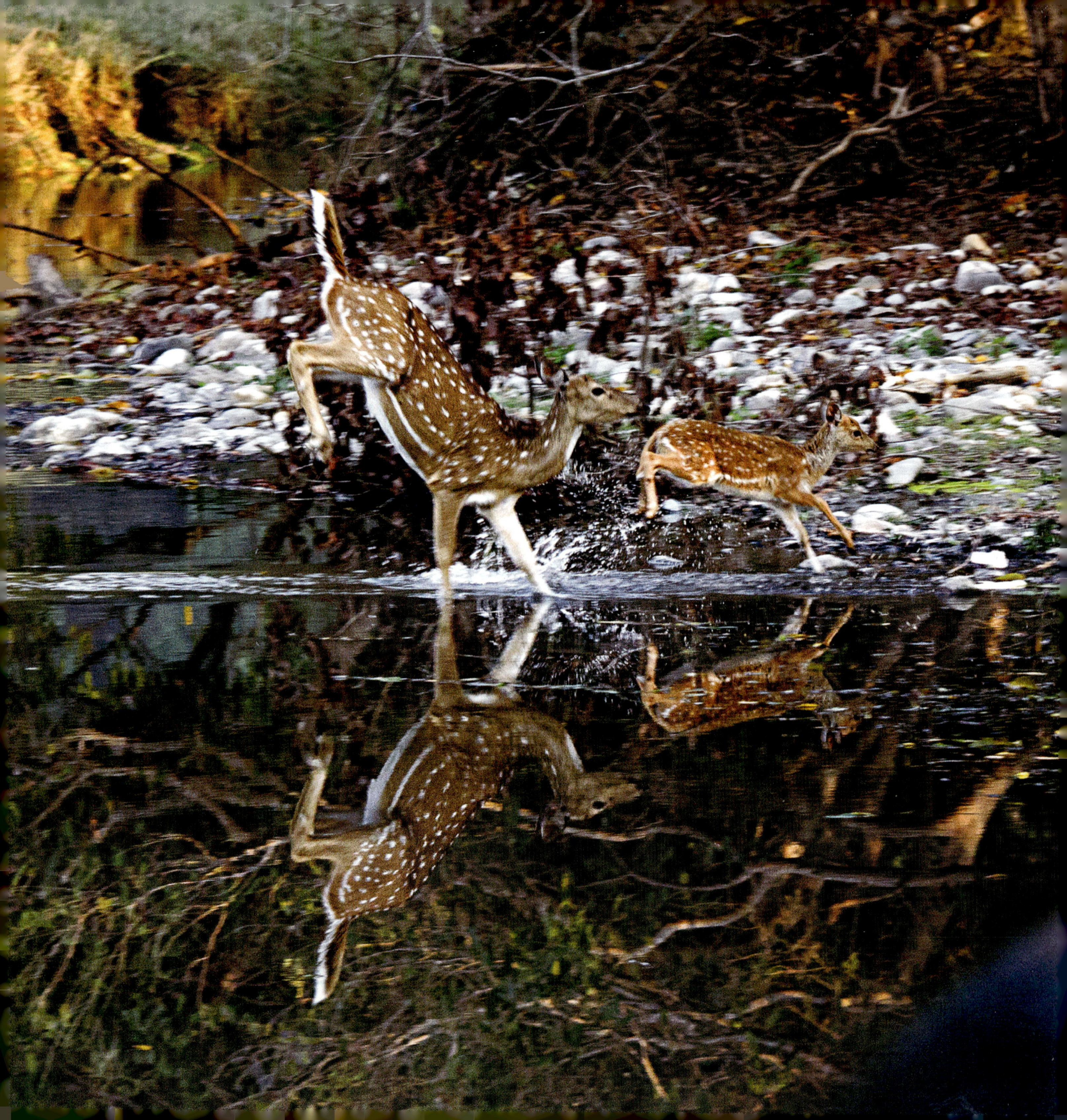

FOREWORD

It's not a mere forest, it's a miracle. A testament to the wonderful world in which we are blessed to live.

Blue rivers, white rocks, verdant and dappled glades, Corbett epitomizes all that is valuable and aesthetic about wild India. This heritage park has something for everyone, ranging from the serious birder to the most casual tiger-centric city dweller. A six-hour drive from India's capital, New Delhi, this is the forest where Project Tiger was launched over three decades ago.

Corbett, long referred to as the 'land of roar and trumpet', is undoubtedly one of India's premier wildlife destinations. It was here, on April 1, 1973, that Project Tiger was launched. And much earlier, it was here, amidst stunning vistas of the Kumaon hills, that Jim Corbett's amazing adventures—including his hunt for the ill-fated Kanda and Mohan maneaters—unfolded. This elephant country also gave rise to some of the world's finest naturalists, such as F.W. Champion, who pioneered wildlife photography in India.

Corbett is tiger country. It is also elephant country. Between them, Corbett and Rajaji hold India's northwestern-most population of tigers, and one of the world's most significant populations of Asiatic elephants. There are also enough adult gharials in the Ramganga river to categorise Corbett as one of the world's most crucial *in situ* gharial breeding sites. But the immense conservation values of this landscape deal only with one aspect of Corbett—its biodiversity. India's art, culture, music, dance, religions and philosophies were all inspired by such forests. This should be reason enough to save the Corbett Tiger Reserve and forests like it across India.

The water of the Ramganga and Kosi, after being 'treated' by the forests of the Corbett Tiger Reserve, flows downstream to slake the thirst of millions, irrigates

Facing page: A Cheetal doe and her fawn dashing across a stream cast a perfect reflection in the blue waters.

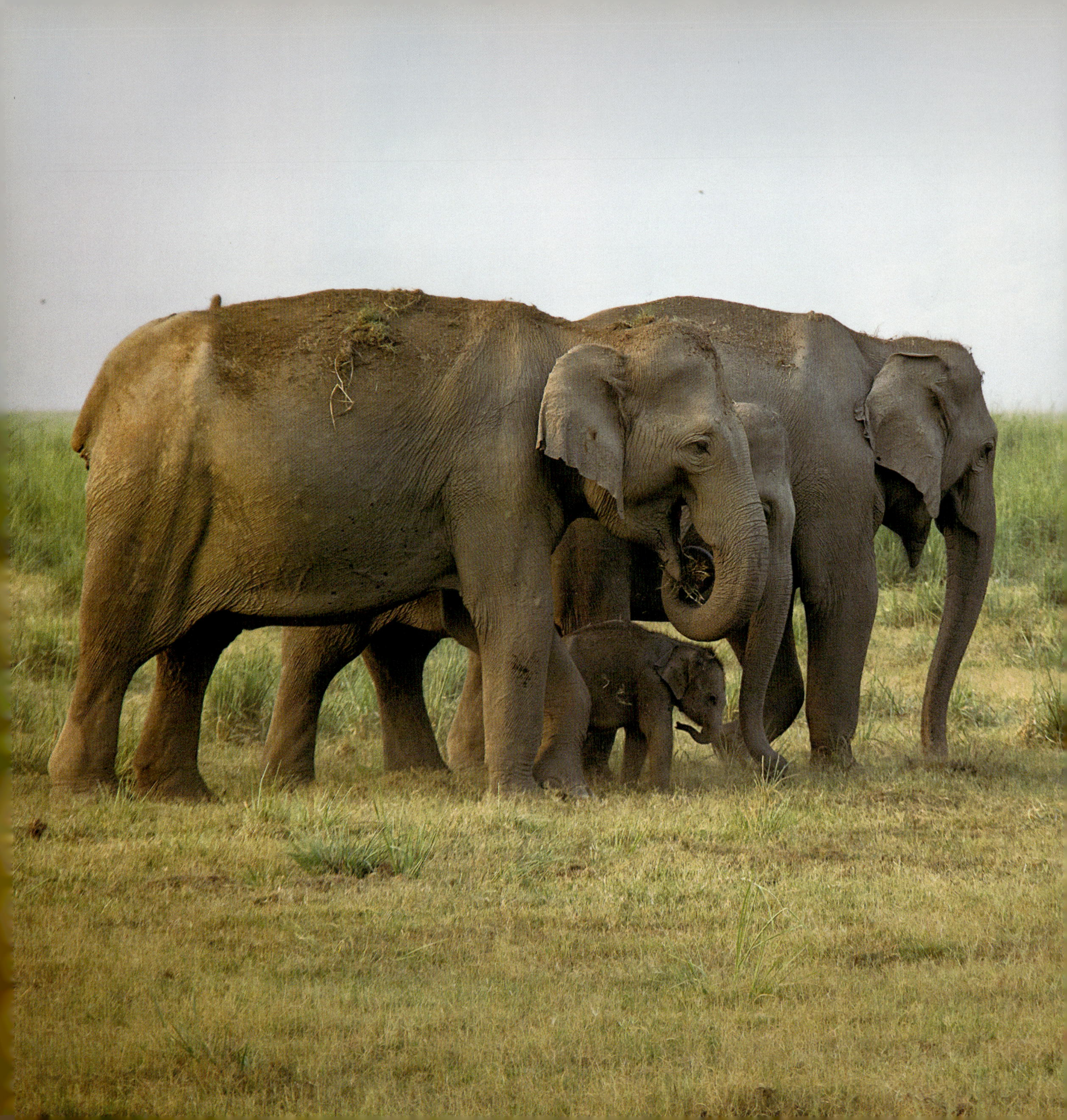

farms and meets the needs of industry. Every single species of plant and animal in the reserve works to enhance the quality of this water in one way or another, through a magical, complicated system that scientists can only guess at, but do not fully comprehend.

This book is a tribute to the wonder that is Corbett. Dushyant Parasher who has spent a lifetime in these forests shares the park's amazing biodiversity through sensitively shot images, which are well supported by Ashima Kumar's lively text. The book straddles conservation and natural history well and reminds us of the fragility of our irreplaceable natural heritage.

May this volume grace the bookshelves of this generation, so that the next can know that some of us worked very, very hard to protect what belongs to generations unborn.

—Bittu Sahgal,
Editor, *Sanctuary Asia*

Facing page: Elephant young always grow in the shadow of their mothers, aunts and elder cousins.

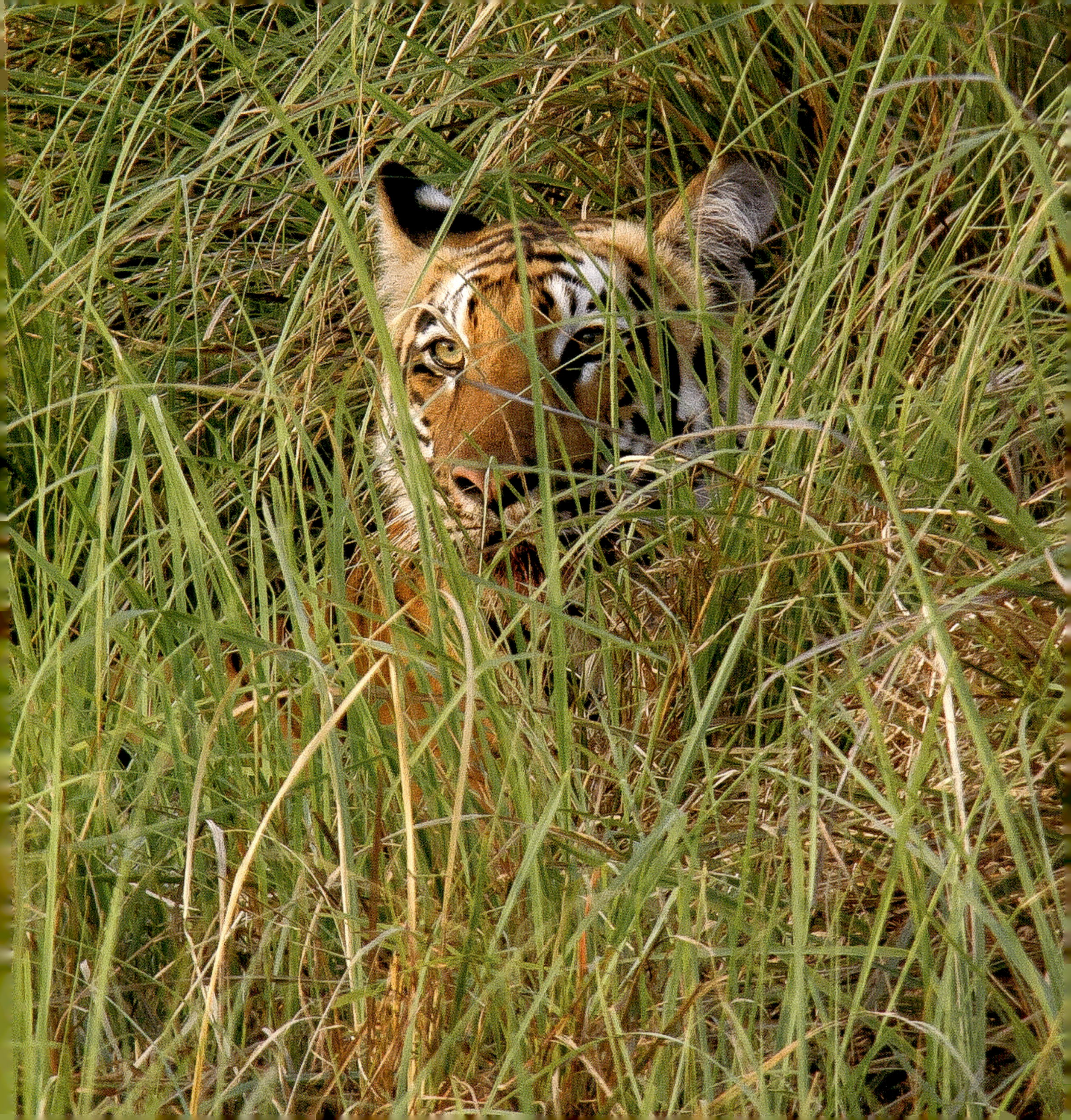

THE CHARISMA OF CORBETT NATIONAL PARK

It was the summer of 2015. The sprawling grassland was shimmering in the golden glow of the morning sun. In the distance a small herd of elephants was lazily plodding through the green landscape, occasionally nibbling at the fresh green shoots. Once in a while, a Black Francolin called in his trademark tune, and another one somewhere in the distance responded with the efficiency of an echo. There was no morning breeze. I was scanning the stillness all around me for any movement that would give away the presence of the many secrets that I knew it held within those green folds. Suddenly, barely ten meters away from me, a blade of grass moved!

All natural horizontal movements in the forest are swaying actions. Grass, bushes and branches move to-and-fro when caressed by wind. If the movement is strongly in one direction, as this one certainly was, it clearly means that something is being pecked at. In this case the pull was strong enough to merit a guess that something was being forcefully tugged at. My heart jumped into my throat. Could it be a tiger feasting on a kill?

Slowly, some of those white streaks that I had earlier presumed to be dry blades of tall grass morphed into parts of a majestic headgear of a male spotted deer. As I strained my eyes to their limit, traces of that unmistakable gleaming golden coat punctuated by black stripes started filtering through the grass. Then, with a sudden jerk, the grass parted like the curtains of a theater and the majestic form of a male tiger raised its proud head. He stood up, leisurely stretched his body and surveyed the surrounding landscape. Breakfast was over, and he was now looking for a safe place to keep the remains of his kill for future meals. He finally grabbed the carcass and started dragging it towards a far-off cluster of trees where he would be able to guard it in shade during the hot summer day. It was hard work and the tiger had to stop every few paces to catch his breath.

Previous double-spread: A herd of elephants at sunset silhouetted against the golden glow of Ramganga river near Dhikala.

Facing page: A majestic male tiger in the Dhikala grassland.

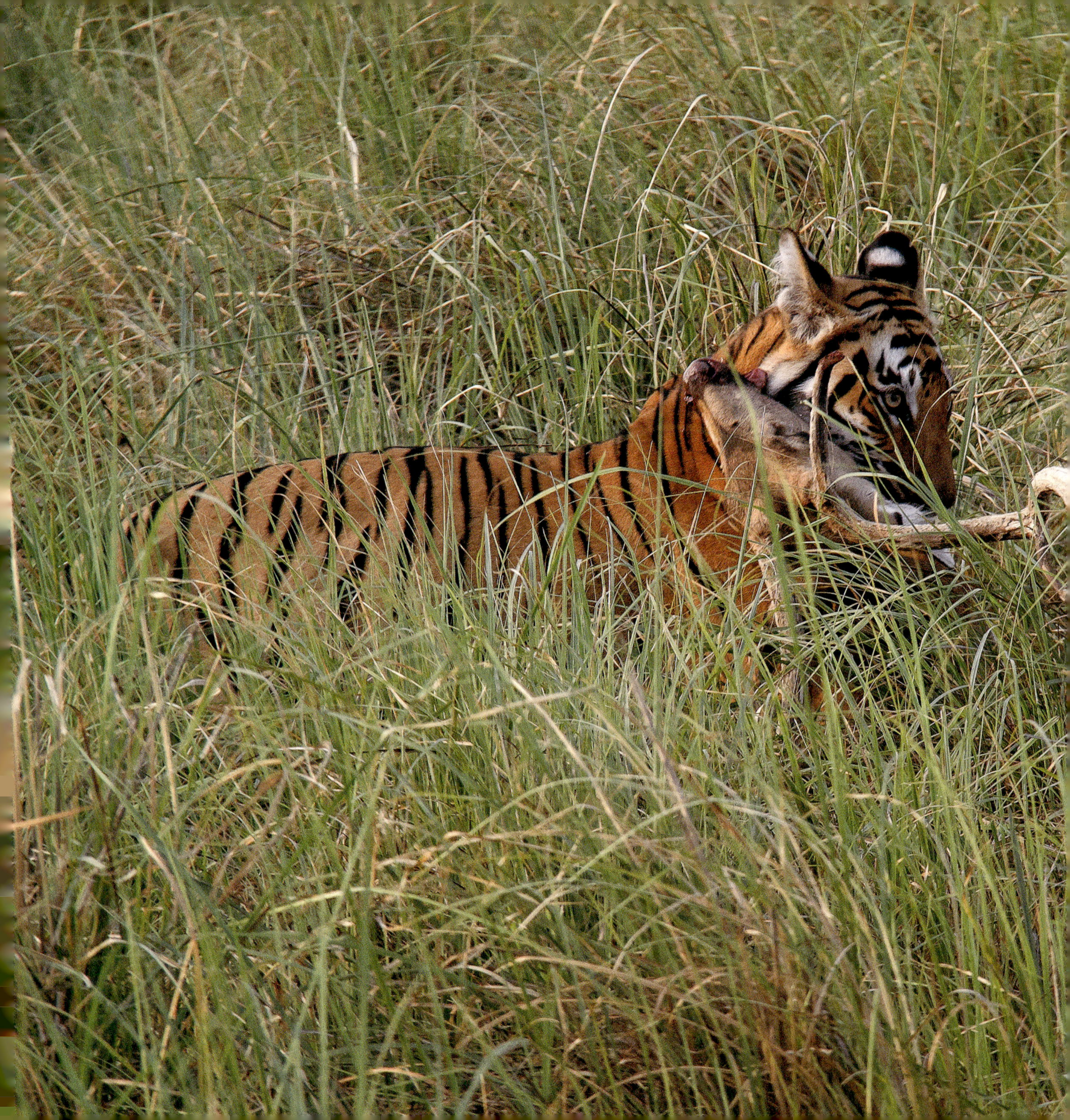

Dragging his meal to safety. Tigers feed on their kill for several days and need to protect them from other animals like jackals, wolves and hyenas.

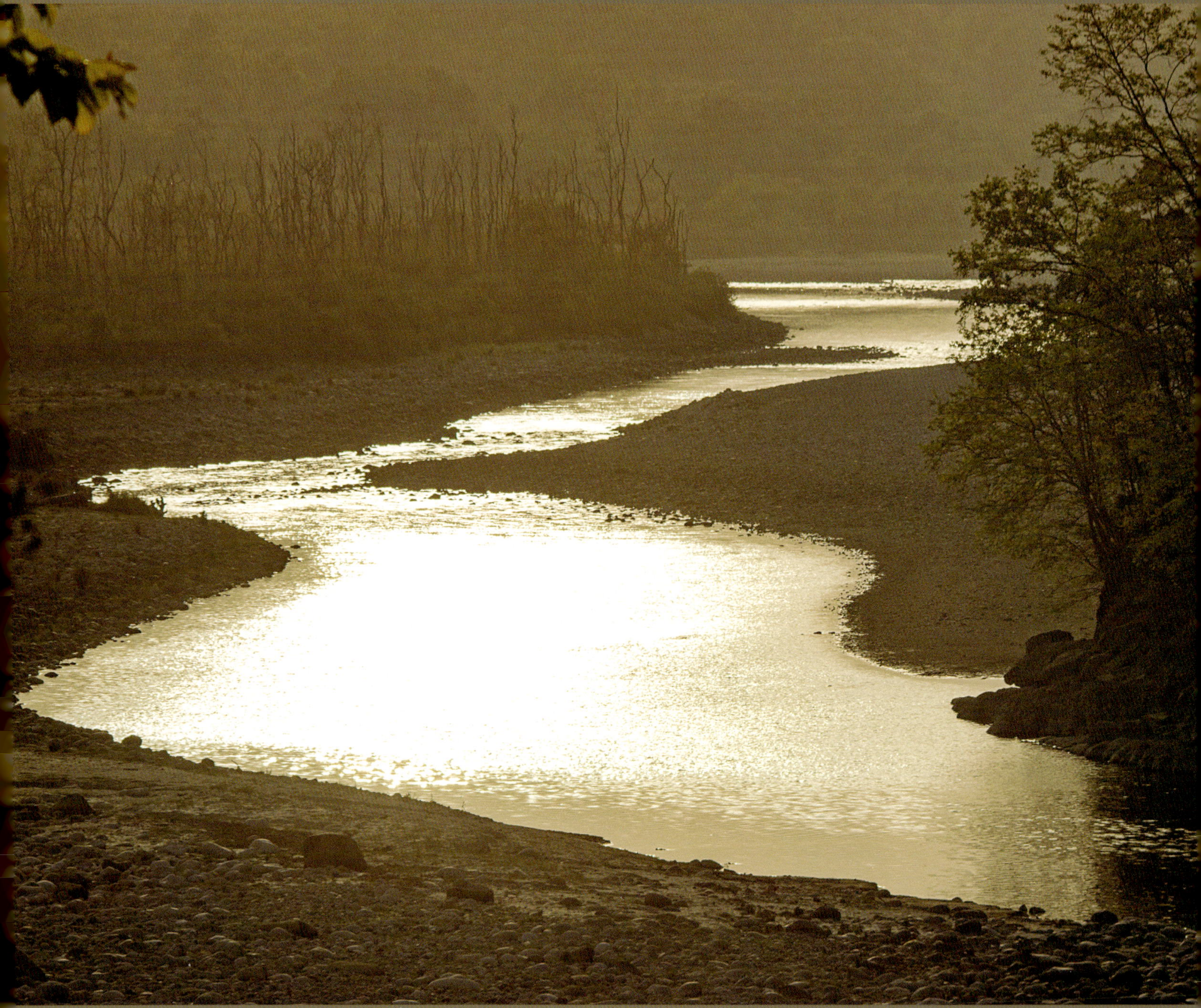

With a smile of satisfaction, we moved on. A tiger sighting can't get better than this. I had just witnessed the charisma of Corbett at its best.

Tigers are truly the phantoms of the forest. You know they are there but seeing one is something that eludes many. There would be hardly any visitor to this tiger-land who would have missed seeing their telltale pug marks on the dirt tracks and soft sand of river beds. They are there, but seeing one in flesh and blood cross your path is a dream. A dream, every visitor to the park has, and only a few return feeling blessed having fulfilled it.

Corbett—the first milestone of conservation history in India

Corbett National Park is a celebrated land. The first seeds of the conservation concept in India were sown here, way back in 1935, when the *National Parks' Act* was passed. It was a hard fought and long drawn battle for the environment conscious people, in which the far-sighted, dedicated lot finally won against the powerful hunting lobby. In 1936, it was here that the first National Park of India was established and most appropriately called 'The Hailey Park'; named so after Sir William Malcolm Hailey, who as Governor of the United Provinces had laid the cornerstone of Indian conservation history by supporting and approving the *National Parks' Act* the previous year. In 1973, when the tiger population of India was virtually at the doorstep of extinction, it was again here at Dhikala that the Project Tiger was launched. A programme that ushered in a new era of hope for the most magnificent big cat—*Panthera tigris tigris*.

Facing page: A shimmering Ramganga river flowing through the Corbett National Park.

Far above: Pug-marks of a tiger on the river-bed.

Above: Portrait of Sir William Malcolm Hailey

Following double-spread: A section of the Sal forest near Dhikala.

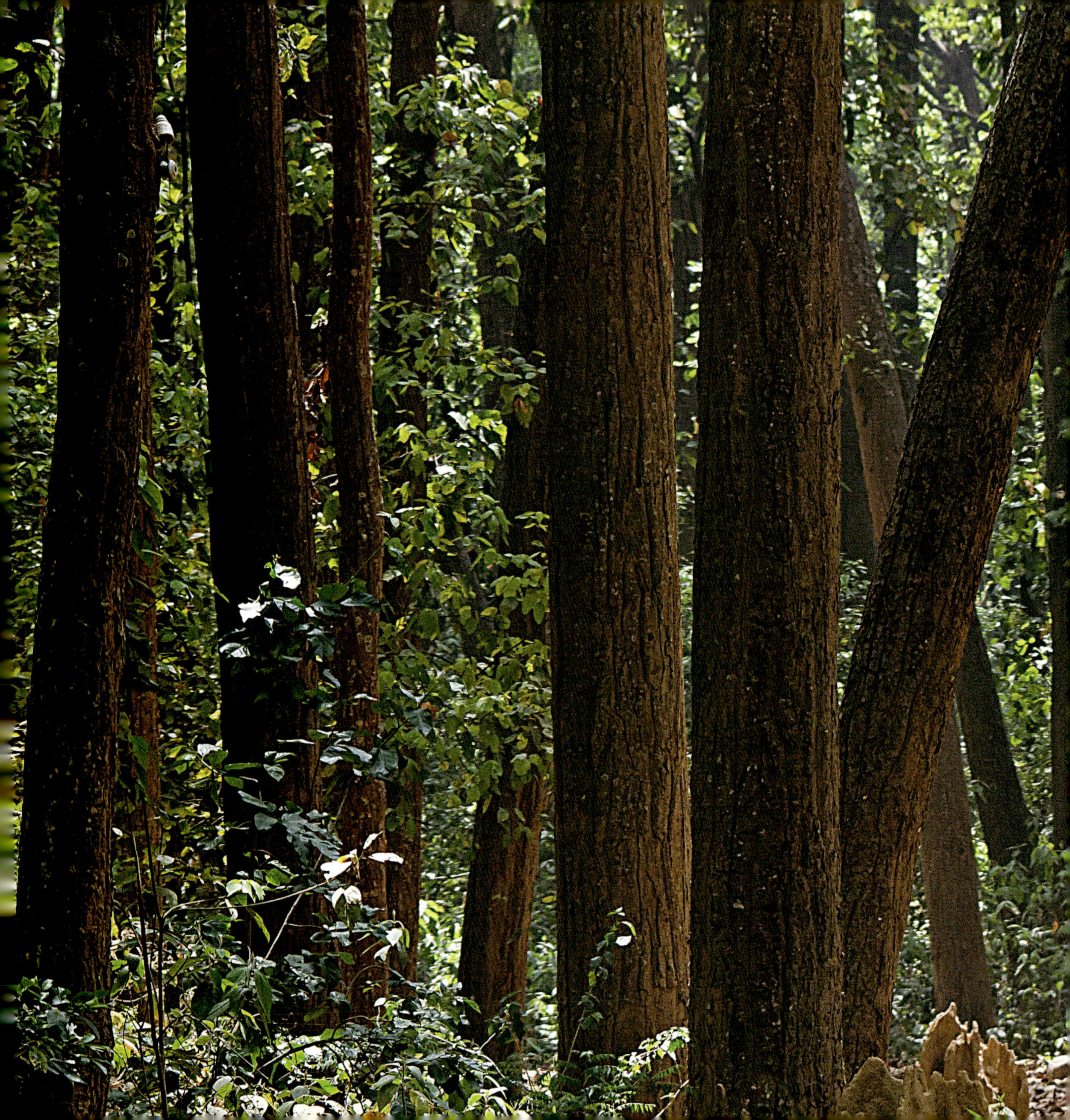

DARK DAYS OF DEFORESTATION
—turning trees into wood

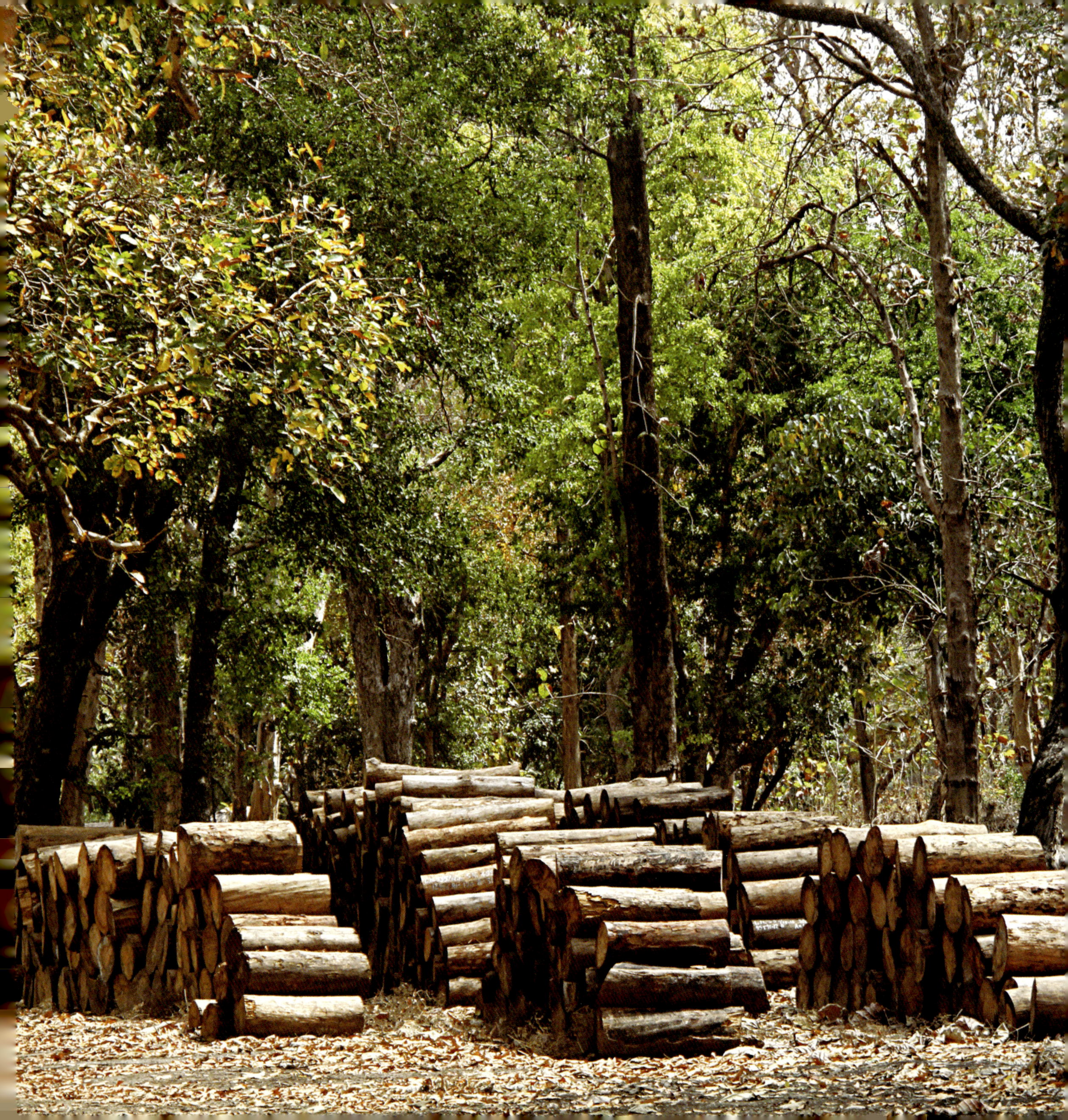

DARK DAYS OF DEFORESTATION
—turning trees into wood

With the coming of the British to India, an unprecedented animosity was unleashed upon the wilds of the country. The British mind-set was one of maximum extraction of forest resources, especially timber, and the mass extermination of wild animals. Land was always required to be cleared for cultivation. In the need to push back the forest, there must have been points of conflict between the people and the mega fauna. Rulers before the British would ask local officials to get rid of tigers and brigands but it had never been on such a massive scale as was seen under the British rule.

Part of the British mind-set towards wild animals and the forests had its roots in the famine of 1770 in Bengal, one of the first areas to be colonised by them. The famines resulted in a high mortality rate. With one in every three people dying, there were fewer hands left to till the farmland. Uncultivated land was soon taken over by nature and slowly reverted to the jungle. With the expanding green cover came deer, wild pigs and predators like the tiger. Bounty hunters eliminated wild animals, especially tigers. Fewer tigers meant more land reclaimed for cultivation and more revenue. Big game hunting thus became an unwritten state policy to make the forests safe for farmers, wood cutters and cattle grazers. This campaign of massive deforestation and elimination of wildlife brought large tracts of land under the plough while environment took a big beating.

Around the same time on the world scale, Europe was on the threshold of the Industrial revolution. With technological advances, a great number of natural resources became commercial commodities as these could now be transported over long distances. Wood, for instance, could be converted into paper, furniture, construction material, fuel for steam engines and building ships for maritime expansion. Revenue orientation of colonial land policy worked towards the

Facing page: Forests are the lungs of our environment. When trees are looked at as timber, our own survival is threatened.

destruction of the forests. The process intensified around the early years of building the railway network around 1853. Large tracts of forests were destroyed to supply the wooden sleepers (to underpin railway tracks). Three species of Indian timber were found to be durable and strong enough—Teak, Sal and Deodar. Dietrich Brandis, the first Inspector General of the Imperial Forest Department observed in *Indian Forester* in 1879 that each mile of railway construction requires 860 sleepers, each sleeper lasting between 12 to 14 years.

The destruction of forests was a pan India phenomenon. However, in 1858, the Governor General of the United Provinces (present day Uttar Pradesh and Uttarakhand), Sir Henry Ramsay, realised the magnitude of the problem and drew up the first comprehensive conservation plan to protect the forest. In 1861-62, farming was banned in the lower Patlidun valley. Cattle sheds were pulled down, domestic animals were driven from the forest, fire-lines were created and a regular cadre of workers was commissioned to fight forest fires and secure them from illegal felling of trees. Licenses were issued for timber and a count of trees was undertaken.

In 1868, the Forest department assumed responsibility for the forests. In 1879, they were declared reserved forest under the *Forest Act*. Reserve forests did not mean that these forests were protected or reserved for wildlife. On the contrary,

Right: Fire-lines are a road-like stretch cleared of all trees and shrubs to prevent forest fires from marching forward, like this one near Mohan.

Below: Fire-lines and forest roads have to be constantly maintained free of leaf litter. Forest department staff ensures that the easily combustible dry leaves are burnt periodically.

these were the forests deemed the most commercially valuable and amenable to sustained exploitation under the control of the state government.

In 1907, Sir Michael Keen suggested the possibilities of creating a game reserve but it was turned down. The strategic value of the Indian forests, which had first emerged during the building of the railway network, again came up during the World Wars. Timber and bamboo were extensively supplied for construction of bridges, piers and ships. The impact was severely felt by the forests of the subcontinent.

This was also the time when the Garhwal and Kumaon hills saw an immense increase in cases of tigers and leopards turning man-eaters. This happened because with the forest cover and prey base gone, animals came in direct conflict with people. Between 1907 and 1938, almost 1,500 human lives were lost to big cats that had turned man-eaters. The menace had never acquired such mammoth proportions anywhere in the world either before or after.

It was not until 1916 that the matter was brought to light through the efforts of two forest officers, E.R. Stevens and his successor E.A. Smythies, but to no substantial result. In the United Provinces, the demand for Chir and Sal was virtually unlimited and the forest department's instructions were to 'produce the maximum outrun possible.'

To fill the demands for commercial timber and revenue the forest department intensified its exploitation by making forests more accessible and improving transportation network. Forest land around railway tracks was done away with and consequently wild animals lost their habitat. This policy is clearly reflected in the writings of Ford Robertson F.C. in *Our Forests*, 1936 where he mentions the following observation by a United Provinces forester,

> '...communications are the veins and arteries along which forest revenue flows and from its earliest days the forest department has been active in opening up the jungles with proper system of cart roads and paths.'

Below: A section of water management infrastructure created by Sir Henry Ramsay in the Pawalgarh area.

Sir Henry Ramsay's work

In the middle of mindless hunting and destruction of forests for timber, there was one man among the British who understood the needs of the land and its people. Sir Henry Ramsay, as Commissioner of Kumaon and Garwhal districts created a brilliant network of canals and aqua ducts in what is today Corbett National Park region. These marvels of civil engineering created in the mid-nineteenth century still survive and serve the Pawalgarh area's rainwater drainage requirements and irrigation needs.

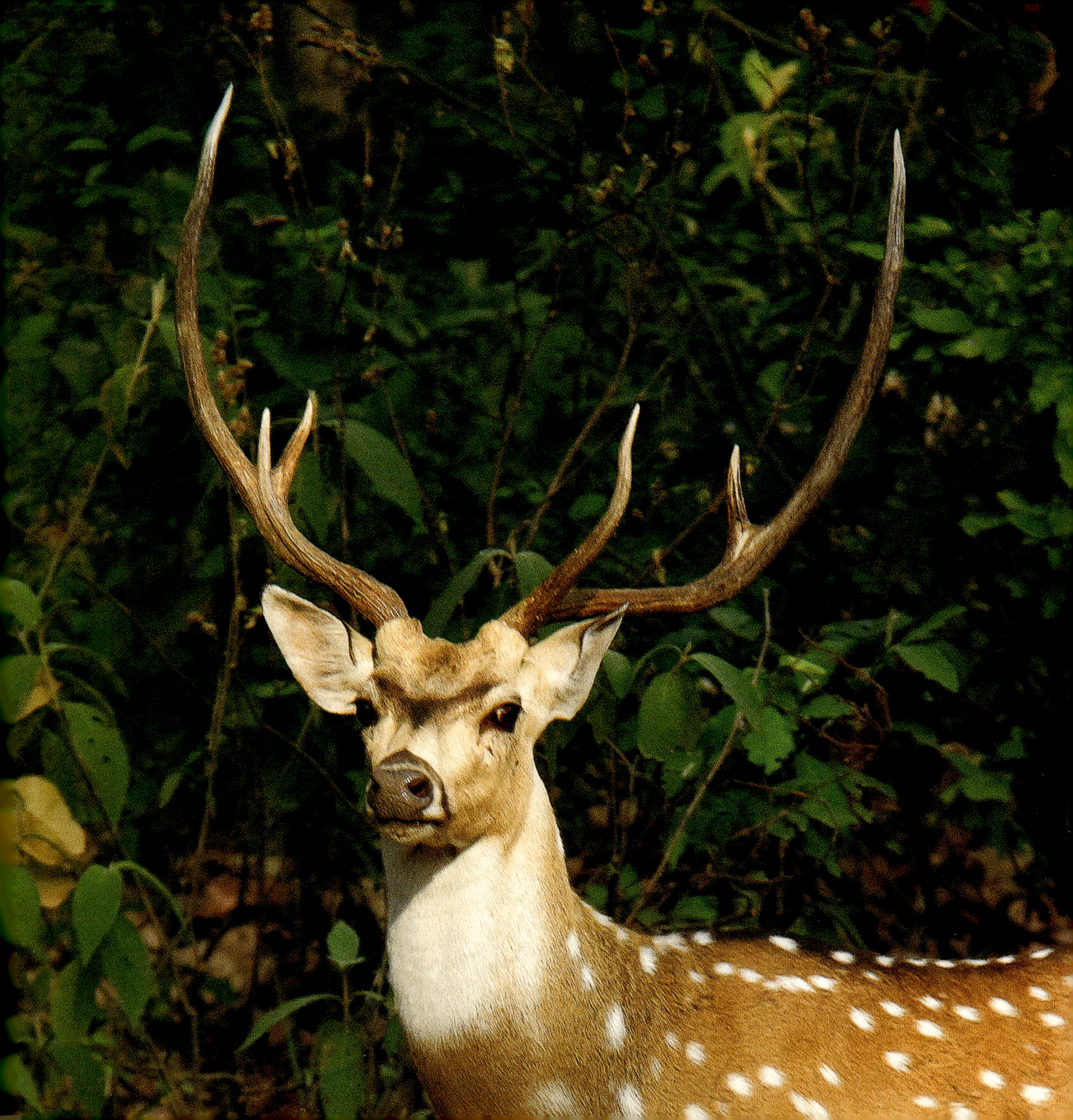

JUNGLE RAJ
—*the race for trophies*

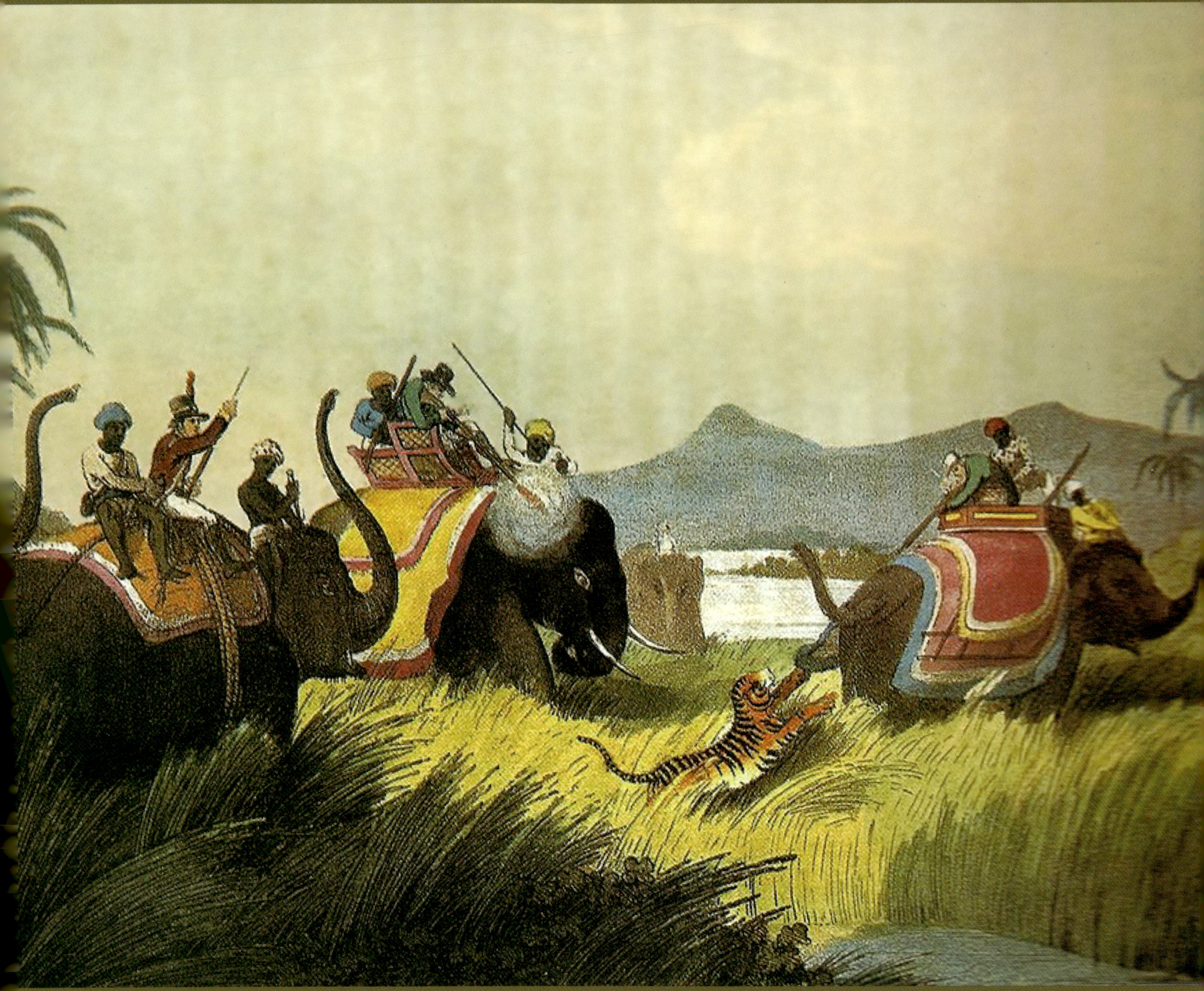

JUNGLE RAJ

—the race for trophies

Big game hunting was a tradition among the Mughals who had developed hunting into a ritualised activity. It was more a means of gathering intelligence about the affairs of the state, than merely for pleasure. The royal hunt was an elaborate affair accompanied by soldiers, elephants and captive cheetahs. Though the size of the bags was usually preposterous there was still enough wild life to go by. Very good at documenting and keeping record, the Mughals were keen hunters who particularly observed what they hunted. There are memoirs with dates, details and paintings illustrating the events. Jahangir's memoirs are replete with descriptions of his hunting expeditions. In the first twelve years of his reign, he had killed over 17,000 animals which included 86 tigers and lions besides others.

The Raj had a close relationship with big game hunting as a sport. Large scale hunting was prevalent at all levels of power from the Viceroy down to the officers of the British Indian Army. Shooting was motivated by the acquisition of hunting trophies and the desire for large 'bags'. Many Indian Princes tried to emulate the *shikar* exploits of the British. The outcome of such unregulated hunting had catastrophic consequences, leading to the steady decline of wild species, especially the tiger, rhino and the wild buffalo.

At the time of the British, big game hunting was considered a gentleman sport. A much favoured recreation for army officers and civil officials, who were encouraged to shoot wild animals for the acquisition of trophies. The British Raj like the Mughals before them, adopted the elephant borne tiger hunts that were grand events much for the show of imperial power and weaponry. The sports hunter vilified wild animals as cunning and blood thirsty beasts and saw his own role as a protector, which is very evident from the writings of Brigadier General

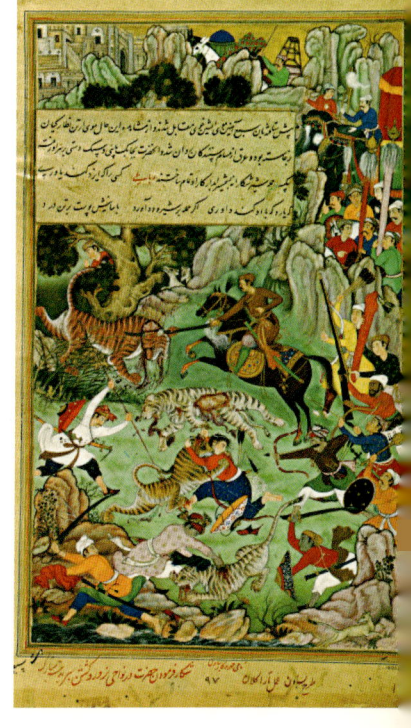

Facing page: Illustration of the unfair game. Scenes of tiger hunts were a favourite subject for the artists and lithographers of the colonial era. This image shows the typical hunting technique of that time—surrounding the animal and gunning it down by a volley of shots from all directions.

Above: A page from Akbarnama *showing the bravado of the emperor. In this fanciful painting while Akbar is slaying a tiger by his sword, some others are engaged in spearing, stabbing and shooting arrows at other tigers.*

R.G. Burton who stated that 'Tigers must have been terribly destructive to both people and cattle before the advent of English sportsmen.' Thus by eliminating a tiger or leopard considered a pest they rendered a service making the jungles safe for the native inhabitants.

In the last quarter of the nineteenth and early into the twentieth century wild pig, porcupine, cheetal, sambar were regarded as common game. The leopard was considered vermin and extensively hunted along with the tiger. Sports hunters baited by tying up a buffalo after ascertaining the presence of a tiger by its fresh pug marks. If the bait be killed and dragged away, they would track the tiger or leopard and after ascertaining his way of escape the hunter would position himself in a place the predator was bound to be driven by a 'beat'. Men on foot would then beat drums or shout loudly to chase the tiger in the direction of his gun. The hunter on the back of an elephant or machan would be well beyond harm. Should the unsuspecting tiger get only wounded he was to be followed at all costs on elephant. Viceroys and governors were supposed to bag the largest trophies of tigers. Sir John Hewitt, Lieutenant Governor of the United Provinces shot at least 150 tigers before 1912.

A classic example of mindless hunting during the British Raj. British Army officers with a stash of trophies from a fortnight's hunt.

The hunt had some rules. The sports man would in his mind give the animal a 'sporting chance' and then do the job with a single shot. An underlying rule was to finish off the beast and not leave a wounded animal in the jungle to die a lingering death. However, this was not always adhered to and many a tiger were left injured only later to take to man slaughter. Hunters also had no qualms in hunting tigresses with cubs. The indigenous ways of hunting by way of traps, nets etc were highly condemned and most local people were excluded from the hunt.

The British had an office of Tiger Slayer, the main object of which was the destruction of animals like the tiger and leopard. Digby Davies as tiger slayer to the Bombay Government who served for over thirty years, stated that during his term in office the figures of tigers shot by him were about two hundred and these did not include the number he killed before being appointed to that office or during periods of leave.

In this race for hunting trophies, Indian princes were measure to measure with their British counterparts. Indian royalty organised elaborate hunts for high British officials to appease them or for favours. Some in order to outdo the British surpassed them in their lust for big bags and trophies. Most rulers had hunting grounds reserved exclusively for the pleasure of the hunt. The jungle was not protected for itself but maintained for enjoyment of a few as a hunting reserve. This was at the cost of denying those who lived close to the forests a source of livelihood. The gentleman hunter though committed to fair play was often prone to hunting excesses. Hunting trophies were displayed on the walls and floors of the residences of the sports men as prized possessions.

The Indian wildlife that seemed limitless and unending was indeed exhaustible. By the second decade of the twentieth century a certain degree of control was exercised through the issue of game licenses for booking forest blocks for shoots with an adherence to 'open' and 'closed' season for shooting game. By this time wildlife had taken a huge hit and its numbers were dwindling at a rapid pace.

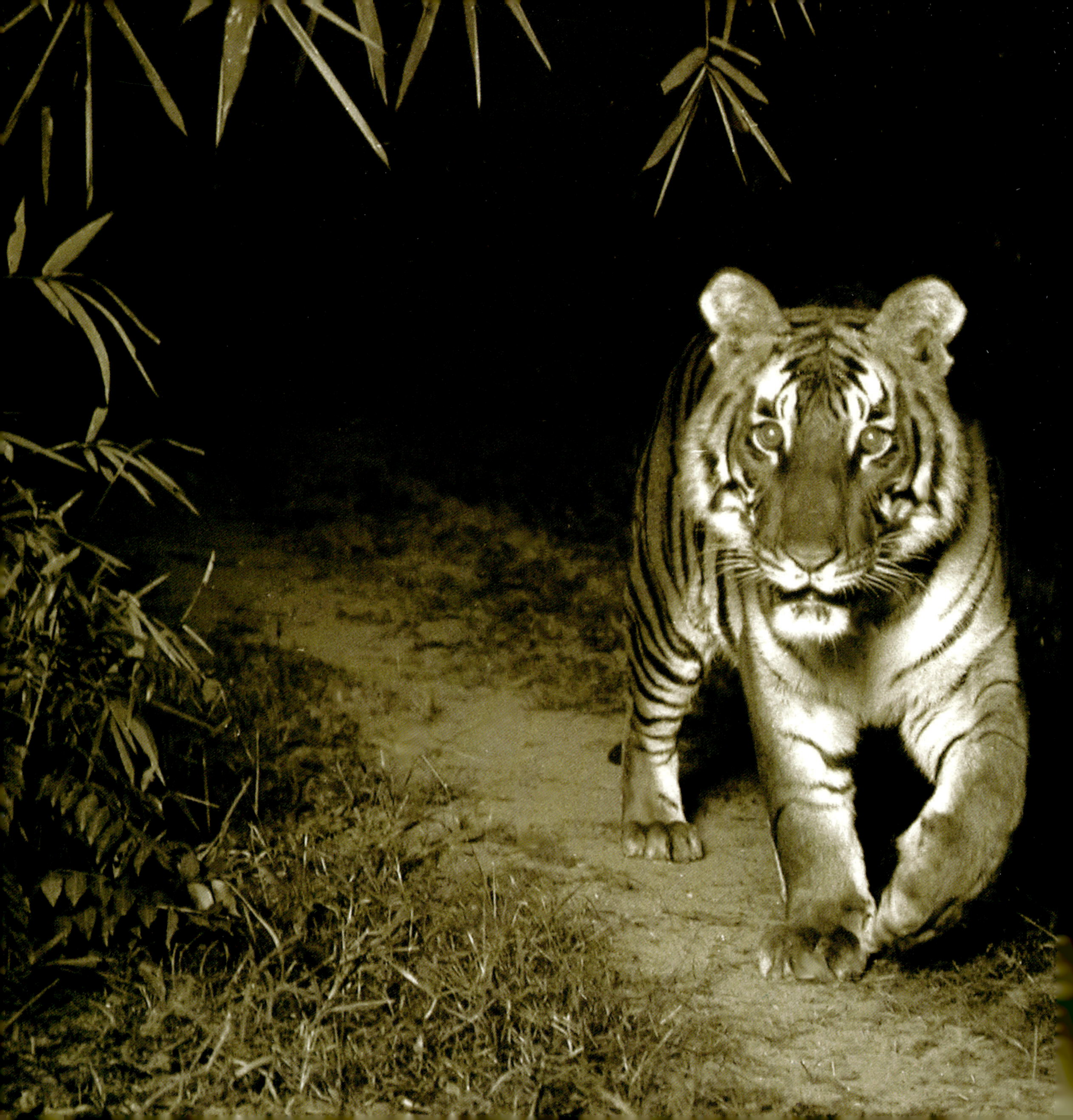

FIRST VOICES
OF CONCERN

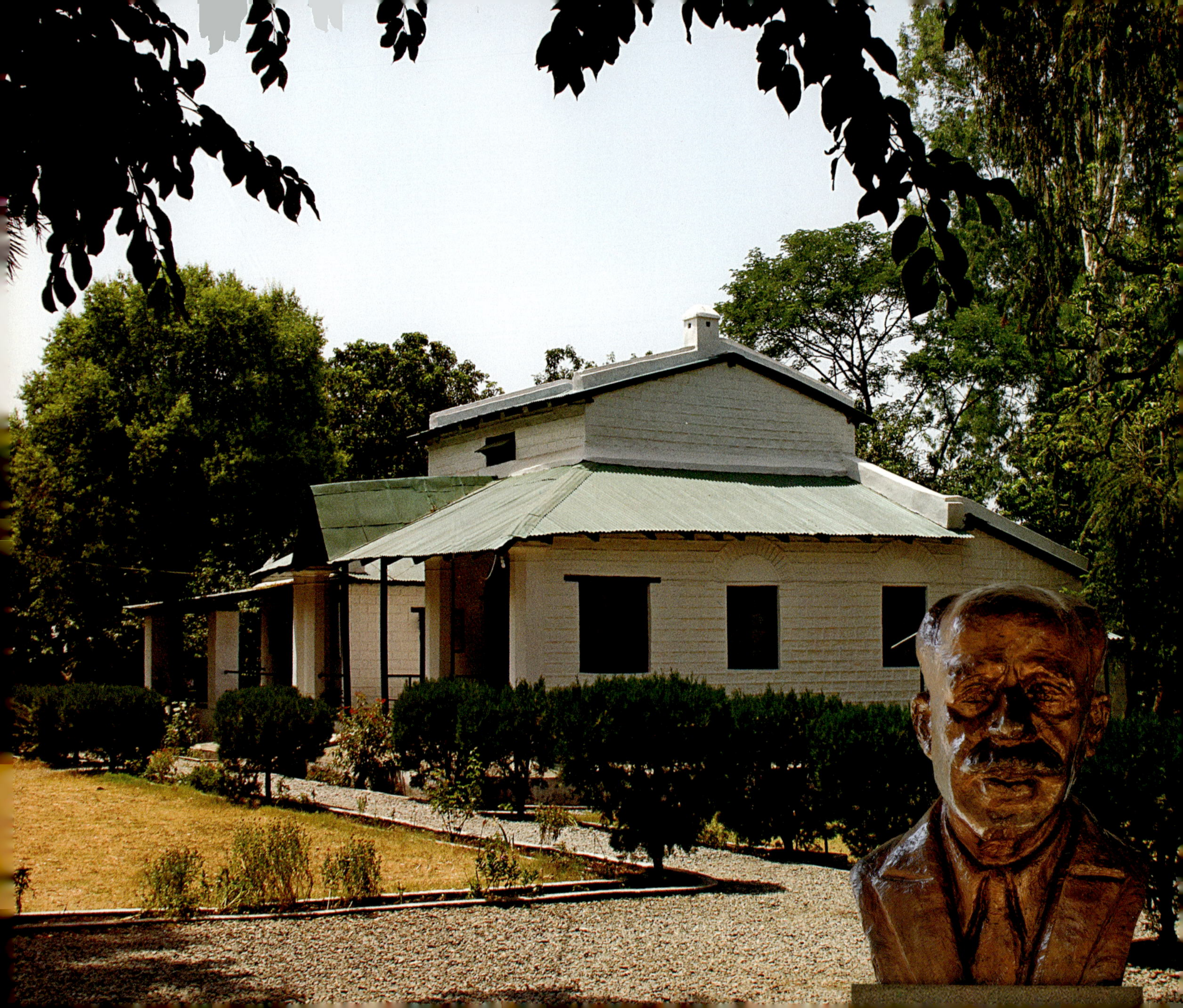

FIRST VOICES OF CONCERN

Jim Corbett

For those who have grown up reading his stories of man eaters, Jim Corbett needs no introduction. A hunter turned conservationist, a naturalist, an accomplished writer and a photographer. His love for the jungles, its wildlife and the people of Kumaon comes through clearly in his writing.

Edward James 'Jim' Corbett was born in 1875 in the hill town of Nainital in the Kumaon hills of the Himalayas. His parents had moved there in 1862 as his father was appointed the post master of the town. Summers were spent at Gurney House in Nainital. In winter the family would move down to the foothills to their cottage at Kaladhungi which has now been converted into a museum.

Jim Corbett lived the better part of his life in the foothills at Kaladhungi and Nainital. One among 13 children, Jim had a keen interest in the forest and wildlife around his home. At a very young age he took to shooting for the pot or for collection. Thus began his education in jungle sights and sounds. He could tell most birds and mammals by their calls. This knowledge that he gained as a child helped him through adult life as he became a master tracker, accomplished sportsman and a wild life photographer.

He was well loved and respected by the people of Kumaon whom he helped from time to time to get rid of man-eating tigers. He shot twelve tigers and leopards that had been documented as man-eaters. This he did after satisfying himself that the animal was indeed seeking humans as food and not killing them by accident. Jim Corbett always tried to look for an explanation, the reasons why they turned to man eating. He took great pains to explain that 'a man eating tiger is a tiger that has been compelled, through stress of circumstances beyond its control, to adopt a diet alien to it.' An animal left injured with a bullet wound, loss of vigour due to old age would turn to an easier prey. He fought in the defence of wild life and pleaded for the preservation of the tiger.

Previous double-spread: F.W. Champion pioneered wildlife photography by using trip wires and remote-controlled cameras, where by the animal would unknowingly take its own picture. This spectacular self portrait of a tiger is a great example of his innovative technique. Photo courtesy: James Champion, grandson of F.W. Champion

Facing page: Jim Corbett's house in Kaladhungi that is now a museum, a visit here sure takes you back in time when Jim roamed the jungle to rid the locals of man-eaters.

Above: Jim as a youngster. (younger boy on the left)

37

Having acquired a camera he set about recording tigers on cine film. This he could do as he had an intimate knowledge of the forest. An avid photographer he vowed never to kill a tiger unless it turned man eater.

A preservationist at heart, over time he became a wild life conservationist, much concerned about the fate of the tiger and its habitat. He tried to bring much awareness among the people about their forest and the need to conserve it along with its wild life. He authored many books of which *Man-Eaters of Kumaon* is perhaps the best known.

In his book *My India* he writes about the simple people of the country who he had lived with and who he loved and who in turn grew to love and respect him. He has many a story to tell about these brave at heart, humble people of the hills who lived their lives in penury and hardships and yet were large-hearted and proud. Jim Corbett had a great deal of concern and sympathy for them and was an astute observer of their lives, traditions and culture.

At the time of the First World War, Jim Corbett had been working for the railways for sixteen years, handling the change of goods from one gauge to the other at Mokameh Ghat. He left first to serve in France and later in Waziristan. But even during his absence, work had continued smoothly without a hitch at the ghat. This says a lot about the kind of man he was although he gives credit for this to his work force. His men were loyal and had so much respect for him because they knew he was honest and hard working. In his own words after he came back after four years, he resumed contact with his people as if just a day had gone by.

Much revered by the local people who lovingly called him 'Carpet sahib', he helped set up a Provincial Association for the Preservation of Wildlife in the 1930s and later stressed upon the creation of a National Park. Both Corbett and F.W.

Above: Jim Corbett
Below: A part of the boundary wall that Corbett had built around Chotti Haldwani.

Jim Corbett heritage trail

A Jim Corbett Heritage Trail has been developed near Kaladhungi in the Chotti Haldwani that was owned by Jim Corbett and later gifted to the villagers. This 2.5 km trail is a peep into Corbett's world as this is the very area Corbett wrote about in his book *My India*. The trail leads to Moti's house, the *chaupal* where the grandson of Trilok Singh will proudly show you the gun Corbett had given to his grandfather. Finally you end up at the masonry wall built by Corbett for the protection of villagers. The wall stood at a height of six feet and was three miles long. Because of the high cost involved it took almost ten years to build. The tour is run by the Community Based Tourism members who also run a souvenir shop here at Jim Corbett's house which is now a museum. Though the interiors don't have much to offer in terms of memorabilia, but just a walk within the walls of the house where Corbett actually lived can be a magical experience.

Champion were harbingers of change first to recognise that if something was not done to preserve the tiger, it would be lost forever. As observed by Corbett in his book *'Man-Eaters of Kumaon'*.

> There is, however, one point on which I am convinced that all sportsmen—no matter whether their view point has been a platform on a tree, the back of an elephant, or their own feet—will agree with me, and that is that a tiger is a large-hearted gentleman with boundless courage and that when he is exterminated—as exterminated he will be unless public opinion rallies to his support—India will be poorer, having lost the finest of her fauna.

A legend in his time, the saga of his life is as fresh and well-remembered today just as it was when Jim roamed the jungle alone with his rifle in hand.

Jim Corbett's books

Corbett was a word weaver. His first book, *Man-eaters of Kumaon* was a huge success and was chosen by book clubs in England and America. His writings reflect his immense knowledge of the Indian jungle and his skill of reading the signs of the jungle to track man eaters. After Independence he moved to Kenya where he wrote five more books, *The Man-Eating Leopard of Rudraprayag* (1948), *My India* (1952), *Jungle Lore* (1953), *The Temple Tigers and More Man-Eaters of Kumaon* (1954) and *Tree Tops* (1955). His books weave a beautiful and descriptive tale of the Indian jungles, its wildlife, the tigers and leopards that he would track and shoot. The Indo-chinese tiger, *Panthera tigris corbetti*, is named after Corbett.

Above: Dust jacket of the first American edition (1946) of Corbett's famous book Man-eaters of Kumaon.

F.W. Champion

We all remember that Neil Armstrong was the first man to step on the moon, but we often forget that Buzz Aldrin also walked the lunar surface along with him on that trip. It is a story often repeated with pioneers that we remember one; while the other conveniently fades from collective public memory. While Jim Corbett's name has become synonymous with Corbett National Park, very few people today remember that there was one more friend of nature—F.W. Champion, who stood along with Jim in the front-line of conservationists and raised the first voice of concern to save the dwindling forests and protect its wildlife.

Frederick Walter Champion lived in a time when shooting wild animals for a trophy was the trend, particularly for the British. Yet he chose to shoot them

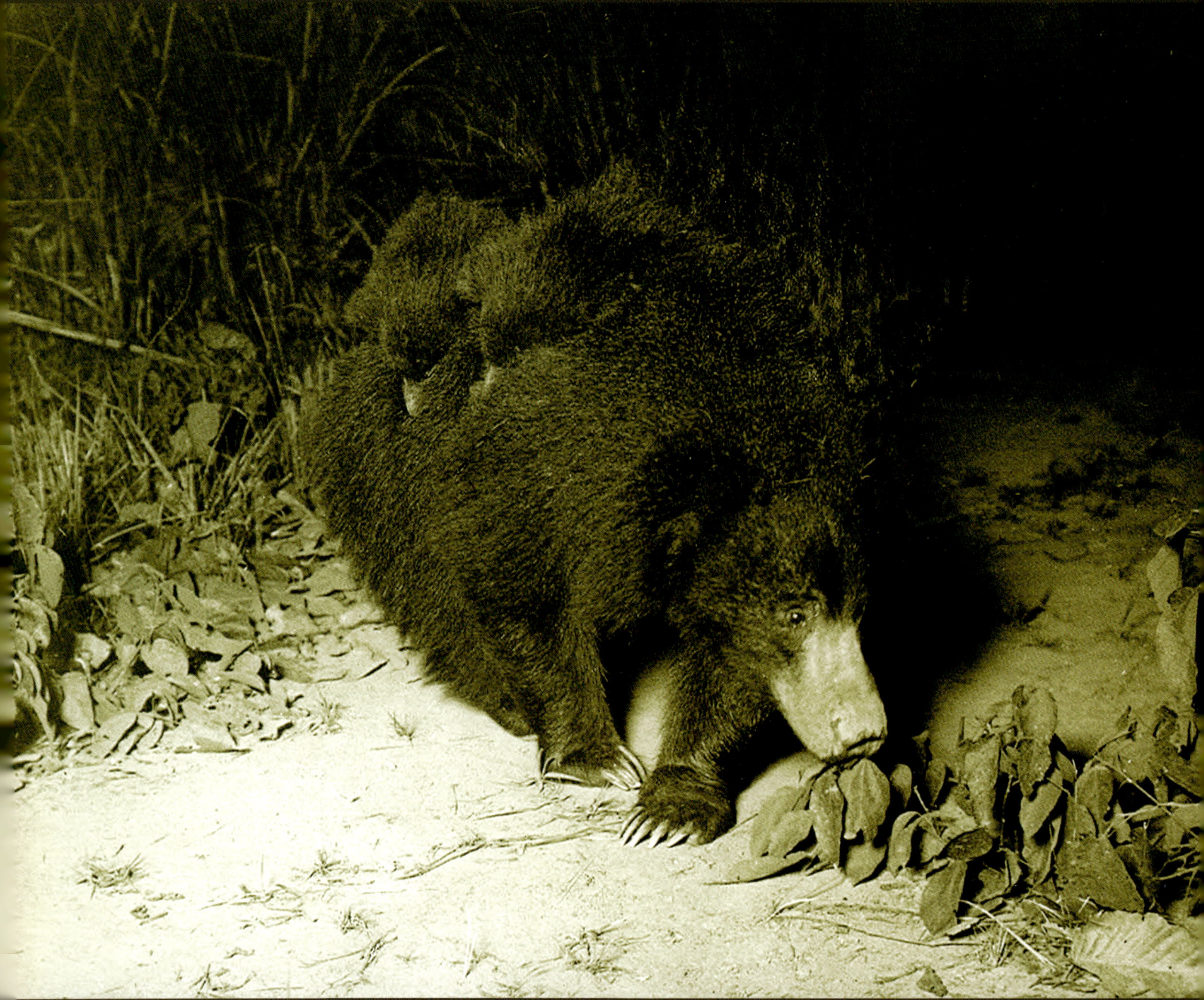

with his camera. Having served in the killing fields of the First World War, he had seen enough senseless bloodshed and had no desire to see any more, in the emerald landscape that was his new chosen field as a forester with the Imperial Forest Service. He was a conservationist to the core and derived immense joy from seeing wild animals thrive in their natural habitat. He also pioneered wildlife photography in India.

Those days, in the context of forests and animals, the role of cameras was usually limited to record the hunt-parties and photograph hunters standing next to the carcasses of the animals. This to Champion's mind 'was not a true representation of the denizens of the Indian jungles'. He wanted people to see animals as they live in their natural habitat. He so beautifully writes in the introduction of his first book, *With a Camera in Tiger-land*,

> '... I believe this to be the first book ever published [in India] which is illustrated throughout with photographs of wild animals, just as they live their everyday lives in the great Indian jungles, away from the ever-destroying hand of man.'

Images on facing page, below and following two pages were taken by F.W. Champion using trip wire technique.
They provide a rare glimpse into the nocturnal happenings of the forest.

Photographs courtesy: James Champion, grandson of F.W. Champion

Facing page: This one of a kind photograph shows a Sloth Bear carrying its young on her back.

Below: A leopard with its prey (left) and a leopard on the prowl at night (below).

Top: A Fishing Cat

Right: Ratels or Honey Badgers merrily moving on the jungle floor caught unaware on camera set off by them. Omnivorous in their feeding habits, they are well known for scavenging.

Many of his pictures were taken using trip wire triggers in which an animal would set off the camera and flash light simultaneously, taking a picture of itself. That was an early version of today's modern camera-traps, using photo-optic switches and thermal sensors. Using his simple equipment, coupled with his immense field knowledge of animal behaviour, he managed to take dozens of beautiful night-time shots. These rare pictures opened a new window into the nocturnal activity of the forest, something that was never visually recorded before. Champion was perhaps the very first photographer who has left behind an immense image bank of professional quality pictures of tigers, leopards, sloth bears, honey badgers, elephants and other wild animals of India.

He shared his images and knowledge in many articles and two books that he wrote. The first, *With a Camera in Tiger-land*, published in 1927, was a pioneering work in a way that it presented the jungle and its wildlife to a layman in an easily understandable manner, without making it too technical and scientific. The second, *The Jungle in Sunlight and Shadow*, published in 1934, further added pictorial treasure and understanding to the early wildlife records of India. In his writings, films and wildlife photography, he was lovingly assisted by his wife Judy, and their work truly reflects the couple's love for Indian wild animals and jungles.

F.W. Champion was a friend and mentor to Corbett. He greatly influenced the latter to take to the camera to shoot tigers in the wild. Corbett bought his first camera in the late 1920s. He had a distinct advantage of knowing the jungle and its denizens well; but even then, by his own admittance,

> 'Photographing tigers was no easy feat. 'Being hunted' the animals were exceedingly shy and it took all of a winter's efforts to get a good picture'.

Champion was also in the forefront along with Jim Corbett in setting up of the Hailey (now Corbett) National Park. He was a strong believer in the role of the Forest Department in the protection of wild life and a critic of the hunters. In the words of his grandson, James Champion, 'As DFO, he would often issue permits to shoot in areas where he knew that his beloved tigers were absent.'

Top: An Indian Jungle Cat
Above: A Leopard Cat

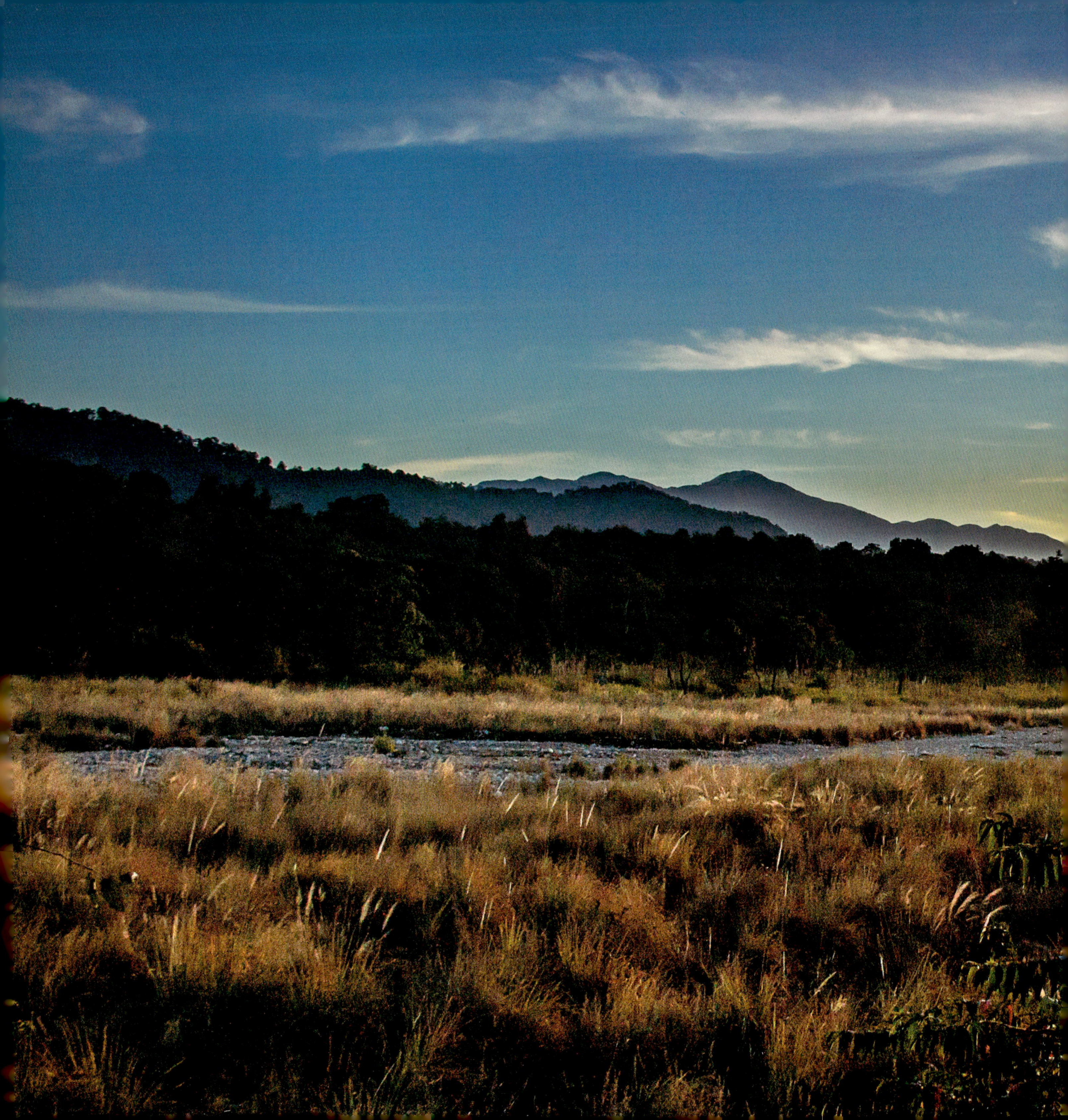

DAWN OF CONSERVATION
—a ray of hope

46

DAWN OF CONSERVATION
—a ray of hope

It was not until 1934 when Sir William Malcolm Hailey, as governor of the United Provinces, approved of a recommendation put forward by a committee of which Jim Corbett was also a part, to demarcate boundaries for a game reserve.

In 1936, under the United Provinces National Parks Act, an area of 323.75 sq km was set aside for the park—and thus the Hailey National Park, the first National park in the country, was set up. The Second World War made its huge demands for raw materials and this area like all forests across India suffered greatly from timber felling and poaching at the hands of contractors.

In 1952, the Hailey National Park was renamed Ramganga National Park after the Ramganga river that flows through it. But in 1957, when Jim Corbett died, the Indian government thought it befitting to name it Corbett National Park in his honour and memory. The fifties were not a time when wildlife was on anybody's priority list. The use of DDT and other chemical pesticides helped control malaria in Terai. Earlier inhabited only by the hunter gatherer community of Bhoksa, the Terai was cleared for agriculture. Land here was distributed to migrating refugees from Pakistan. In the post-independence years the government's thrust was on agriculture and hydro-electric power which further took a toll on the forests.

Previous double-spread: A crystal clear morning in Bijrani. Dawn is the best time to get out in the forest to spot wildlife.

Below: View of the reservoir from the heights of Kanda. On a clear day one can see the little islands formed by the rising water as it inundated the hilly area around the dam.

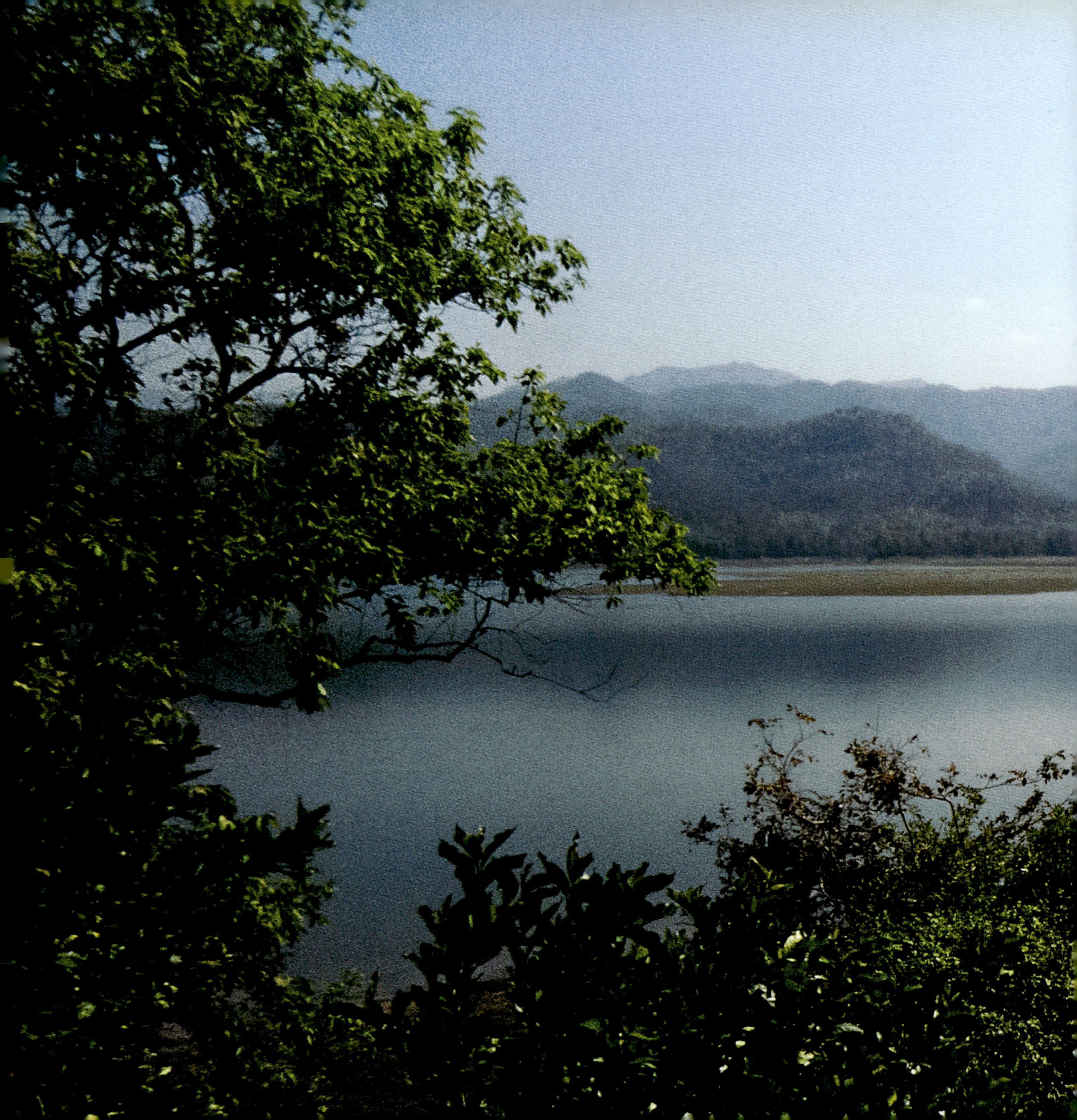

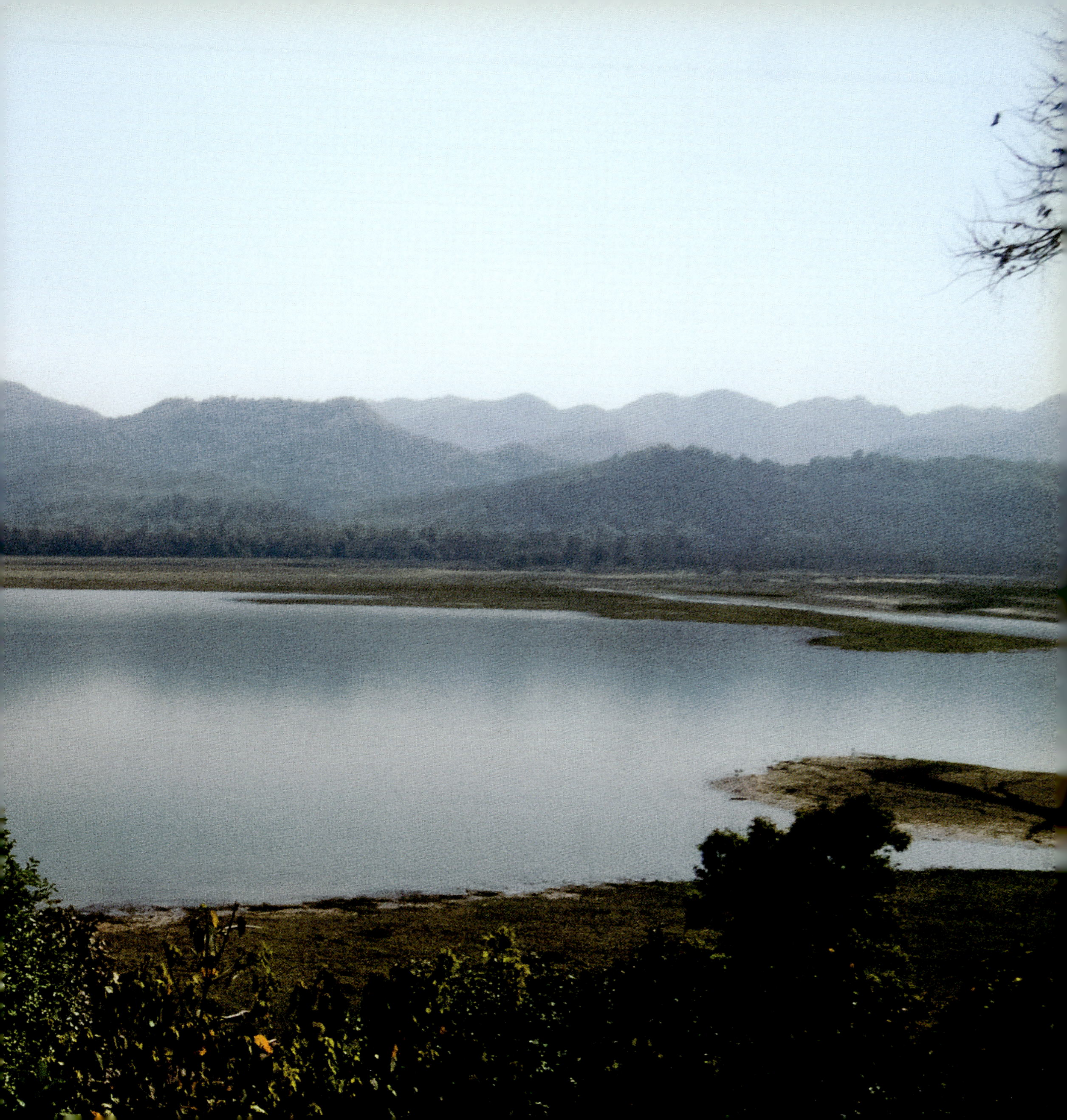

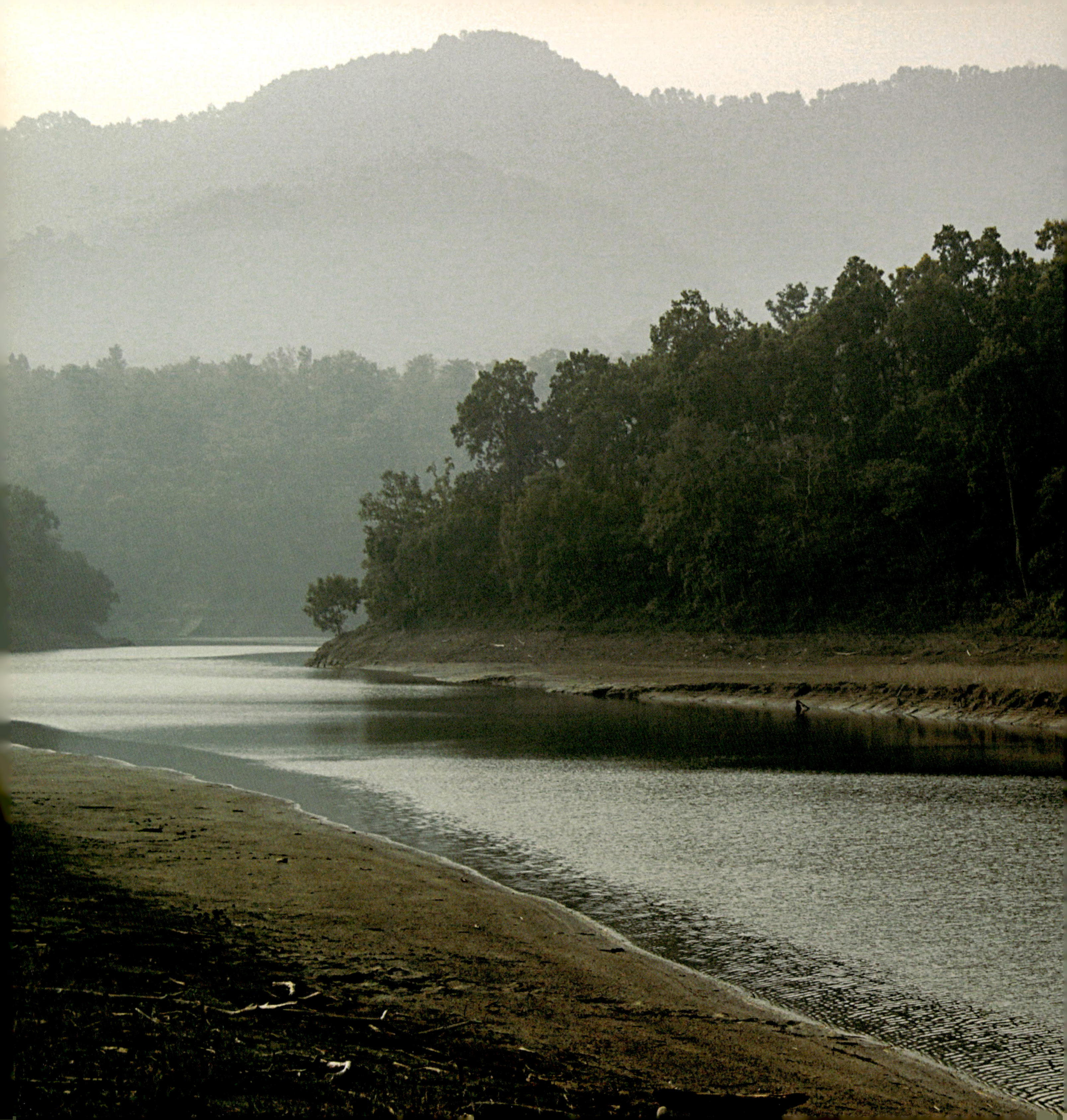

In 1966, the area of the park was increased to 520.82 sq km but the tigers were quickly disappearing. It was not until 1969 that the International Union for the Conservation of Nature held its tenth meeting and agreed to put the tiger on the endangered list. This was much opposed by commercial safari operators and hunters who insisted that the situation was not that bad. Indira Gandhi, the prime minister of India then, was clear in her intention to save India's dwindling tiger numbers. This paved the way for 'Project Tiger'—a new era in safeguarding the tiger was born.

CNP TODAY—eighty years and surviving

What started in 1936 as a 300 sq km park is today a 1,318.54 sq km area. In 1991, through the initiative of Prime Minister Rajiv Gandhi a huge chunk was added to the Corbett Tiger Reserve that included 301.18 sq km of the Sonanadi Wildlife Sanctuary, 496.54 sq km of Reserved Forests and Corbett National Park at 520.82 sq km.

Previous double-spread: Tail-end of the reservoir at Dhikala where Ramganga drains into the water-body.

Facing page: Beautiful Sonanadi, as seen in the Halduparao area.

Below: Unlike crocodiles, gharials spend less time out of water and never venture far away from the safety of their aquatic habitat. This makes them a difficult subject to photograph on land. This one slithered away into the river just as we noticed him on the shore.

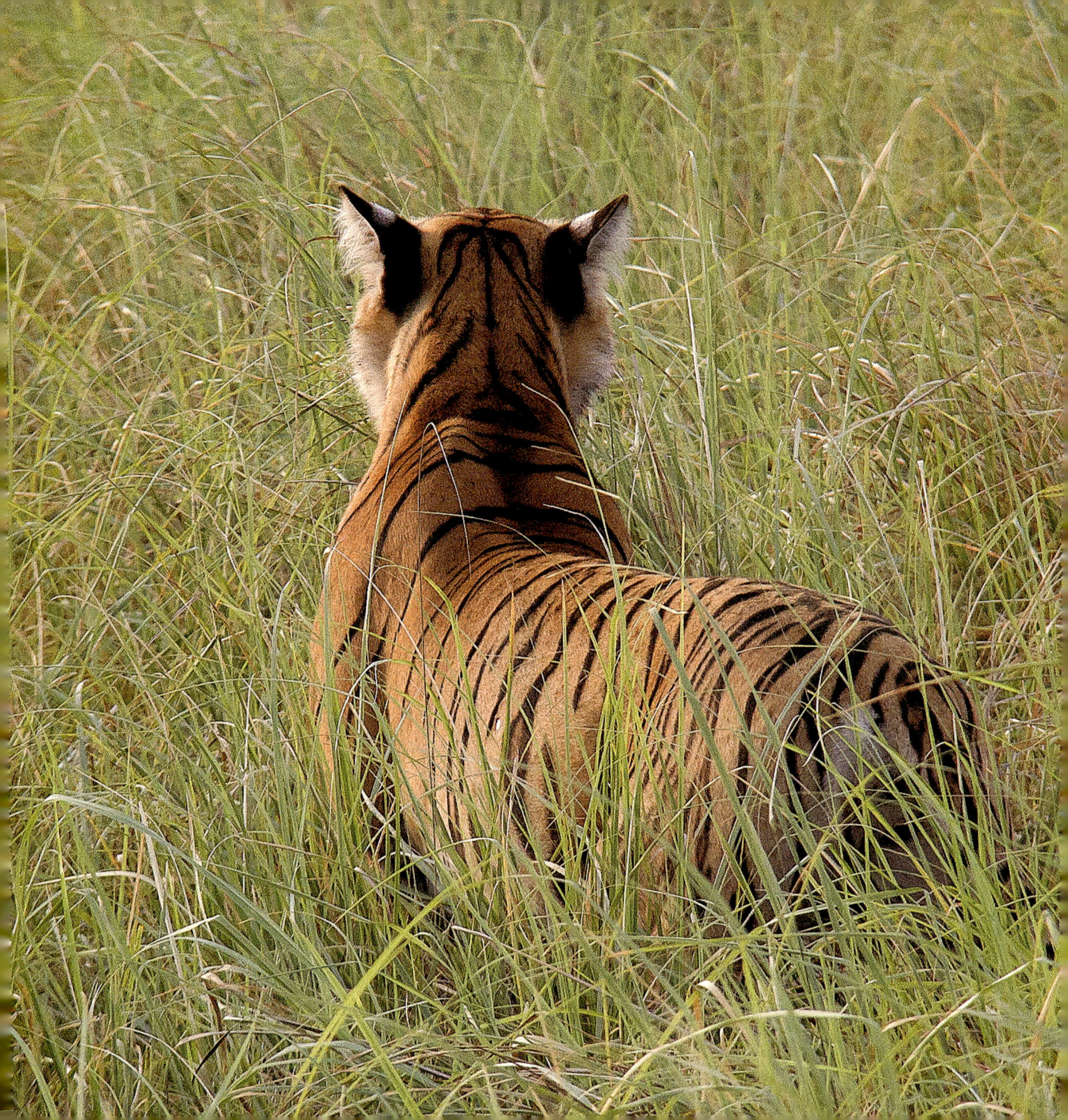

PROJECT TIGER
—*an effort to save the tiger
from extinction*

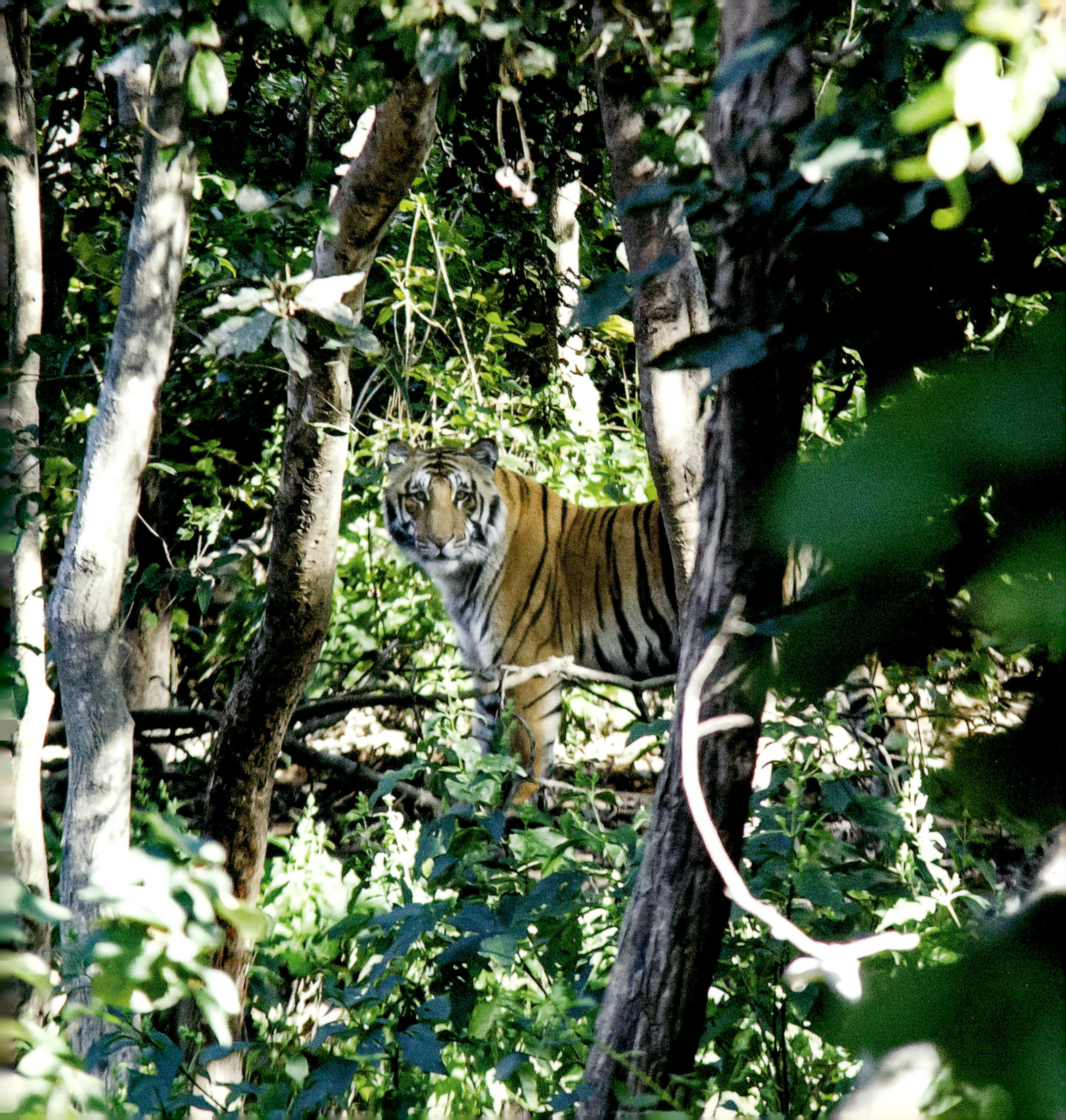

PROJECT TIGER

—an effort to save the tiger from extinction

Guy Mountford of the WWF was convinced that there was still a fair chance to save tigers and he brought his proposals to Prime Minister Indira Gandhi. He wanted her government to create a number of Tiger reserves where legislation against poaching and the black market of tiger skin and bones could be enforced and the tiger be saved from extinction. She readily agreed and set up a Tiger Task Force that included stalwarts like Dr. Karan Singh, Duleep Mathia, M. Krishnan, Salim Ali and Anne Wright, that was to report to her directly, to draft the plan for setting up Project Tiger.

Thus, Project Tiger became a reality. Its objective was to protect tigers and their habitat. By preserving areas of biological importance in Tiger Reserves, it would not only save the tiger but also safeguard other species of flora and fauna in these areas. Corbett National Park was the first Tiger Reserve along with nine others in the country. Today the number of such reserves has increased to fifty.

By the turn of the 20th century, it was estimated that India still had twenty to forty thousand tigers in the wild, despite merciless hunting by the Indian royals, the British and the trophy hunters. After India gained independence, the situation for the tiger only became worse as huge tracts of forest land were cleared to make way for irrigation projects, hydroelectric dams and roads and railways. With growing pressure of human need for fuel, fodder and extraction of forest products, there was further degradation and fragmentation of wildlife habitat.

The depleting tiger population was a cause of great concern and in 1970 a ban on hunting of tigers was imposed. A tiger count was done across the entire country that led to the discovery of a pitiable fact that not more than 1,800 tigers remained in the wild. This jolted the authorities to put in some serious efforts to save the

Previous double-spread: A tiger surveying his domain. With the conservation efforts, tiger numbers as of now are showing a promising increase but the crisis of tiger conservation is far from over.

Facing page: The stripes of a tiger play a light and shade dance just as the dappled light of the sun falls on the leaves, making it hard to spot tigers in the undergrowth.

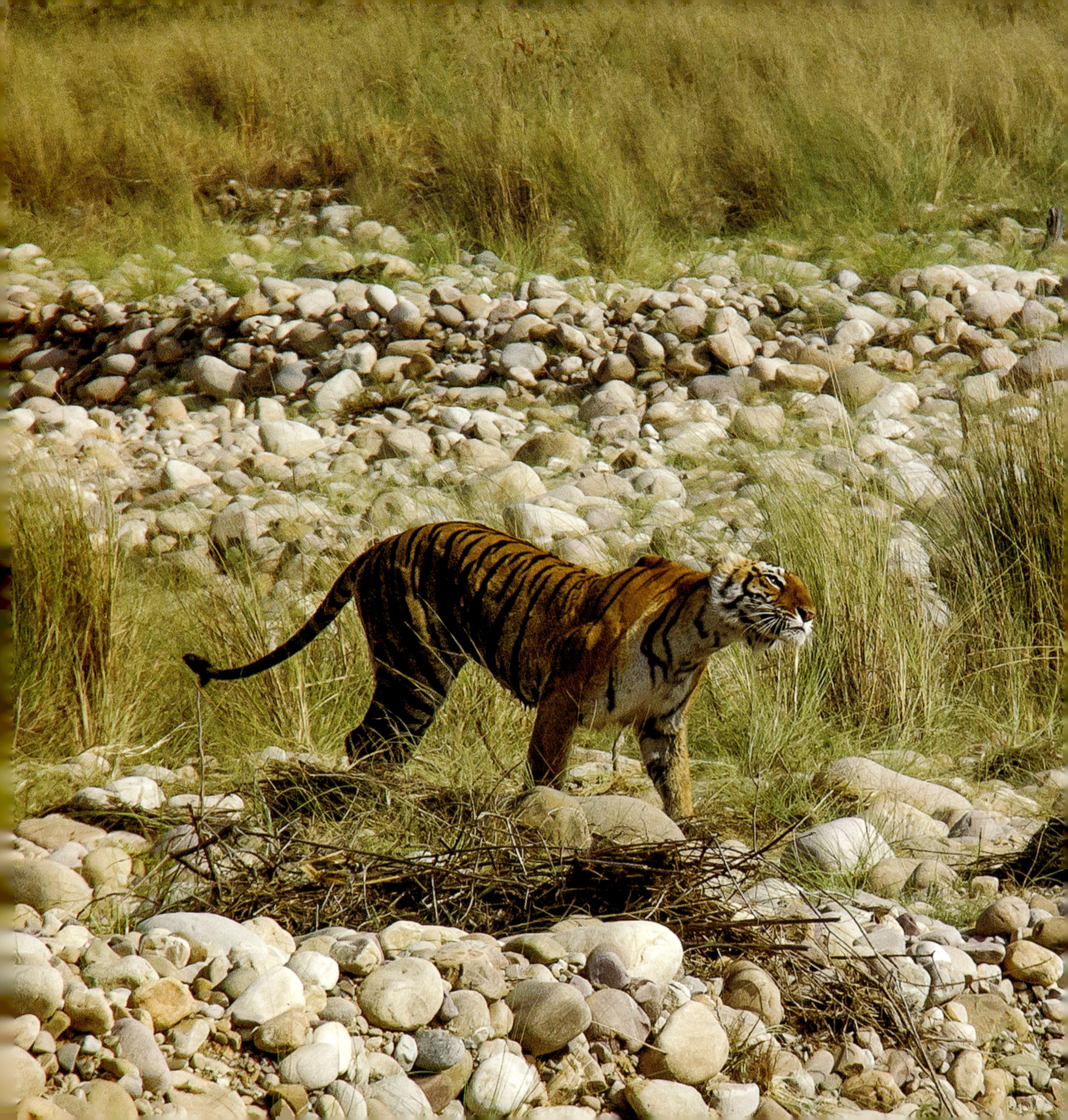

tiger from extinction. In 1972, the Wild Life Protection Act was laid down and the plan formulated by the Task Force for the conservation of tigers in India was set into motion. On 1st April 1973, Project Tiger was launched from the Dhikala Forest Rest House in Corbett National Park.

The main aim was to create Tiger Reserves that would be safe havens for tigers and thereby ebb their declining numbers. Initially, nine Tiger Reserves were formed in different states Manas (Assam), Palamau (Bihar), Simlipal (Odisha), Corbett (U.P.), Kanha (M.P.), Melghat (Maharashtra), Bandipur (Karnataka), Ranthambhore (Rajasthan) and Sunderbans (West Bengal) The idea was to create optimum environmental conditions for the survival of tigers and its prey species. The Tiger Reserves were constituted on the core/buffer strategy in which the core is kept free from all biotic disturbances, forestry operations and human intervention through grazing animals and collecting non wood produce and timber. The buffer zone is the 'multiple use zone' which supports the spillover of animals from the core area and also provides some sustainable eco-developmental activities to villagers from the surrounding areas.

Project Tiger specifically works to prevent habitat loss, forestry disturbances, loss of prey and most importantly loss of tigers to poaching.

A lot has been achieved and a lot needs to be done to safeguard the existence of the tiger—our national animal and pride of our wilds.

Facing page: Tigers are sometimes caught on camera with very interesting expressions, like this female in the Bijrani zone.

Left: The Old colonial Forest Rest House at Dhikala. This heritage structure provides a panoramic view of the Ramganga river and hills beyond.

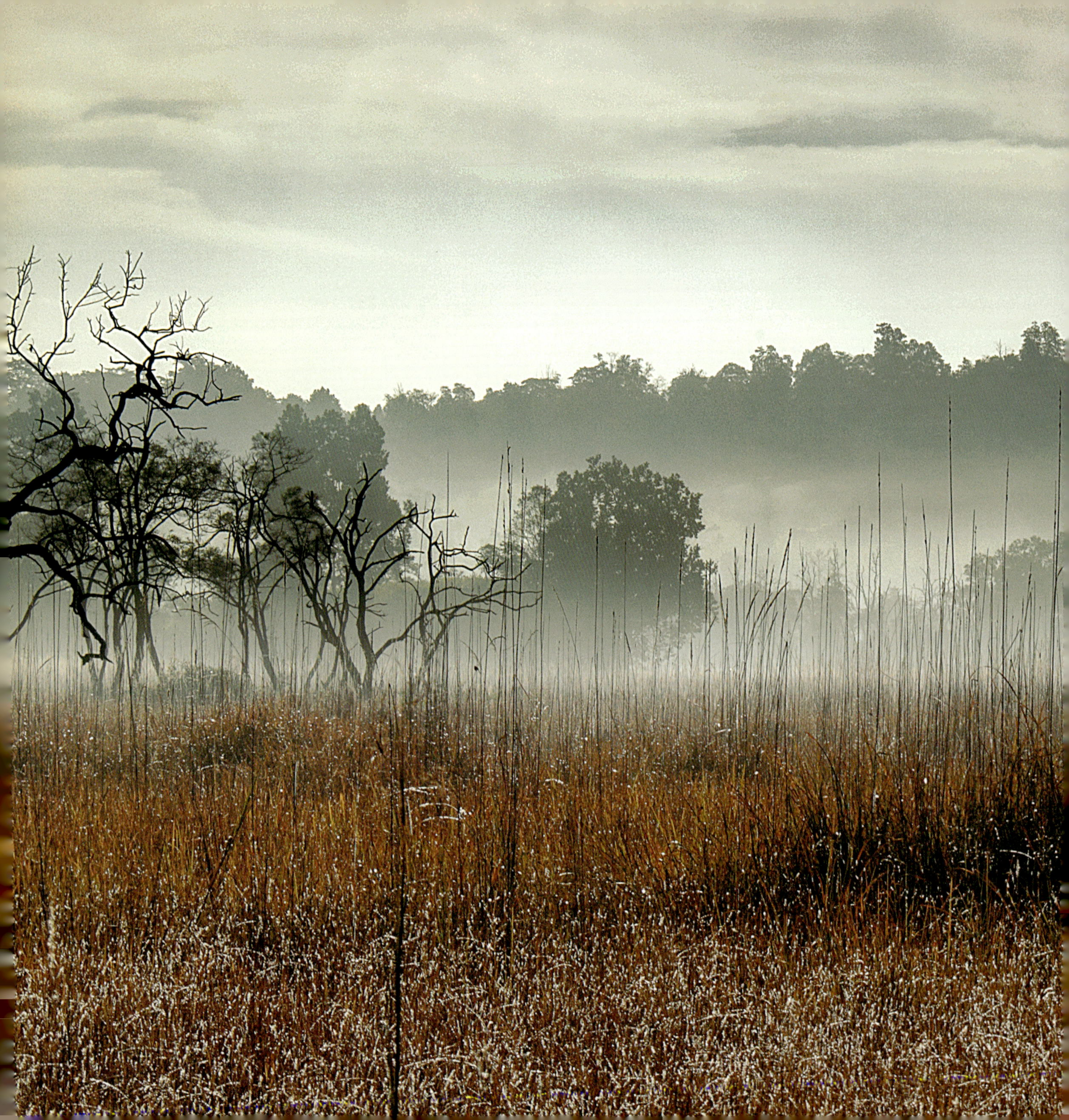

UNDERSTANDING OUR LANDSCAPE
—*tracing the journey of natural history*

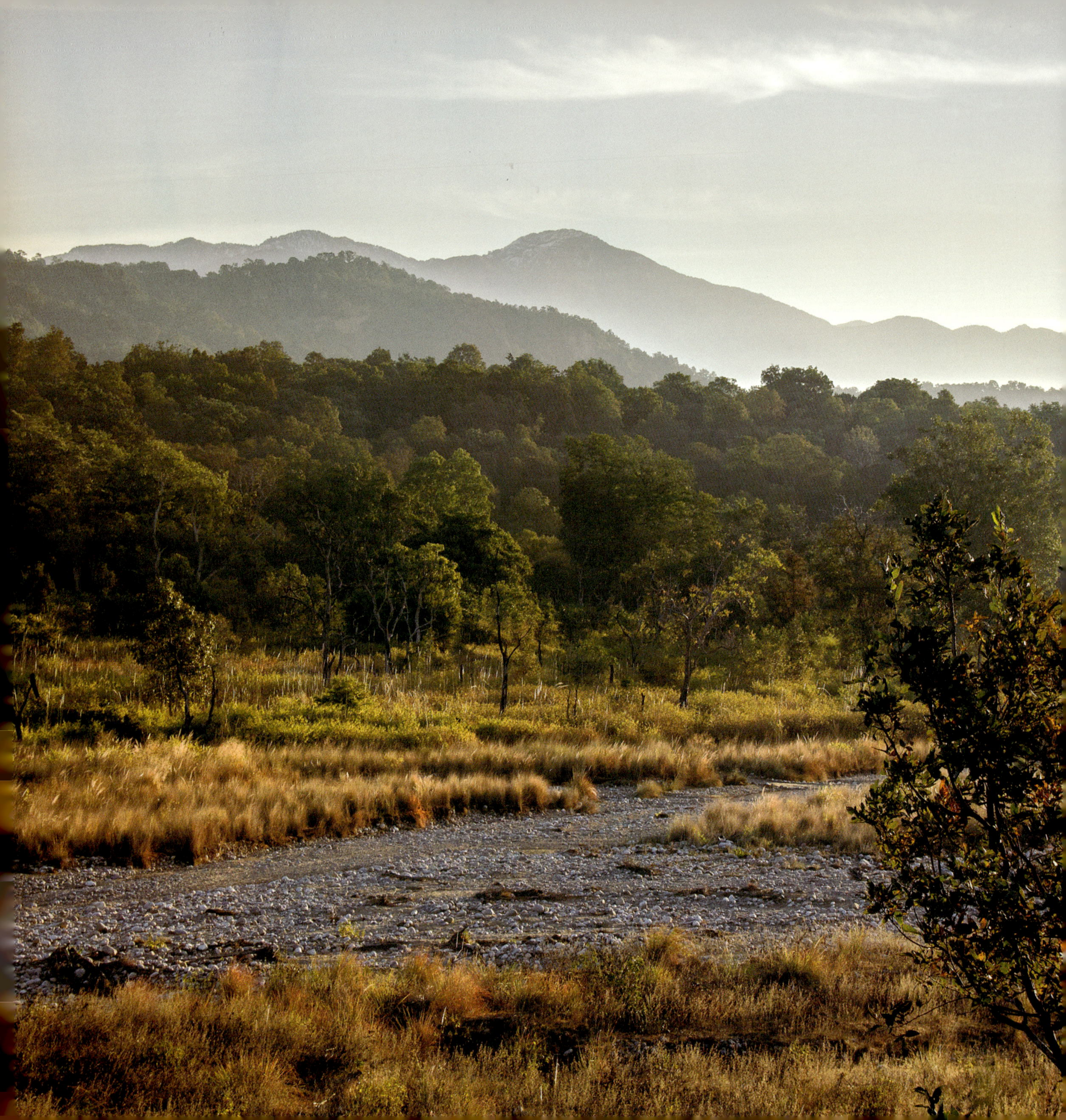

UNDERSTANDING OUR LANDSCAPE
—tracing the journey of natural history

Over the years I have seen Corbett landscape in many moods—waking up to the spring season, as the warmth after the winter months sprinkles its leaf-less trees with various hues of fresh green. Sizzling under the summer heat when it's deeply wooded areas provide balm to the scorching skin. In autumn I have enjoyed the rustle of falling leaves piling up a thick golden carpet all over the forest floor. I have also braved the winters here, when the park reopens after the monsoon months and the fog plays a game of hide and seek every morning.

It was one such winter morning and a low mist hung in the air. The Himalayan foothills in the distance stood like rows of sentinels silently watching over the vast open grassland spread before us. The sun was rising but its warmth had not yet touched the moist earth below. The mist seemed to have settled on the golden dry grass and there were countless droplets clinging to the blades. The shimmering landscape looked as if a crop of pearls was waiting to be harvested. I could hear the soft ripples of the Ramganga river flowing beyond, but it was completely enveloped in the morning mist. Only the calls of some Red-wattled Lapwings and River Terns were filtering through from the river front to us. The few trees that punctuated the grassland here and there seemed to be floating over the blanket of mist. Some spotted deer and a few wild pigs were grazing nearby. Suddenly the ethereal silence was broken by the alarm call of a sambar. Soon a langur somewhere from his high perch confirmed that within the white folds of morning mist a tiger was moving nearby. The whole atmosphere was so tranquil yet so vibrant with life. Instead of thinking of a sighting and racing towards the call I decided to just soak in the moment and was transported to a different time zone—before we *homo sapiens* had arrived—there would have been a time when the whole earth would have been all like this—pristine, balanced and perfect.

Previous double-spread: A misty winter morning at the grassland with Himalayan foothills forming the backdrop. Night dew had settled on the golden dry grass and there were countless droplets clinging to the blades.

Above: Multiple hues of the tree foliage create a colourful image.

Facing page: Bijrani landscape. Hills, forests, river-beds and grasslands are the main components of the Corbett matrix.

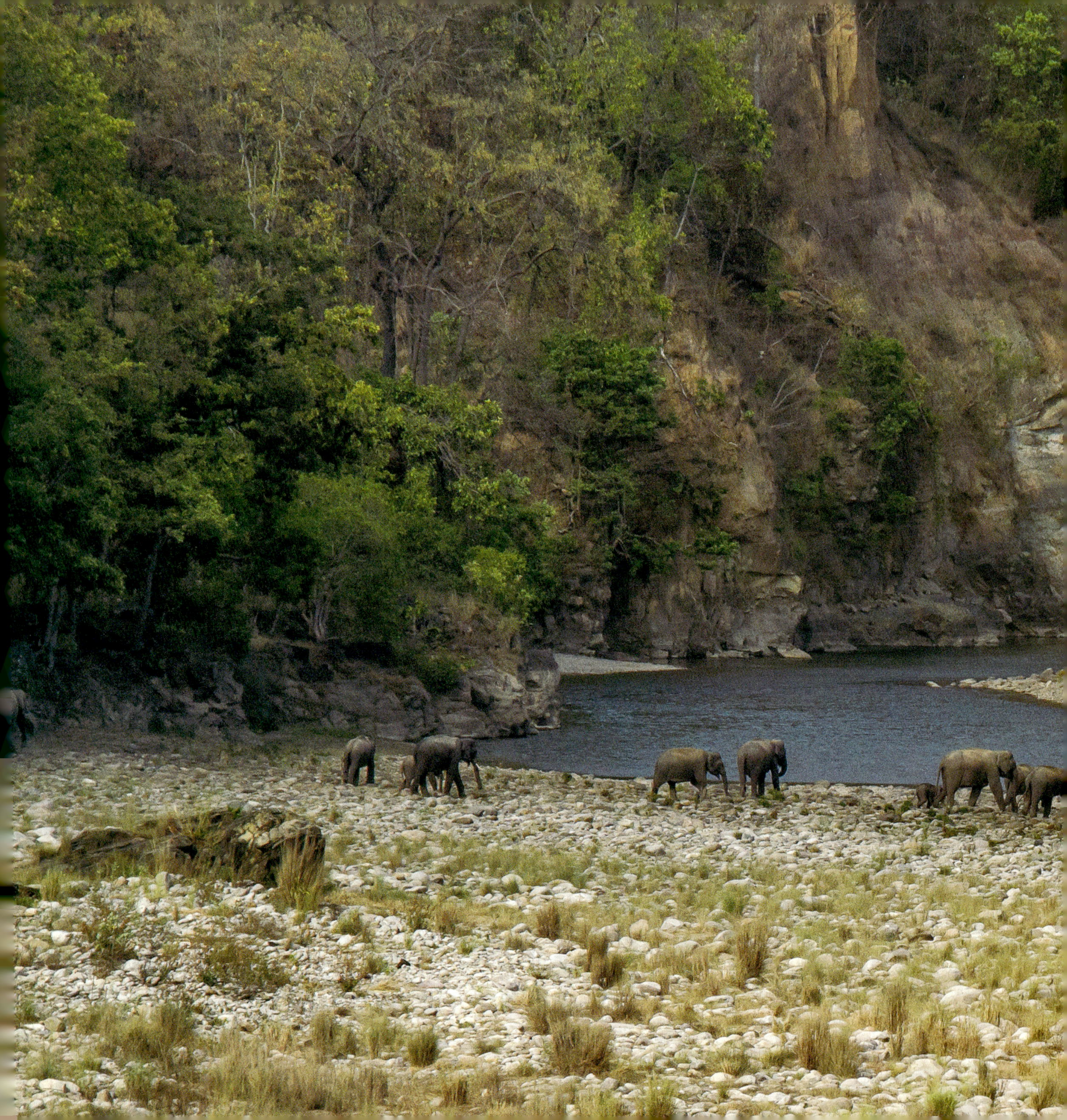

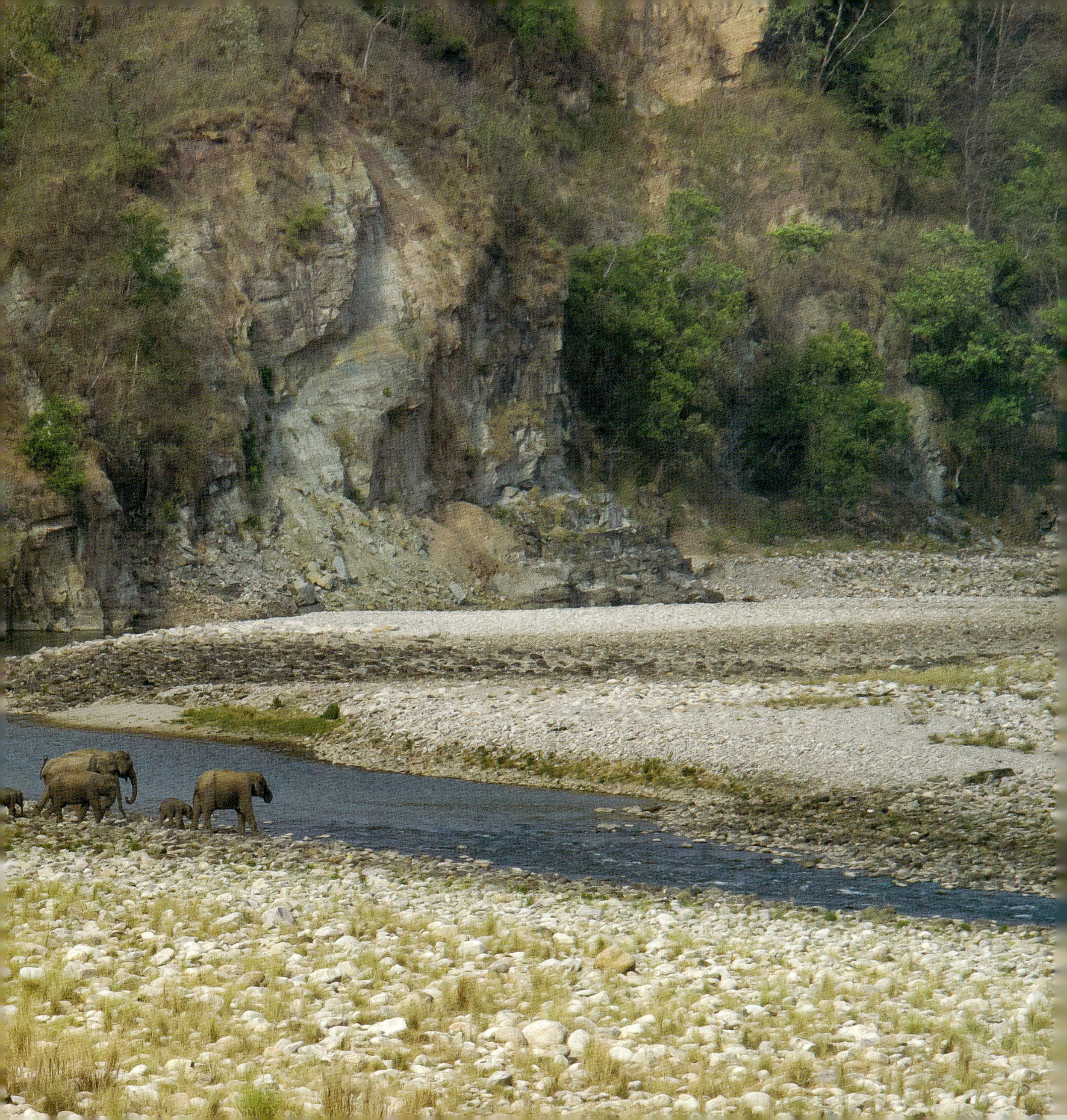

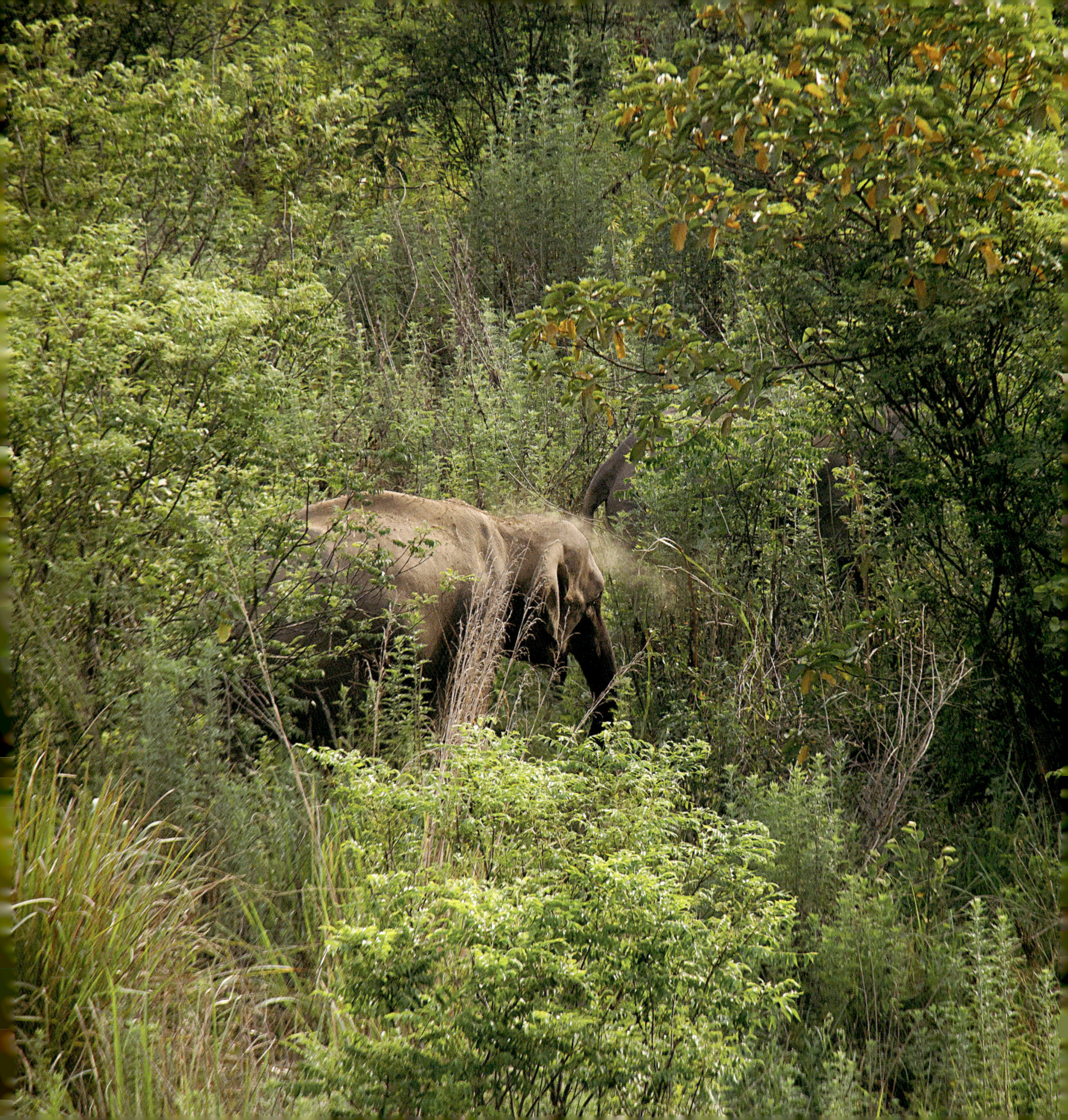

To understand this landscape better, let's take a step back in time, following the footsteps of natural history on the time-line of the Indian subcontinent, we arrive at an event that changed the face of the earth. About 50 million years ago, a roughly triangular plate which was to be the Indian subcontinent separated from the Gondwana land mass and crashed into Asia, the impact fused the two and the earth folded upwards to form the Tibetan Plateau, Great Himalaya, Outer Himalaya and the Shivaliks. Ice caps and glaciers on the newly formed mountain range eventually gave birth to rivers flowing south. The mountains on the lower slopes got covered with lush forests collecting rain water and channelising it into countless streams and rivers that was the perfect habitat for wild animals. Some plants and animals on our subcontinent like the gharial are descendants of those that travelled with the separated land mass and evolved in isolation during their epic journey. Others like tigers, elephants, wild pigs, monkeys came from the faunal exchange between Africa and Eurasia.

Between the outer Himalayas that form its northern boundary and the Shivaliks in the south, in an area called the Terai-Bhabar region is Corbett National Park. Bhabar is a narrow tract of land, barely 8-16 km wide; running along the southern part of the foothills from the Indus river in the west to the Tista in the east. Mountain rivers of the northern region running down from the steep slopes of the Himalayas descend with a heavy flow and bring along a lot of mountain debris. These boulders and mineral rich gravel make the Bhabar a region of high porosity where many streams disappear as they sink underground. As a result of this phenomenon, Bhabar has acquired a character of dry river courses.

The underground streams of the Bhabar belt reappear as they come down further south in the Terai region and make it a swampy humid landscape. This Terai belt is about 15-30 km wide and is an area of high dampness and warmer climate. An ideal recipe for the growth of thick forests—an ideal habitat for many species of wild life.

Corbett is a mosaic of varied terrains. It has sprawling grasslands called *chaurs*, thickly wooded forest areas, hilly terrain, riverine landscape, marshy plains, plateaus and ravines.

In this myriad landscape there is a series of somewhat parallel ridges that run North-West to South-East. They are steep in some parts and gently undulating in others. At places they give way to longitudinal flat bottomed valleys of open grasslands called the 'Duns'. Corbett is located in one such region known as the south Patlidun valley.

Previous double-spread: A view from the High Bank—An elephant herd at the Ramganga river.

Facing page: A solitary elephant in the dense foliage.

Above: Many faces of Corbett landscape—Dense green forest (top) sprawling grasslands (middle) and rivers (above).

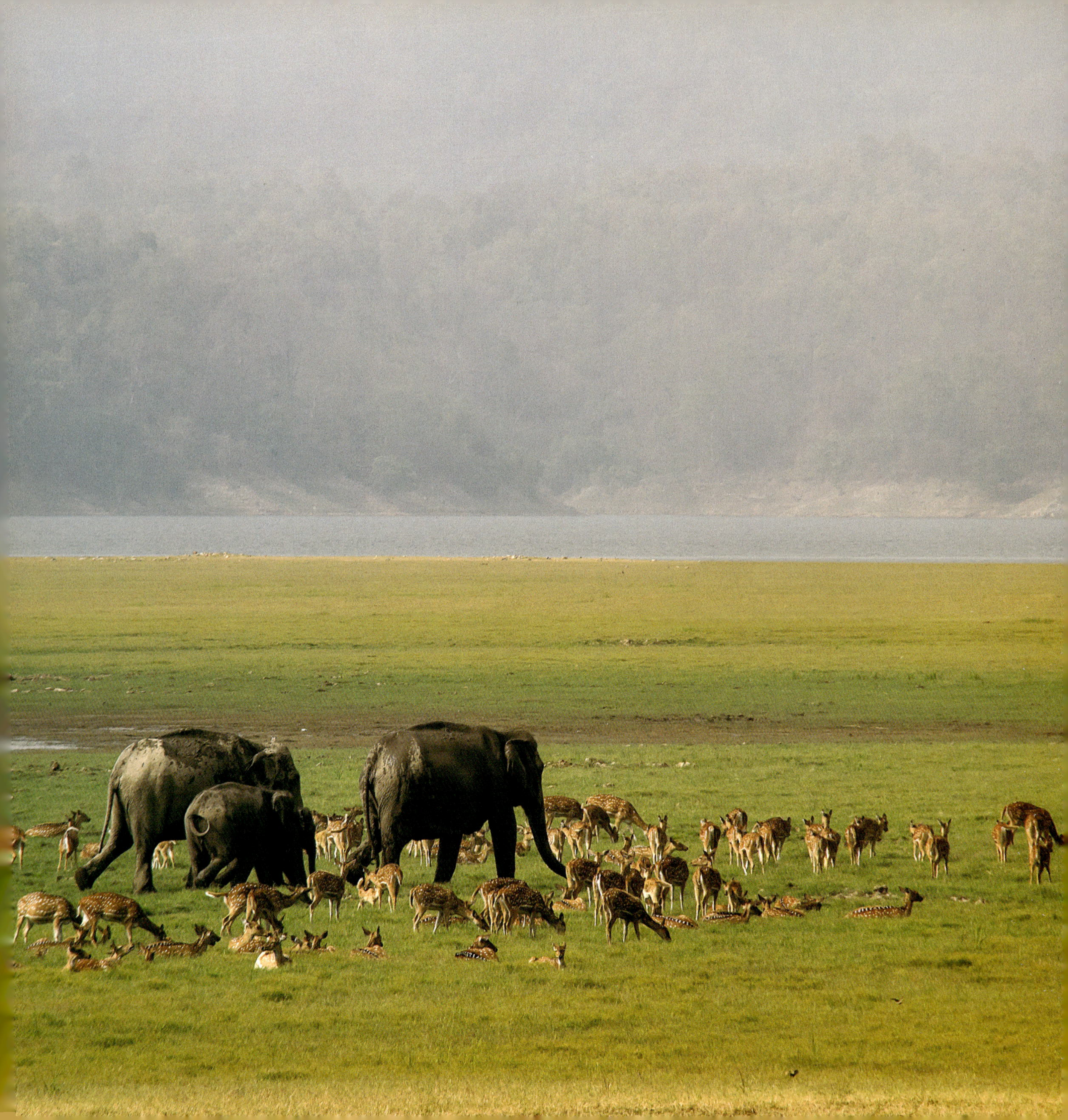

Offshoots of these ridges run north to south and create deep ravines, a landscape feature that has contributed greatly in making Corbett a safe haven for tigers to raise their cubs. Tiger cubs are very vulnerable in early life. They are threatened not only by small predators but tiger mothers keep them hidden from male tigers too. In tiger land it is a common practice for grown up males to kill offspring of other males to pursue the tigress for mating. This zeal of the big cat to propagate his own seed in the largest possible numbers has cost many a young ones their life at an infant stage. The ravines of Corbett provide safe hideouts for the young, particularly when their mothers are away to grab a quick bite for themselves.

The Northern ridge that forms the outer boundary of the park in that direction has its highest point at Kanda. Between this ridge and the median ridge watered by the Ramganga river lies scenic Dhikala *chaur*. The southern ridge is an area that is drier and has the deciduous type of vegetation, with broad grasslands as the Paterpani and Jamuna Gwar *chaur*.

In 1974, a significant topographical change took place in Corbett with the completion of the hydroelectric dam at Kalagarh on the Ramganga river. The Ramganga rises in the Dudatoli range and flows through Kumaon and Garhwal and enters the park at Marchula. It flows through the Patlidun and exits from Kalagarh towards the South West. Asia's largest earth-filled dam was built across the Ramganga seven kilometers upstream of Kalagarh. With its construction for irrigation and power generation, an area of 42 sq km of riverine forest and grassland was submerged by the reservoir, the back waters of which reach up to Dhikala. When full, the reservoir spreads for 80 sq km inundating Boxar and Phulai *chaur* on both banks of the Ramganga north of Dhikala. Many species were adversely affected by the water of the reservoir, leading to the extinction of the swamp deer from the park. Cheetal, hog deer, wild boar numbers also suffered. Grass dependent hog deer were pushed into the forest where their numbers fell as they were unable to survive. This also resulted in a change in the movement patterns of the predators. The worst sufferers were the elephants as their migratory corridors along their traditional routes were cut off. The northwestern boundary of the park that was contiguous with the eastern zone of Rajaji National Park got disconnected, along with the grasslands of Sona and Ramganga rivers. However nature has an amazing way of bouncing back. With the passage of time, Corbett recovered. The elephants established other routes. The lake formed by the dam attracted a large number of migratory and other bird species and now, it is also a perfect habitat for gharial.

Facing page: Coexistence in the wild—a herd of deer respects the elephants' right of way.

Above: Sunset over the tail end of the Kalagarh dam reservoir in Dhikala zone.

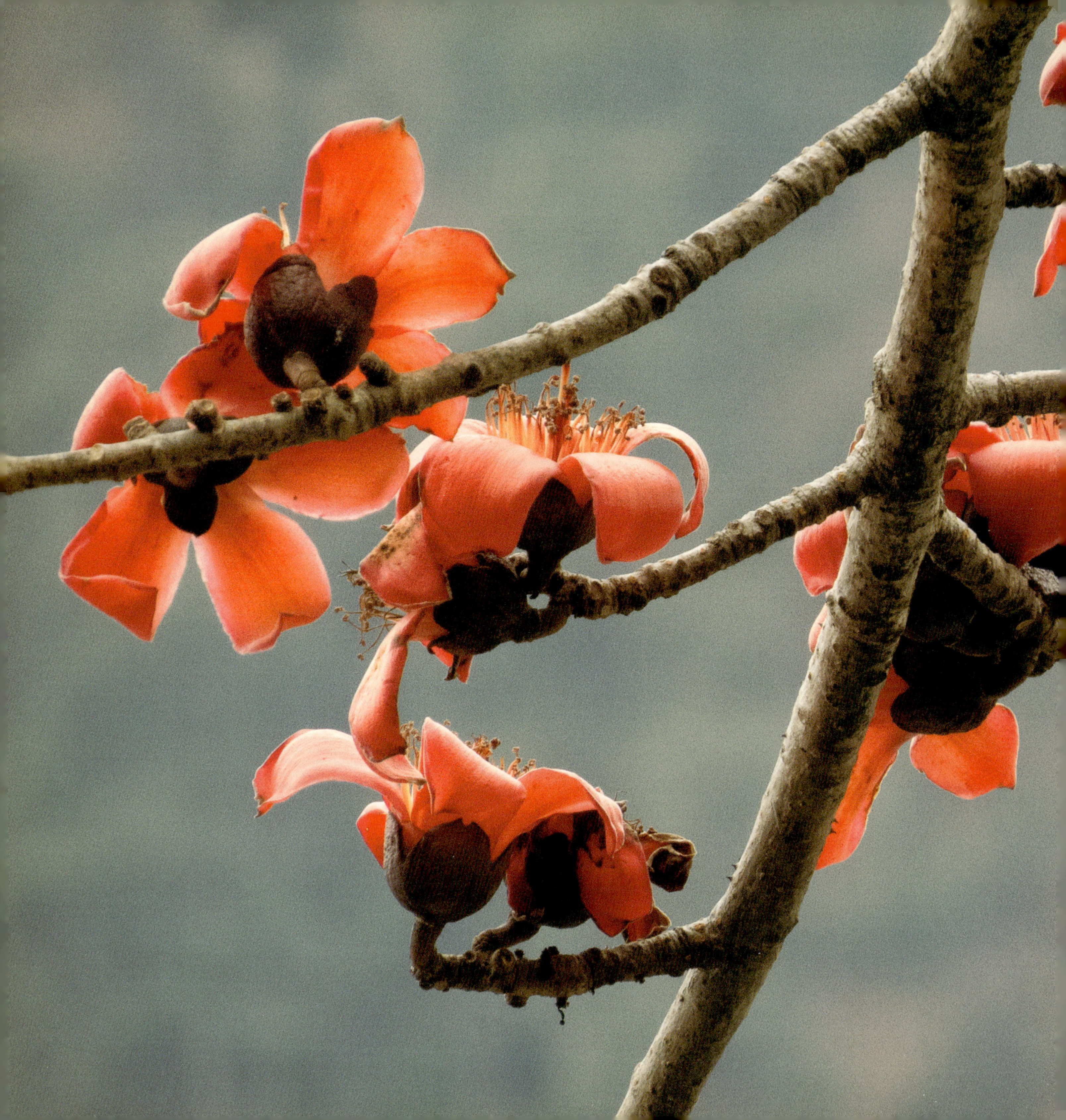

Corbett's varied terrain allows for a rich diversity of vegetation. Sal (*Shorea robusta*) grows on the lower slopes of the hills and in the valleys, along with species like Haldu (*Adina cordifolia*), Rohini (*Mallotus philippensis*) and Karipak (*Murraya koenigi*). The large tracts of Sal forests are some of the finest found anywhere in the country. Sal mostly grows in pure stands. Its leaves have a high tannin content which renders them unpalatable to insects; so you will not find very many insectivorous birds in the Sal dominated forest. Though there is limited under growth in the shade of the Sal, it attracts herbivores. Good visibility of this open forest makes it ideal for big cats to spot and chase their prey. No wonder the Sal dominated areas of Corbett and other such landscape in India have always been a traditional home for the tigers.

On the higher ridges grows Bakli (*Anogeissus latifolia*) easily discernible in the month of April by its pale yellow-brown of new leaf with a tinge of pink, along with Chir (*Pinus roxburghii*) and Anauri (*Legestroemia parviflora*) and Bamboo.

Grass that is a staple for herbivores is an ancient flora. Recent discovery of fossilised grass embedded in Amber found in Myanmar has pushed its date of existence to a 100 million years to the Cretaceous period. The grasslands of Corbett have a variety of grass species such as *Cymbopogan flexuosus* commomly known as Lemon Grass, *Themeda arundinacea*, *Vetiveria zizanioides* which we know as Khas, *Eulaliopsic binata* popularly known as Bhabar, *Thysanulena maxima* (Jharu Ghas), *Saccharum benghalense* etc.

At the Dhikala complex the forest department has a patch of land that has all these grass varieties planted in small beds. You can distinguish between the different species by observation and name. The grasslands are the favourite feeding grounds of cheetal, hog deer and elephants, particularly after the late winter fires that are deliberately set by the Forest Department. This helps to regenerate fresh growth of protein rich grass shoots and keep the wooded species at bay.

In spring the Semul (*Bombax ceiba*) or Silk Cotton tree is in full bloom, its large waxy scarlet flowers on leafless branches are a riot of colour in the jungle, visually enticing to humans and a gastronomical treat for birds like parakeets, sunbirds and a host of other species that descend to its branches by the hundreds for the sweet nectar. The seeds get dispersed on white silky fibers that get air borne and travel far, sometimes taking root in the grasslands. Semul is a prolific breeder, almost invasive, as it tries its best to march on to the grasslands. Elephants feed and prune the young saplings. An elephant safari in the grasslands reveals a relevant gardening nature of the elephants; it is a common sight to find your

Facing page: Waxy blossoms of Semul on leafless branches in the months of March and April are a riot of colour in the forest. The flowers are a feast for parakeets, sunbirds and a host of other species.

Above: A tendu tree (Diospyros melanoxylon) also known as the Coromandel ebony or East Indian ebony, loaded with fruits that are relished by birds and animals.

mount uprooting young Semul tree saplings and feasting on them while walking in the grassland. A practice also followed by the wild herds of elephants to ensure that the tree cover does not overtake their favourite feeding grounds.

If you happen to be in Corbett in March-April you will be a witness to one of nature's most colourful phenomenon—the blooming of Dhak (*Butea monosperma*), also known as Flame of the Forest. It thrives in areas of less shade, like the grasslands and open patches in the forest. While still leafless in March, the flowers appear on the lower branches. Like a spreading flame they bloom upwards till the whole tree is covered by the bright orange clusters by end April. The flowers are the source of colour that has traditionally been used as the fragrant natural orange-yellow dye used in colours on the festival of Holi.

The mauve blossoms of the *Bauhinia* and pale rose of Sandan (*Desmodium oojeinense*) along with the lovely crimson reds of Kosam (*Schleichera oleosa*) in new leaf are no less beautiful. Kosam is distinctly noticeable from the green hues of the forest in the month of March-April due to the bright red colour of its new leaf foliage. A scattered tree mixed in with other deciduous trees, it grows on low foothills in dry, bouldery, well-drained soil. This is also the time for Sal to bloom. The honeyed fragrance renders the air with a heavenly smell.

Far above: Palash (Butea monosperma) or 'Flame of the Forest' has fiery orange blossoms that start to bloom on the lower branches and spread upwards covering the entire tree.

Above: Clusters of Palash flowers that look like multiple tongues of a flame adorning leafless branches of the tree.

Why the leaves of Kosam are red?

If you happen to be in the forest in the month of March-April, a most wonderful sight hard to miss is the Kosam trees all dressed in red. In some trees, like the Kosam, the new leaf foliage start their life cycle from a deep red colour and change hues over time to the chlorophyll green. One theory that exists is that the anthocyanin that gives the leaves their vibrant red colour is less nutritious, and unpalatable to invertebrate predators and browsers. This gives the leaves a better chance of survival. Another theory is that the red colour is not discernible to bugs and beetles that cannot see the colour red. So the new red leaves go unnoticed when they are most vulnerable.

The rivers and streams have distinct vegetation that grows on their margins. Riverine landscape is perfect habitat for ground nesting birds like River Lapwings. Vegetation next to water bodies has strong root structures to withstand flooding. Besides Khair (*Acacia catechu*) and Shisham (*Dalbergia sissoo*), Jamun (*Syzygium cumini*) trees are partial to moisture and seek out places like river banks and grow to very large sizes. The Jamun fruit is greedily eaten by monkeys, jackals, bears, civets and bats. This habitat is also home to otters, large number of migratory birds and reptiles like the Gharial and Crocodile.

A lot of stony water courses crisscross Corbett. These boulder laden seasonal streams called '*raos*' or *sots* are a great attraction to wild animals and birds and it is here that most of the *machans*—the watch towers, have been built.

As you drive around in the forest you might chance to see two trees entwined with one another. As if one has taken hold of another. Figs sometimes take root on hosts that will eventually be overwhelmed. *Ficus*, a generic term used for trees of the fig family are 'stranglers' that sometimes start life as a small seed that germinates on the branch of the host tree and draws sustenance through air and rain. From its hold, it sends down long thin roots to the ground and finally after many years strangles the host tree. Fruit of these trees is relished by birds and animals. Park your vehicle by a fig, when in fruit and you will see various species of birds and mammals delightfully enjoying the fruit. Not always starting life as a parasite, figs are magnificent large shady trees that are universes unto themselves, providing sustenance for birds and animals alike.

Teak or *Sagon-tectona grandis* has been grown in the buffer zones by the forest department. This species is not indigenous to the area and it has resulted almost in a monoculture of the species all the way from Bijrani to Dhangari.

Above: A classic example of a host tree in the deadly embrace of a strangler.

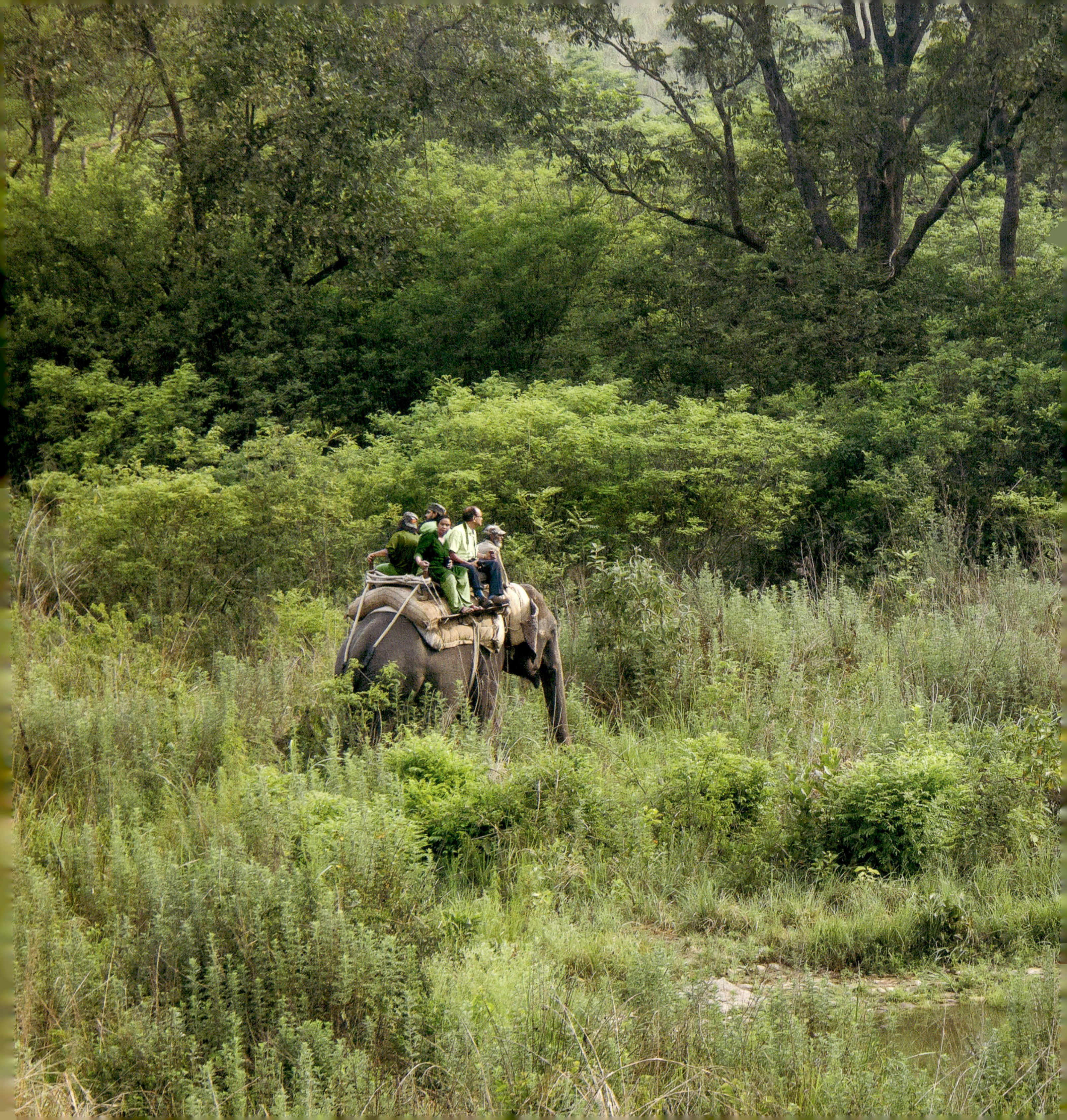

CORBETT MATRIX
—*the green grid*

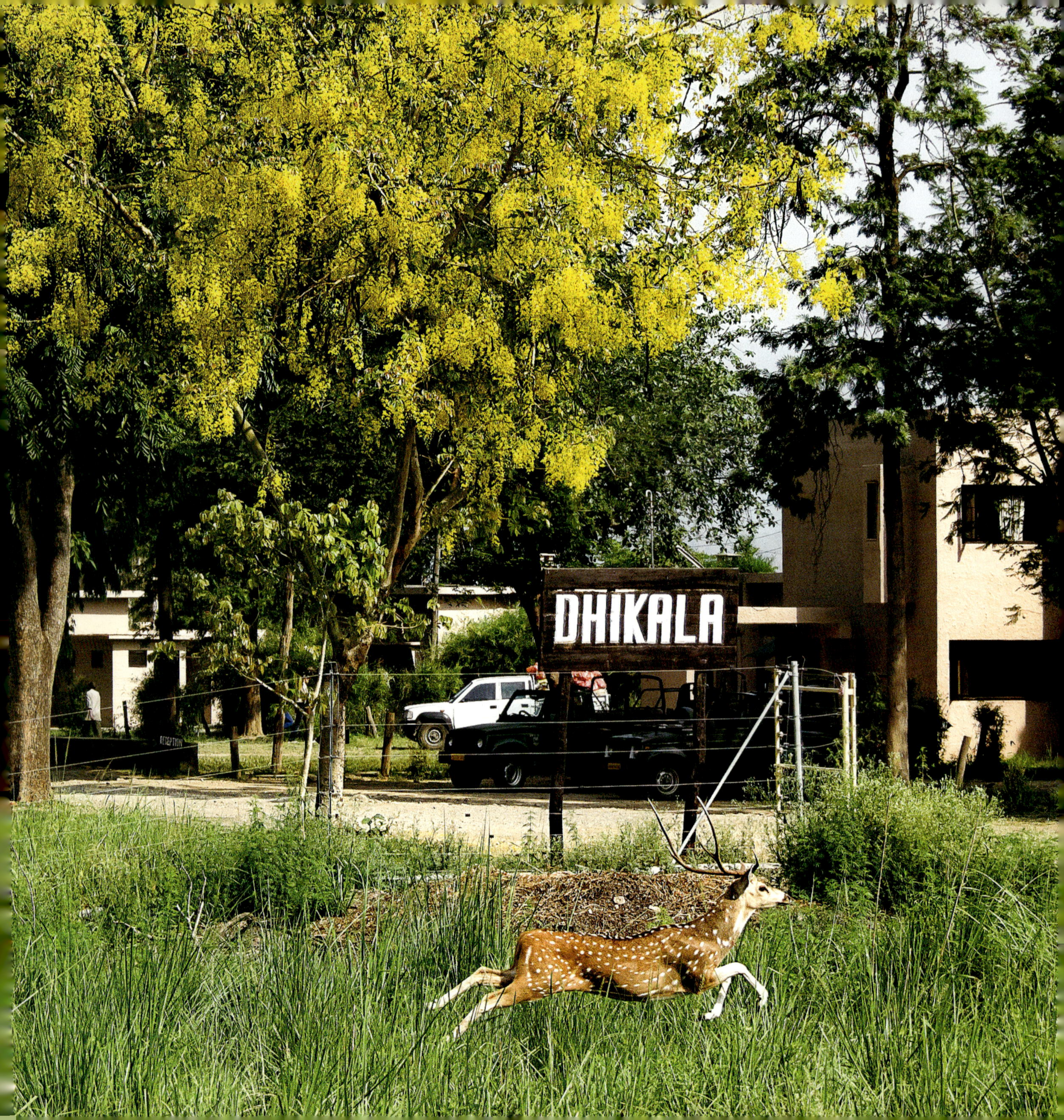
DHIKALA

CORBETT MATRIX
—the green grid

For better habitat protection and wildlife management the Corbett matrix has been divided into zones. These are Dhikala, Jhirna, Bijrani, Domunda, Sona nadi and recently, Dhela has been added towards the southern periphery of the Corbett National Park.

Dhikala

The heart of Corbett is Dhikala. A 30 km drive from the Dhangari gate takes a visitor through some of the finest wooded areas of the park. From the elevated road, one gets a bird's eye view of the majestic Ramganga river flowing below. The experience is richly rewarded by sightings of countless birds and animals. Finally, as you arrive at the great sal forest and drive through the broad fire line, you get a glimpse of the Dhikala complex. Across this distance is a diversity of terrain of hills with deep *nullahs* and the grasslands or *chaurs*. Dhikala overlooks the magnificent Ramganga just before it drains into the Kalagarh dam reservoir.

Today Dhikala is a large complex but the old Forest Rest House, where Jim Corbett used to stay is still there. The beauty of Dhikala *chaur* is an experience with very few parallels. The openness of the grassland that drops right up to the river's edge and the Sal forest on the other side gives it a grand panoramic view.

A drive into the *chaur* never fails to spring surprises. As we crisscrossed the grassland we came across a young jackal lazing in the soft grass next to his den while the mother was away. A Black Francolin sat on a termite-hill just a little distance from a flock of Blue-tailed Bee-eaters sitting right on the road. It was on the Kamarpatta road here that we came across a lone tusker in musth. Animals have right of way in the jungle, especially tuskers. Their sheer size and strength commands respect. Undoubtedly the most dangerous animal in the jungle and

Previous double-spread: An elephant safari in the Dhikala area is a great way to experience the grassland and the forest off the beaten track. Elephants can take you where the safari gypsy cannot.

Facing page: A handsome male spotted deer dashing across the main gate of Dhikala complex. Dhikala, the most favoured accommodation in Corbett is now a large complex overlooking the Ramganga river. It certainly is an ideal base to explore this wildlife rich zone.

Below: Just before you reach Dhikala complex the jungle track goes through a grand Sal forest.

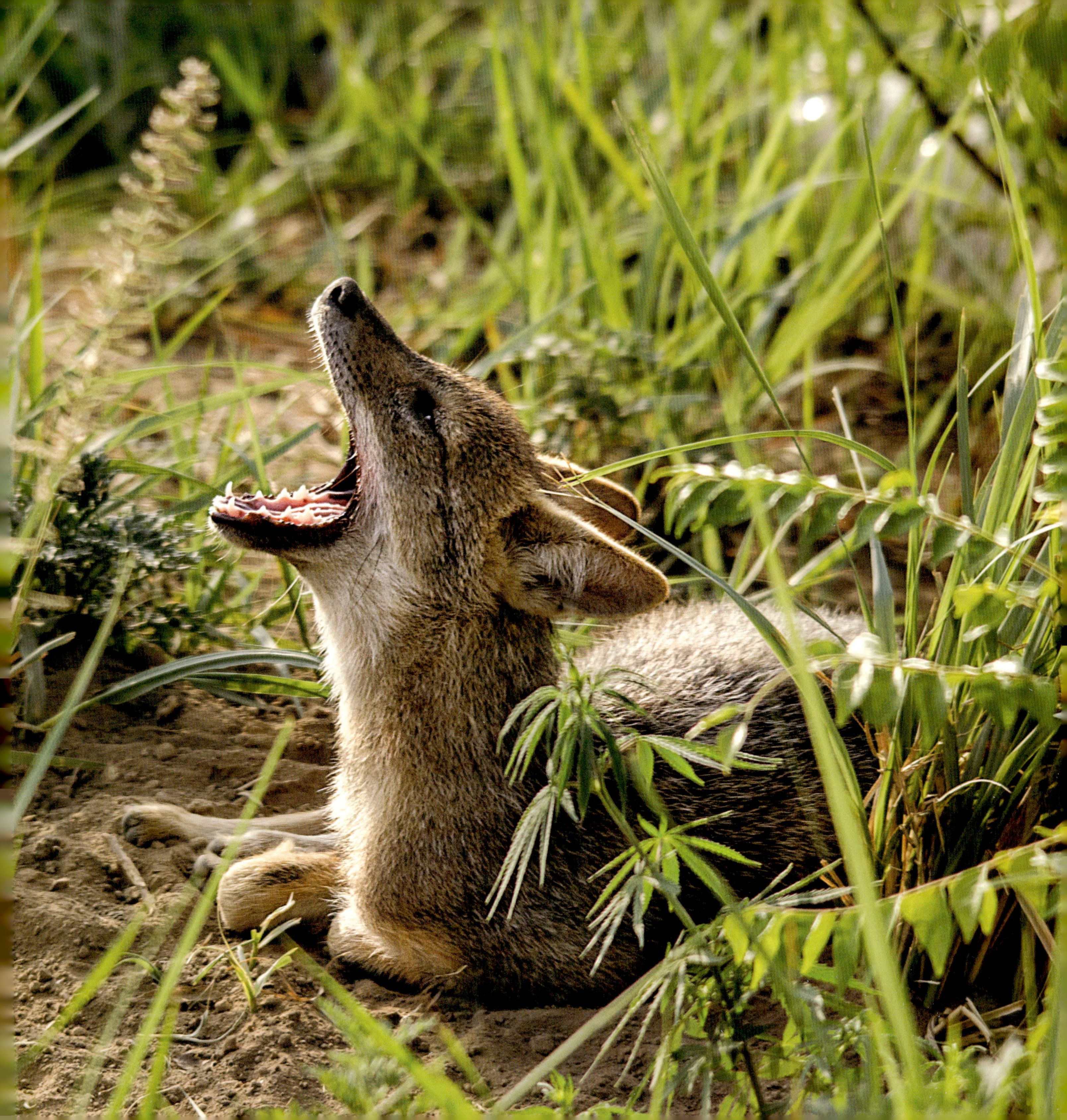

yet nothing else will get your adrenaline flowing more, than coming face to face in a close encounter with a tusker in musth. It is a condition when the temporal glands of adult male elephants become swollen and secrete a pungent smelling fluid. It is a time when the elephants become highly aggressive towards other male elephants and are actively looking for females in oestrus to mate.

The safety of the open grassland gives the Cheetal and Hog Deer clear and long visibility, and they gather in large numbers here. In early June, male bayas are busy making nests to impress the females that are highly critical of their skills and quick to reject the handiwork of a novice. In summer, a drive towards Leed Khalia at the water edge is just the place to see elephants in large numbers.

Facing page: A jackal pup lazing in the grass next to his den.

Above: Baya Weavers' nests on a tree in Dhikala chaur. Baya's prefer to make their nests on isolated trees in the grassland areas, like this one at Dhikala that is a host to their elaborate colony of hanging dwellings. It is highly entertaining to watch the males hard at work building nests to impress the females.

Left: An encounter with a tusker in musth can be a moment charged with adrenaline. Musth is a state of heightened sexual activity. The male elephants are highly aggressive at this time towards other males and are keen on proximity to females in oestrus. In this condition the temporal glands of the male elephants secrete a pungent smelling fluid that is easily discernible on observation.

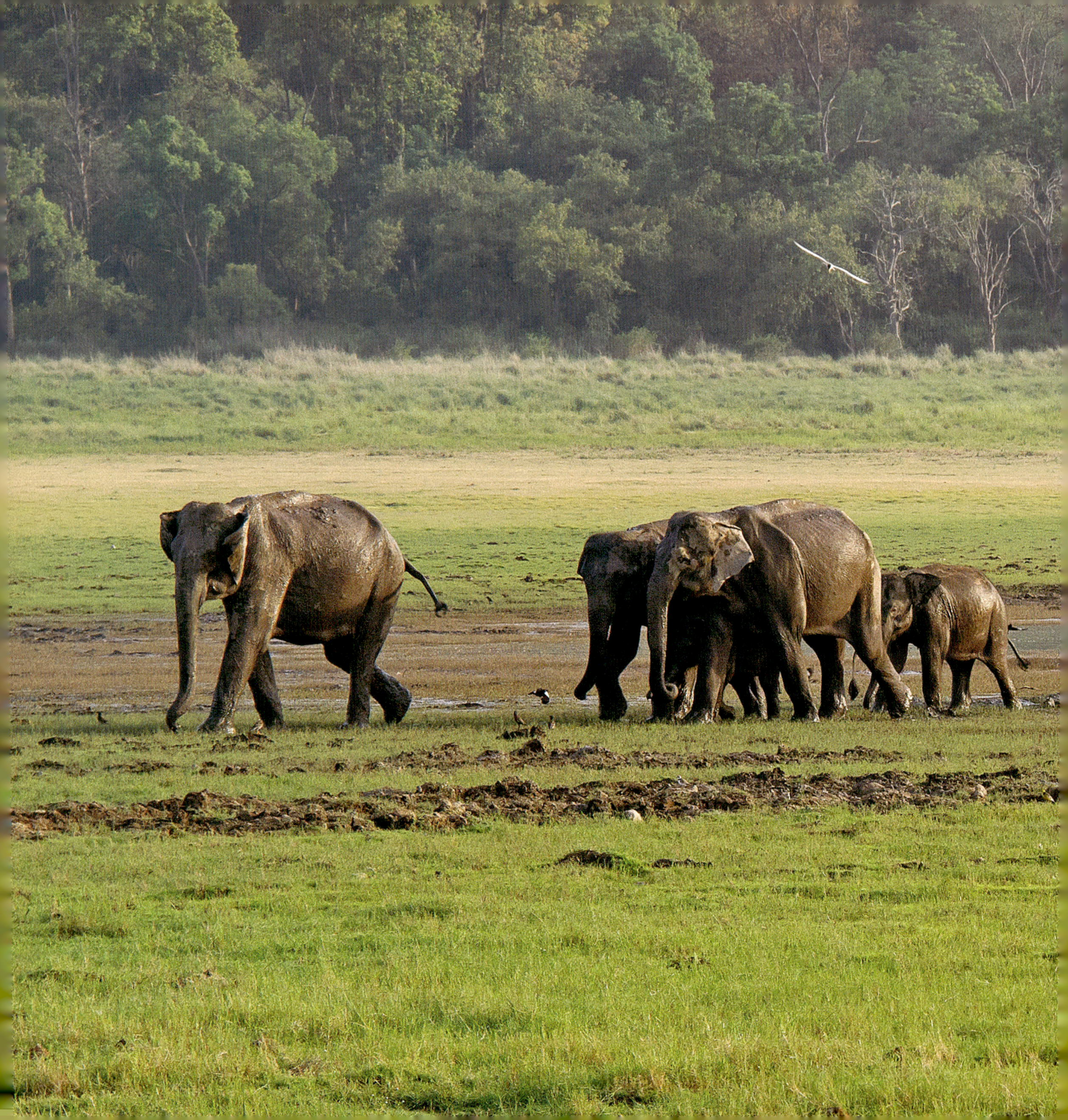

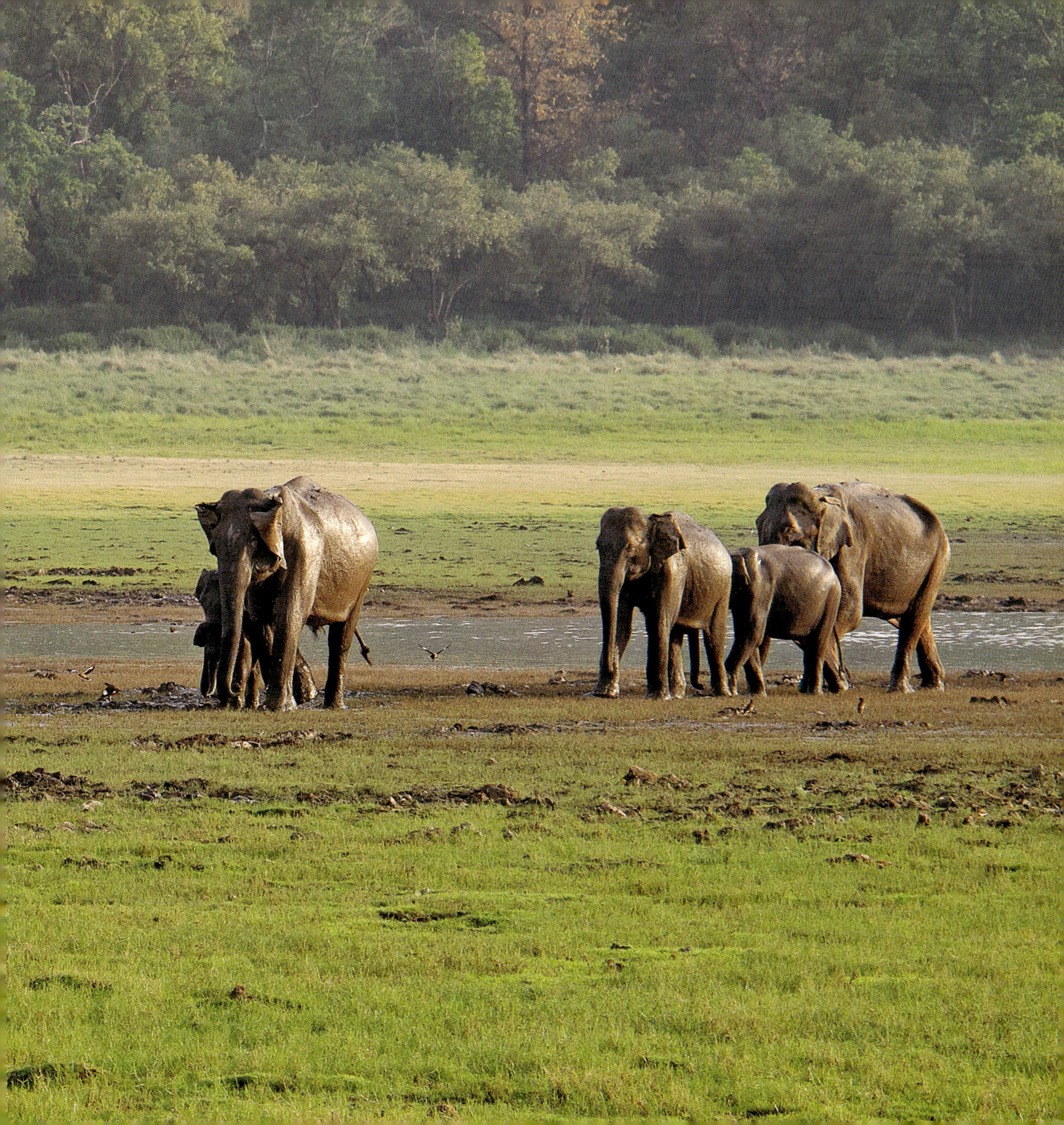

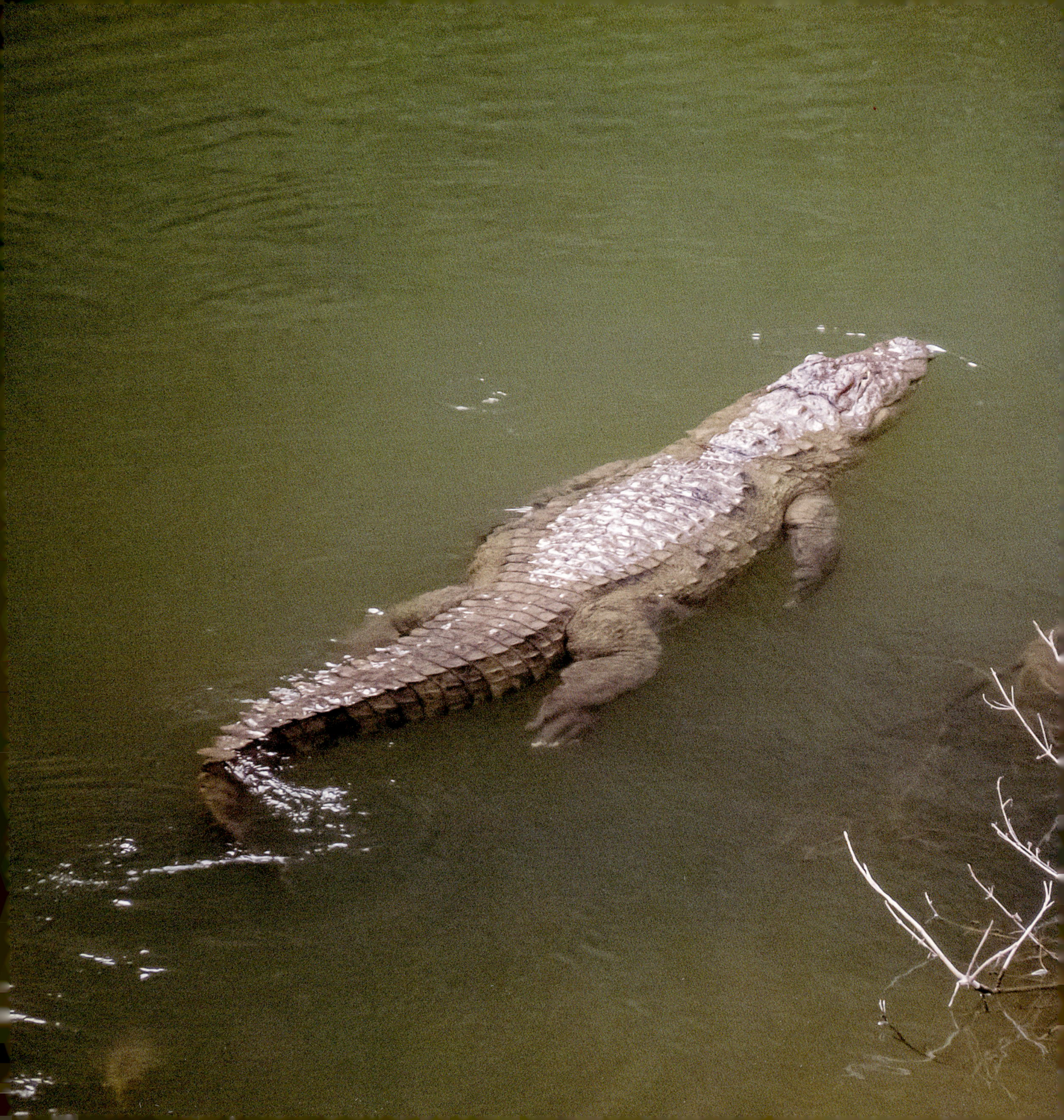

The drive from Dhangari towards Dhikala almost transports you to a time when this is how it all was before human greed and need cut down the forests squeezing the wildlife and habitats such as this to fragmented disconnected patches. The very first forest rest house on this route is Sultan, in the middle of a beautiful patch of the forest. Not many people prefer to stay here, which makes it a great place away from the crowd, ideal to enjoy the quiet and solitude of the forest. The Sajgarhi Nallah in the cool shade of the trees can always spring a surprise. Once, on our way back from a stay at Dhikala during the summer of 2015, we found a male tiger cooling off in a small water body.

Everybody vies for a stay at Dhikala. Gairal and Sarapduli are also great places to soak in the beauty of the river, the forest and the wildlife. At Saparduli and Gairal the low gurgling of the Ramganga will keep you company. While at Gairal you see a fast flowing river, frequented by many species for a cool drink of water. Champion's pool, a little drive from Gairal forest rest house, is a lovely spot to sight Gharials sunning themselves on the banks or in the waters. Off the Gairal road is High bank where tourists are allowed to disembark from their vehicles. As you look down from here, sometimes you can see Mahseer by the hundreds and Crocodiles soaking in the sun on the river banks.

Previous double-spread: A small group of elephants returning from the river still glistening with wet mud.

Facing page: A crocodile lazily swimming in the cool waters of Ramganga river.

Above: The Forest Rest House at Sultan. A stay here can spring delightful surprises of wildlife sightings.

Mota Sal

Mota Sal is a landmark in itself. A safari through Dhikala *chaur* is sure to bring you to this monument of what certainly must have been a very handsome Sal tree. In its hay days it was the tallest and the biggest Sal in the area. This botanical giant is said to have once stood at a height of 47.34 meters with a girth of 6.58 meters. It was however struck by lightning and what stands today is the mere stump of that tree, a miniscule remnant of its original self. However, still a prominent marker and a fine example of how large and grand these Sal trees are.

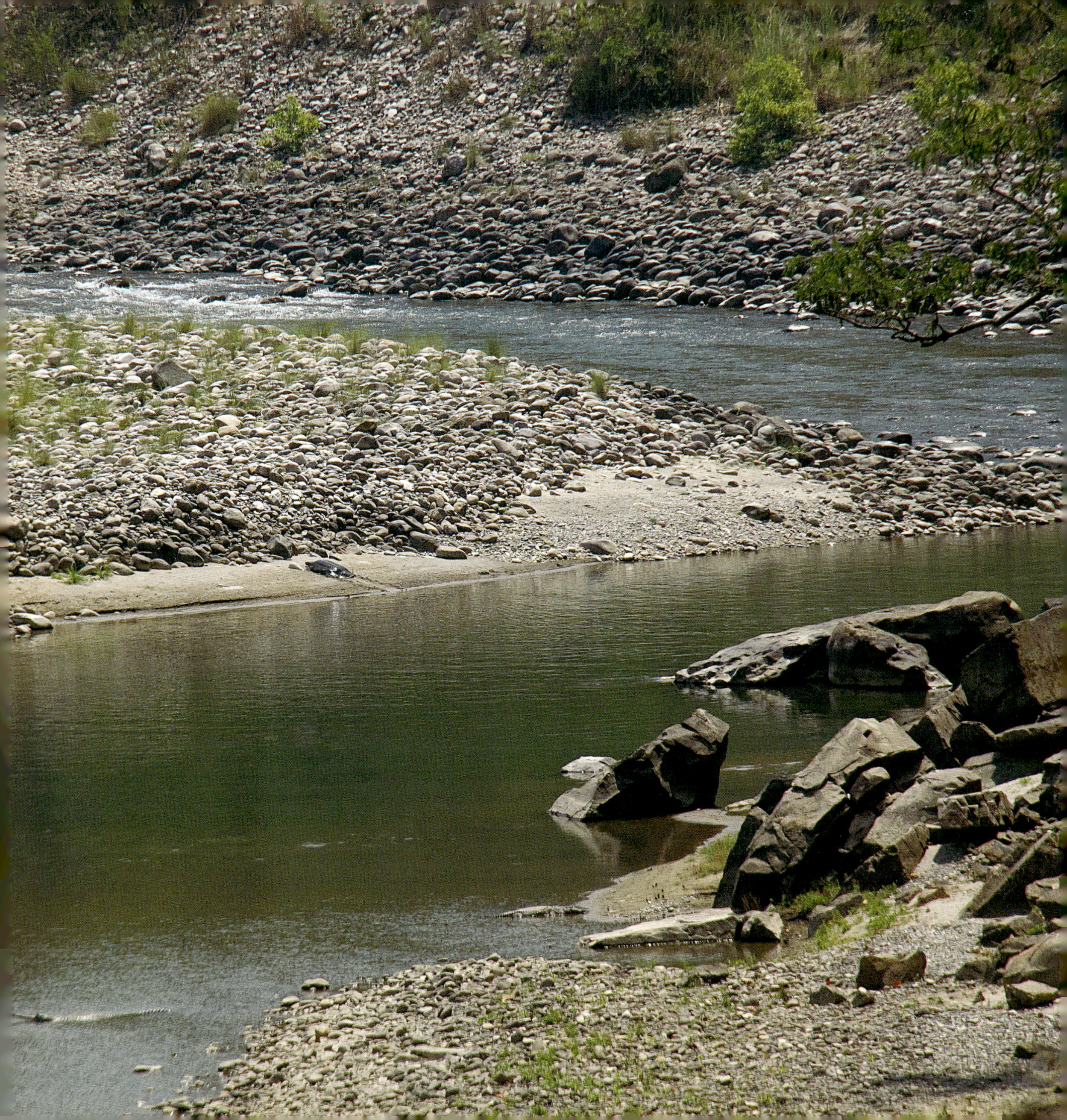

Jhirna

Jhirna towards the southern extremities of the park is a zone kept open to visitors throughout the year. Jhirna is a mix of deciduous forest, grassland and the soft sand gravel of dry seasonal streams. Even before entering we were greeted by the sight of three jackals sitting out in the adjoining fields in the wee hours of the morning. Jackals are successful hunters of rodents and are also known to scavenge on the kills of other predators.

As you try to spot animals in the undergrowth don't forget to look up at the tree tops, particularly in spring when Semul trees are in full bloom. The red waxy flowers attract a large number of birds, insects and even primates. Down in the soft sand animals leave telltale signs of their presence and you may find along with pug marks of a tiger, prints left behind by sloth bears, porcupines, jackals, civets and sometimes even the track of a snake. An experienced guide can easily decode these graphics of the forest floor for you.

The watch tower of Jhirna above the tree canopy gives an excellent aerial view. From this vantage point one can spot many species of woodland birds and photograph them at eye-level.

Facing page: A pristine view of Ramganga river from the High Bank with a Gharial and a Crocodile in the foreground; and a turtle hauling itself up the sandy river beach on the other side.

Above: Jhirna rest house. Jhirna zone is accessible throughout the year even when the other areas are closed for tourists.

Left: An Asian-barred Owl, one of the most commonly seen member of the family.

83

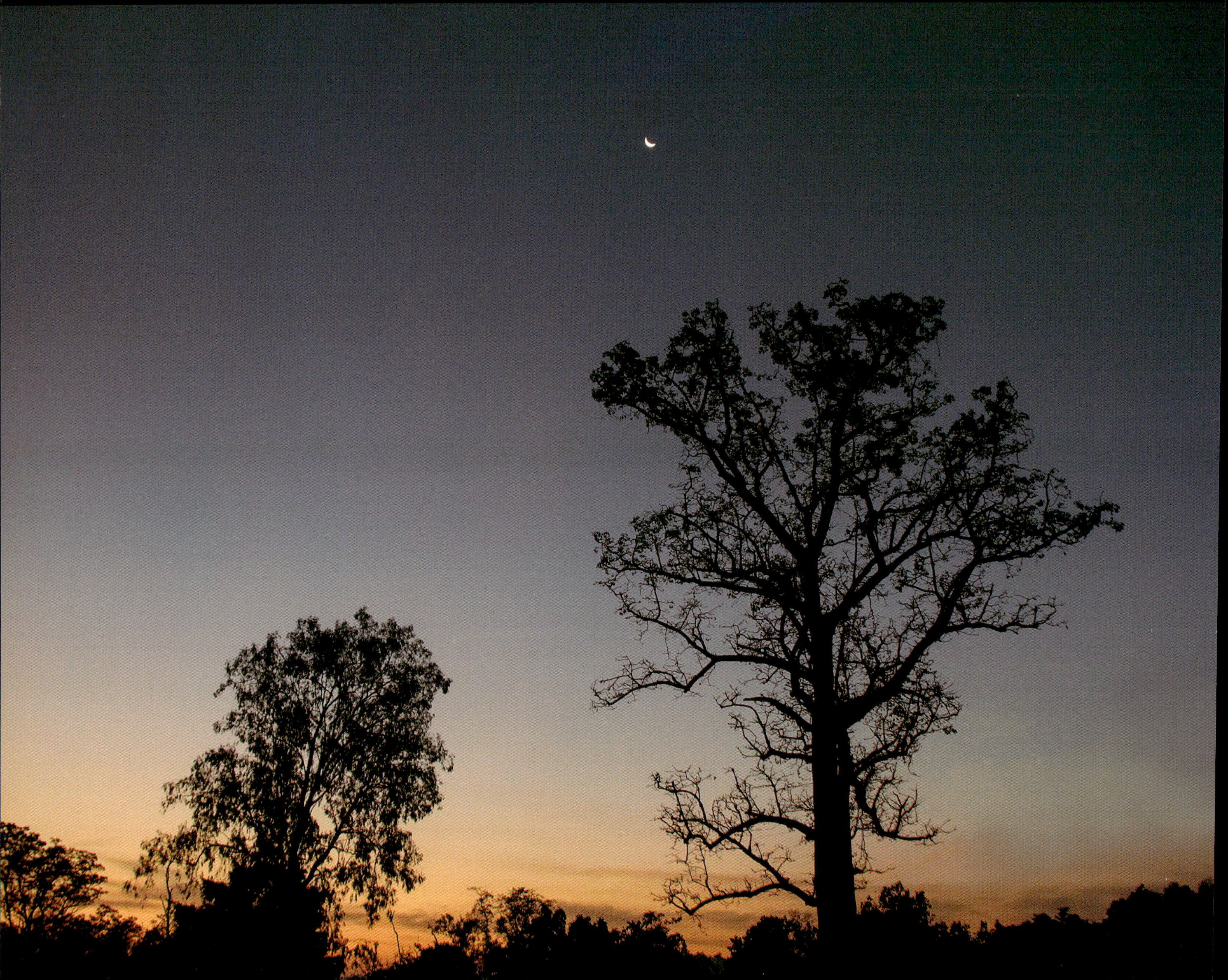

Bijrani

It was 6:30 am on a cold winter morning. Darkness was giving way to light that seemed to be a little weary of the cold and was taking its time to spread out. The moon still lazily hung in the sky as if it too was in no hurry to leave. We were rushing to our jeep ready to leave for the morning safari in the Bijrani zone.

There is always a little excitement at this point at the prospect of meeting the jungle folk waking up to usher in a new day. This is how it has always been, animals going about their business of life, foraging for food, taking care of their young, mating for the enhancement of their species. Though hard to spot, there are a hundred peering eyes and though our human eyes may fail to see them, one knows they are there. The jungle is their home and for us humans it is a new experience every time.

Bijrani lies towards the southern periphery of the park which is drier than the other zones. It is watered only by seasonal streams. In the shallow pools formed by the water, algae had been quick to grow. At this time of the year there is plenty of water, and the under growth was thick and dense in full leaf.

There was a mist rising from the water of the first stream that we crossed, giving it an almost eerie feel. Besides a stone chat in the grass and a jungle owlet settled on the branch of a tree, planning to snooze away the day after perhaps a long night, it was all still very quiet. We casually took a round of Kichaar road—the wooded part of this zone. At this time of the year when it is cold and wet, not many animals are seen here. Although the opposite is true during summers, because then this area remains cool.

The sun was now beginning to rise over the horizon as a light breeze picked up. The forest was slowly waking up as the warmth of the sun reached the ground. At Badhai *chaur* a Changeable Hawk Eagle was perched on the branch of a dry tree; its whistling call mesmerizing and melodious, kept us rooted to the spot for a great photo opportunity. Just as we crossed Badhai *chaur* and entered the forest on the other side, we stopped to photograph the lantana that had grown profusely on the side of the road.

Lantana has become a pest and noxious weed in the forests. Introduced as an ornamental plant, it threatens the native bio-diversity of forest ecosystems. It grows rapidly and chokes the native plants in their fight for sunlight and survival. However biologists have discovered that the best way to rid the land of Lantana is by cutting the main root 3-5cms below the soil at the transition zone between

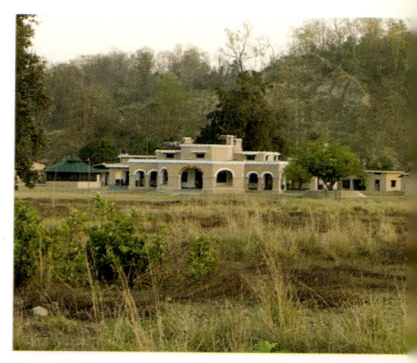

Facing page: Dawn on a cold winter morning in the Bijrani zone with the moon still visible in the sky.

Far above: Bijrani rest house. This zone was one of the shooting blocks where shikar was allowed way into the 1960's.

Above: A Jungle Owlet. These tiny birds sit so still and camouflaged among the branches that only an expert spotter can point them out.

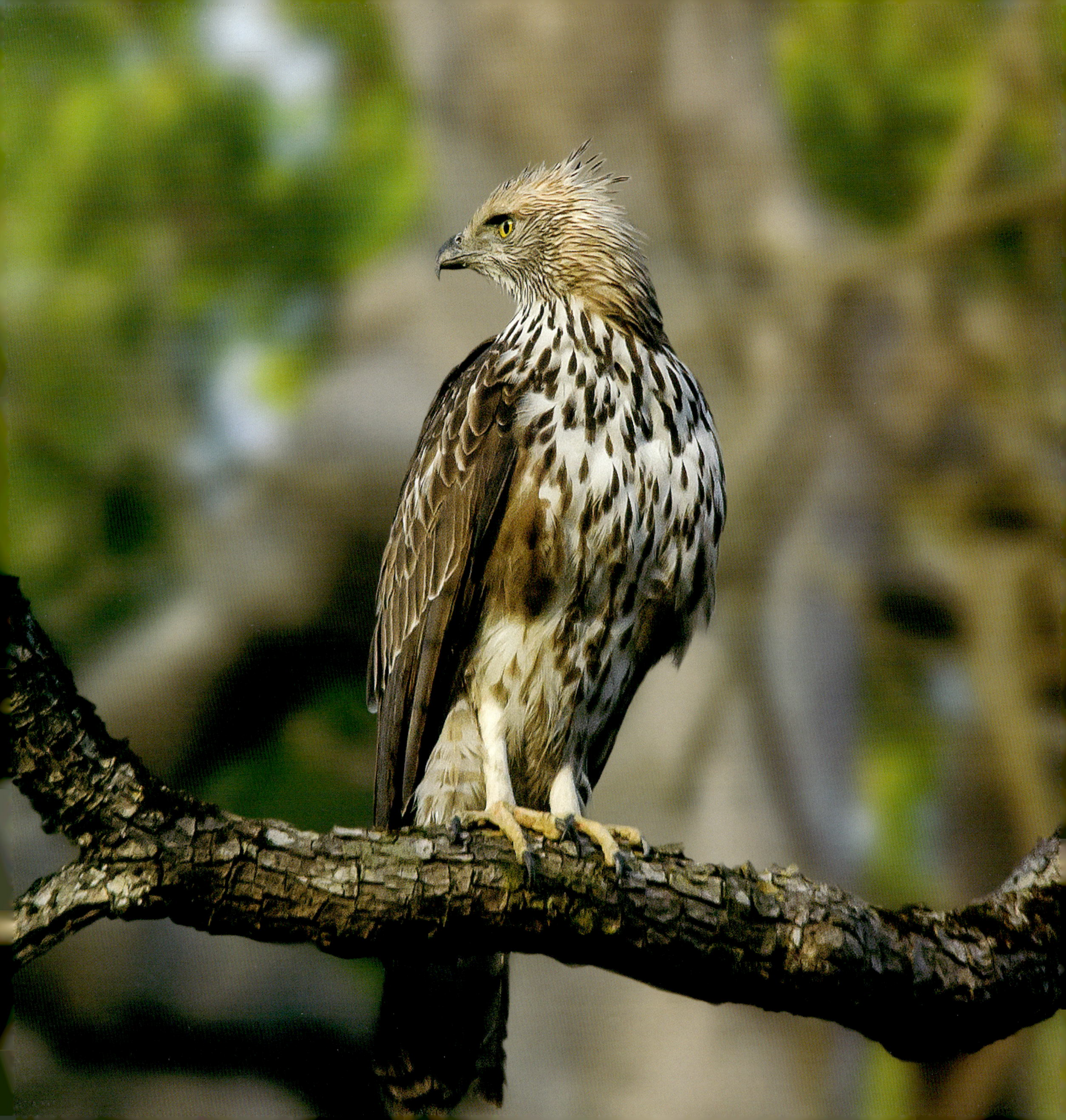

stem base and the root stock, then upturning the entire plant to ensure that this zone dries first. This prevents the plants from propagating by way of fallen shoots. These are then burnt to make way for grasses.

As we moved a few feet ahead, a full grown tigress crossed the road. She looked straight at us but neither the hum of the engine nor our presence was any sort of a deterrent as she continued to the other side. No matter how many times you see a tiger in the jungle its mere presence makes the heart race as you are filled with awe and reverence for this magnificent creature. A streamlined body built for speed and agility, a killer machine in the presence of prey, this tigress however displayed another quality, that of a caring mother, a teacher and guide to her cubs that she will lovingly nurture till they are almost two years old.

Over the years this famous tigress has been given various names. I would like to call her *Bijrani ki Rani* or queen of Bijrani. This particular tigress has mothered three litters over the years. Recently she raised four cubs, who are now almost a year and a half old. It is rare to have all the cubs reach adulthood as they are vulnerable to attacks by male tigers.

As the jeep came to a halt she had vanished into the under growth then she gave a call, we saw her cubs come to her one by one, now almost her size they were

Facing page: Changeable Hawk Eagle—a truly regal bird of Corbett. Elegant and graceful they spend much of the day perched on the branches of leafless trees from where they make short dashes to pounce on prey on the ground.

Far above: A male Peafowl framed among the bright flowers of the Latana bushes. In the Corbett landscape Lantana has become a noxious and invasive weed that chokes the native plants in their fight for sunlight. However biologists have discovered that by cutting the main root 3-5 cms below the soil at the transition zone between stem base and the root stock and upturning the entire plant (above) prevents it from propagating.

Left: A relaxed tigress busy grooming herself on the forest road.

87

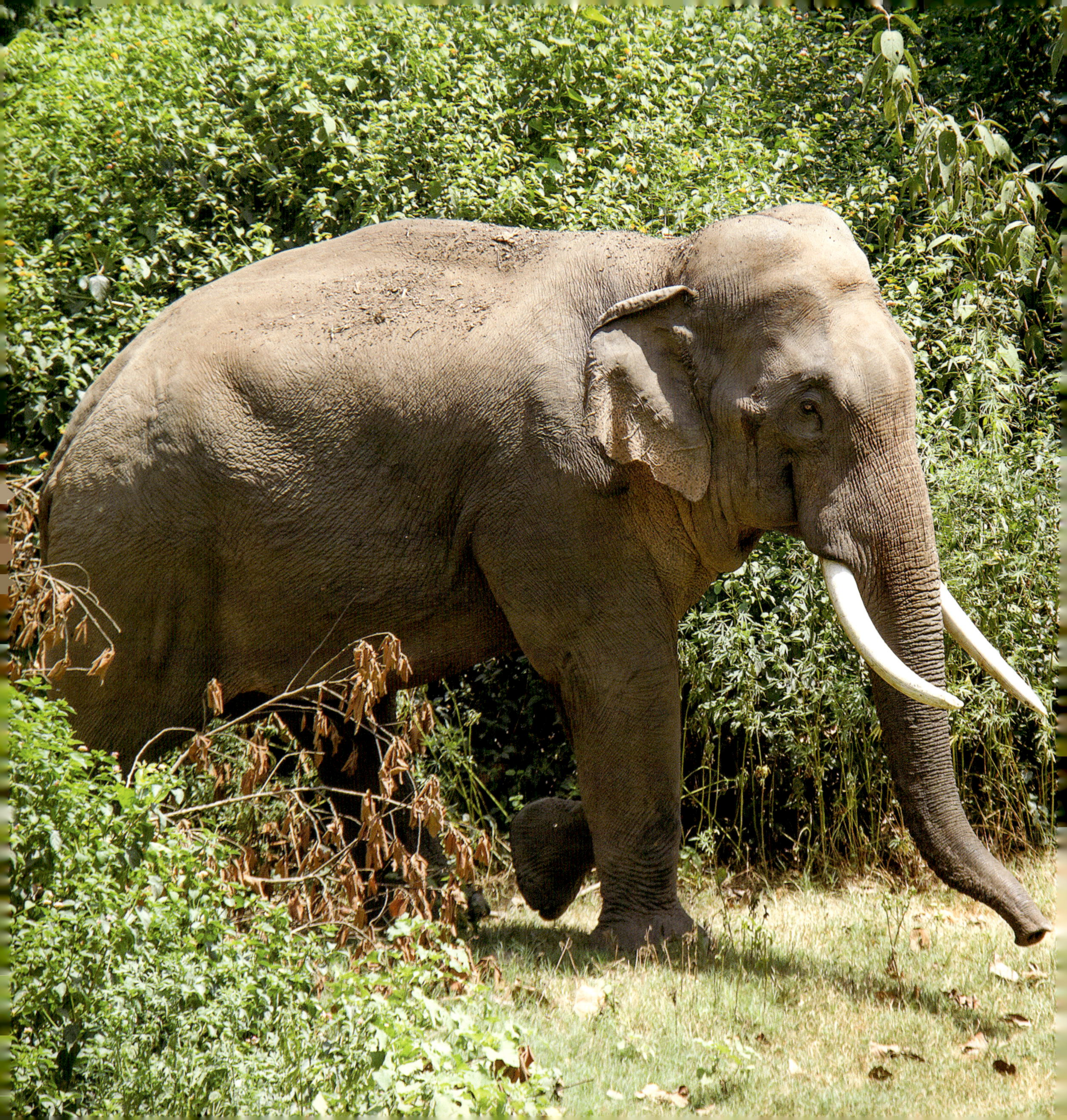

a little apprehensive of our presence. Well camouflaged in the under growth their stripes catching the light of the sun in fiery orange hues. The tigers stayed with us for over ten minutes, till they finally disappeared into the forest to live another day and hopefully a lifetime in the secure haven of Corbett National Park.

Sonanadi and Domunda

It was June 2011. The overcast sky was waiting to usher in the rain, a light fog hung in the dense under growth. It was early dawn but the sun was still hidden behind the clouds. Huddled in the jeep, we strained to see any movement. On taking a turn on a dirt road towards Kakri dang, we came face to face with a group of elephants some fifteen feet from us. This is Halduparao in the Sona nadi wildlife sanctuary, part of the Corbett Tiger Reserve. It's famous for elephant sightings. However during a visit in February 2015, while there was plenty evidence of elephant presence by way of fresh dung, peeled barks and broken branches, we had no sighting. In this game of hide and seek, there is really no predicting whether one will be able to see anything or not. It is a matter of sheer providence to be exactly at the same spot, at the same time, as a wild animal. One considers oneself blessed to have a sighting. More so, because elephant population is dynamic and elephant herds are constantly on the move.

Halduparao purely on conjecture gets its name from the abundance of Haldu trees in the area. The tree is so named because its wood is of a rich yellow colour

Facing page: A tusker in musth coming in for a quick drink of water at the water hole. Elephants have a keen sense of smell and this tusker emerged from the foliage very noiselessly, smelt us out and did not stay in the vicinity for long.

Above: Stripes of a tiger camouflage them so well in the light and shade patterns of undergrowth that sometimes in spite of their bright colour, it becomes difficult to spot them even at close quarters.

Below left: The bark of a tree stripped by an elephant. Elephants eat all sorts of plant matter; they will eat twigs, bark, grass, whole plants, fruits and roots.

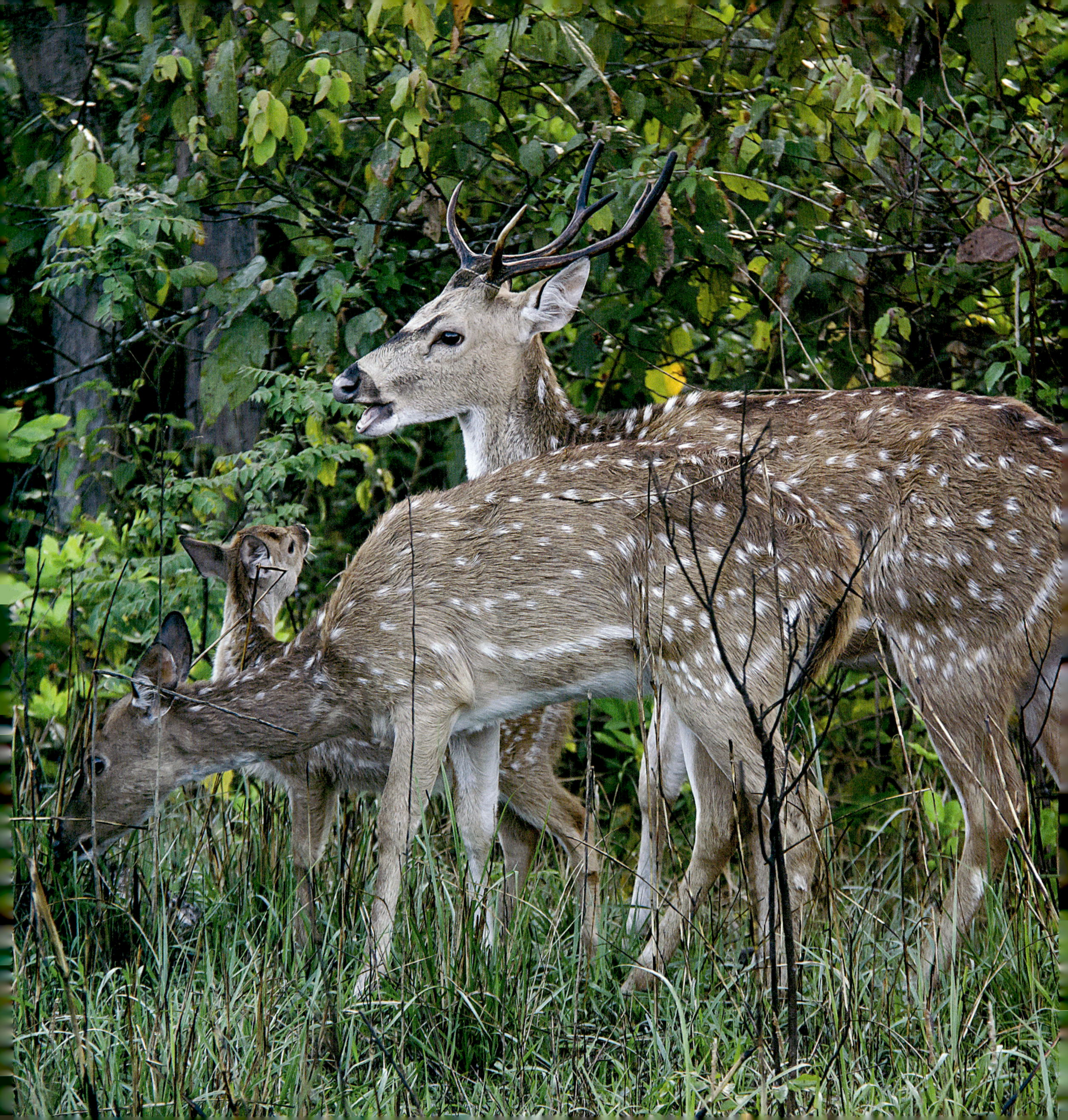

like turmeric powder, which is called *Haldi* in Hindi. Haldu are tall trees with a commanding presence in the forest and are at their blossoming best in winters.

To get to Halduparao you drive along the northern periphery of the reserve via Kotdwar and Dugadda. As you reach the Vatanvasa gate, you leave the metal road behind and take the dirt track into the forest. After fording the first stream, the road starts to climb up a narrow cliff, with a sheer drop down to the right into a gorge cut out by the river Palain, an important tributary of the Ramganga. The Palain enters the park from the North and meets with the Ramganga about 3 km north of the reservoir.

A descent back to the valley floor and you are faced by another expanse of water. Wild life abounds in this area, wild boar rummage in the streams and herds of spotted deer stand alert to the sounds and smells of the forest.

A light drizzle was no deterrent to the drive. In the full spate of monsoons, this area is cut off and is impossible to reach by foot let alone by jeep. The guards, who keep vigil here throughout the year, have to depend on elephants as their only means of transport for provisions and medical emergencies.

The rest house at Halduparao has a watch tower at the edge of a cliff, a great place to hang out in the mornings and observe the life on the river-bed below during the day. A solar fence is all that stands between you and the wild forest beyond, which is rife with calls of sambar, monkeys and maybe even a tiger. A haven for the shutter bugs, there is never a dull moment between the excitement of spotting something and the stories told by the guards, you are kept on your toes least you miss out on the action.

Facing page: A Cheetal family—stag, doe and fawn. Cheetal are found in large numbers in Corbett and form the main prey base of the larger predators.

Above: The Halduparao Forest Rest House was built in 1892. It has a watch tower on the edge of a cliff overlooking the river and the forest beyond. A lot of animals can be spotted from here as they come for a drink of water or searching for food, like these otters (below left) spotted while hunting for a 'fishy' meal.

91

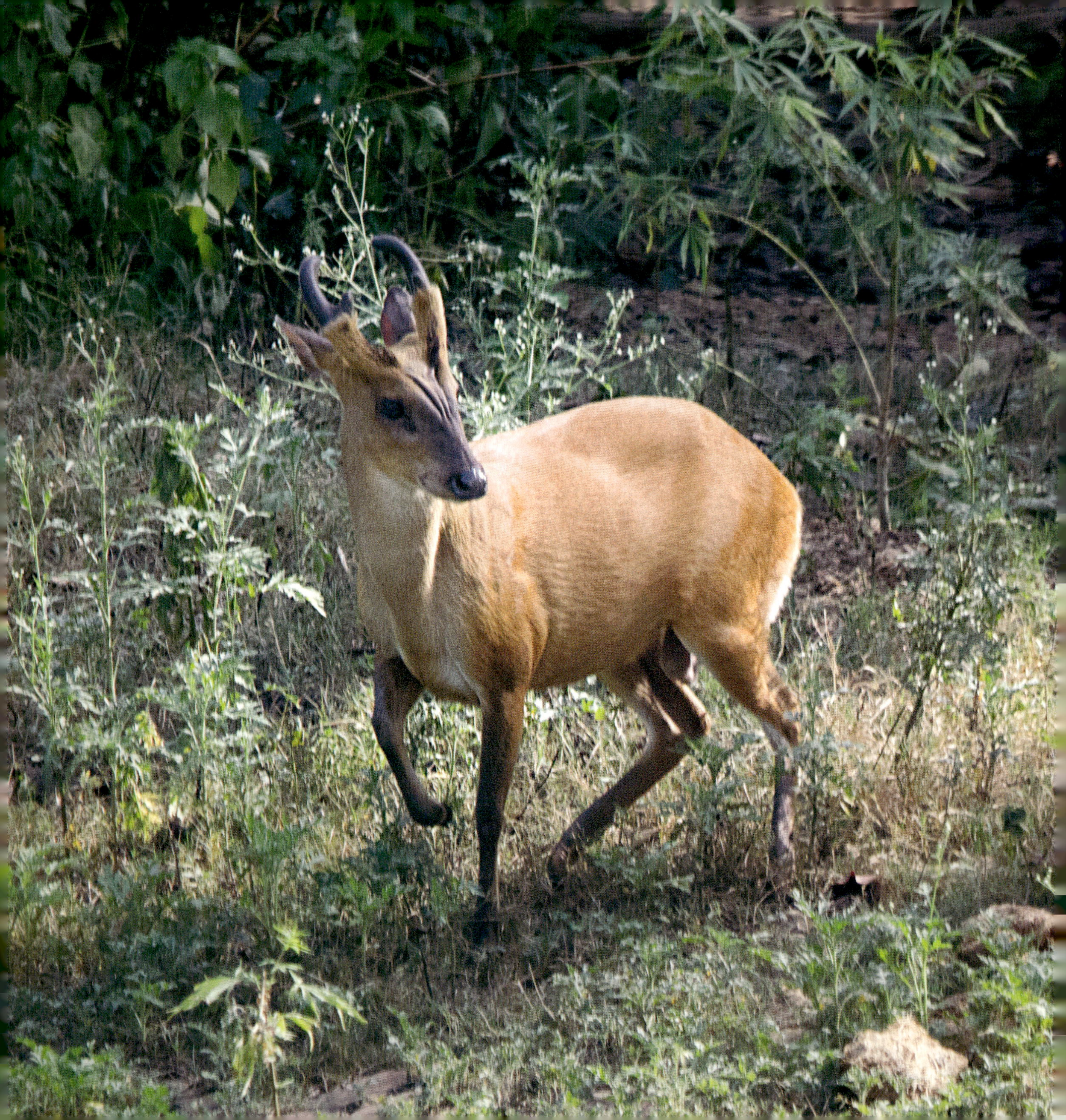

On retracing steps back to the metal road, a short drive brought us to Kanda, the highest point in Corbett National Park at a height of 3,397 feet. The forest rest house here is over a century old and the very same one in which Jim Corbett stayed in May 1933 while in pursuit of the man-eating tiger of Kanda. It has two rooms with a common sitting area. Worth a mention here is that these rest houses being in the remotest parts of the forest offer only basic amenities. One has to carry all provisions. Utensils are usually available and one can request the caretaker to cook for you. The rooms are clean but very basic with no electricity or provision for warm water.

Kanda gives you a 180 degree view of the plains and the reservoir. On a clear day the Dhikala *chaur* is easily visible from here. Earlier one could drive from Kanda to Dhikala. But this road was closed after it faced extensive damage during the 2010 rains. A look at the old visitor's log reveals the wealth of wild life that existed in this area, which unfortunately has seen a steady decline over the years. This is leopard country; if you are lucky you might just see one. Sambar, Ghoral and Barking Deer walk right up to the grounds surrounding the rest house. The value of the Tiger Reserve cannot be underestimated when it comes to bird life.

As you descend the slopes one can drive to Lohachaur, of course with proper permits in hand. While this can be done from both sides, a safer bet is to do it from the Durga Devi gate as most of the wood bridges get washed away during the monsoons.

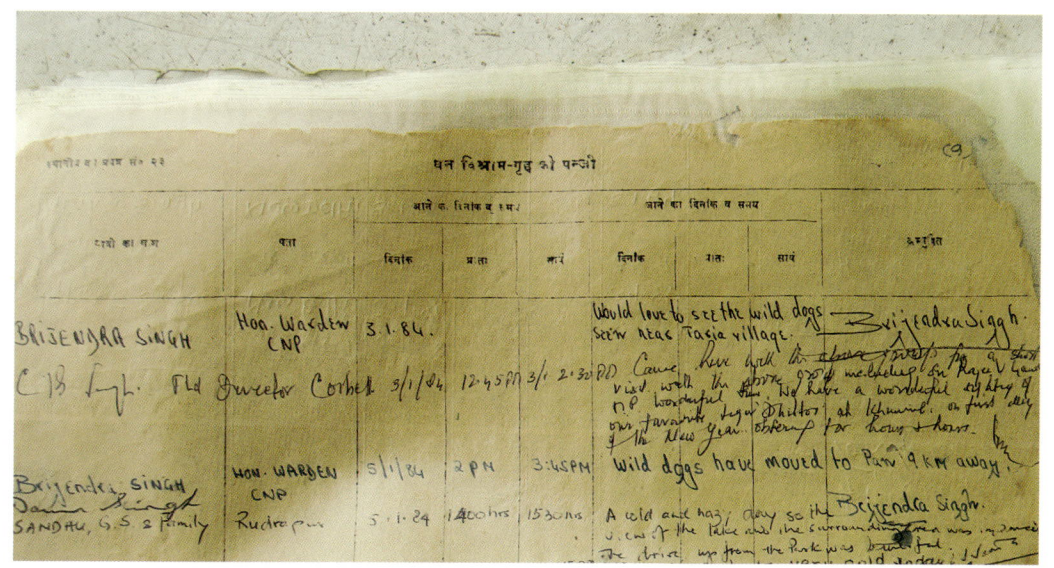

Facing page: Barking Deer is one of the most vocal of alarm systems against tigers in the jungle. They are found in the hilly as well as grassland areas.

Top: Kanda Forest Rest House

Above: A pair of Sambar females stand alert.

Left: The visitors log book at Kanda records the sighting of Dholes—the Indian Wild Dogs in Corbett in 1984.

93

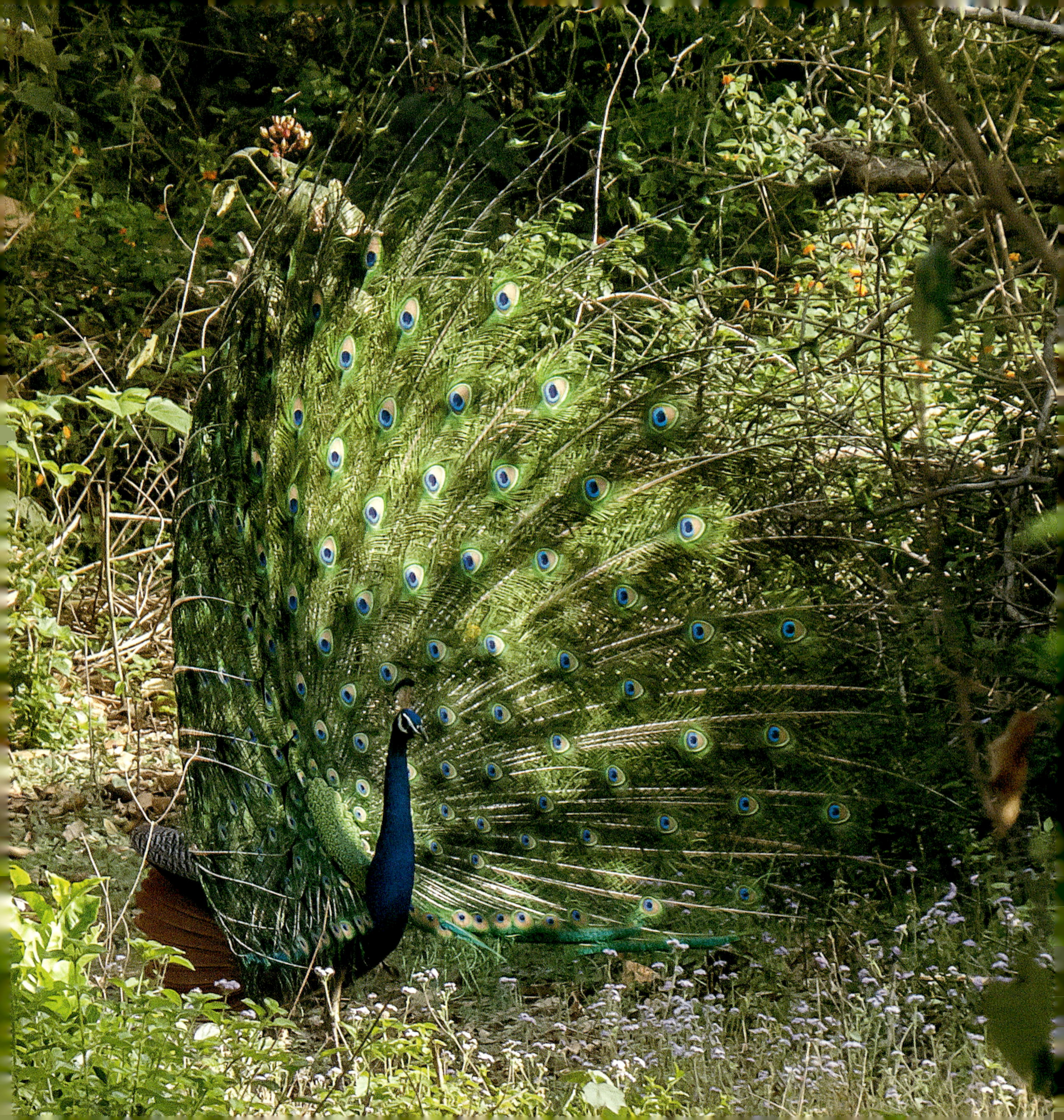

When driving in from Durga Devi you are in Domunda zone. It is here that the Ramganga meets with the Mandal, a small stream during most of the year till monsoon turns it into a torrential river. Mandal river forms the north-eastern boundary of Corbett National Park. It flows for 32 km before joining the Ramganga on the western bank at the head of the Patlidun at Domunda, a little distance above Gairal. It is an important breeding ground for the Mahseer. On crossing the little bridge some way ahead we caught up with a tusker heading in a direction away from us. Just as we stopped the jeep so did he, trunk raised high, testing the air. This is a no move situation; you let the animal decide and accordingly proceed or retreat. He soon gauged we were no real threat and carried on his way. We saw him again crossing the river. Lohachaur also offers some excellent birding opportunities.

This is hilly terrain that is very different from Dhikala. If you happen to be here in March-April, the reds of the Kosam trees in new leaf foliage are hard to miss.

Dhela

This newly added zone is fast recovering under the umbrella of protection. A deeper look reveals how promising this area is. It has a rich bird life. Sighting Spotted Deer and Wild Boar is common and with a little luck one might even spot a leopard, elephants and jackals. I even came across pug marks of a tiger in the area.

Here at Laldhang *chaur* one can see the grassland reclaiming the once cultivated land. The site of the village by the same name is now slowly reverting back to a state of wild. An old village temple and some parts of the school building are the only remnants of its past still standing in the middle of this fast changing landscape. Peafowl are plenty in this area, perhaps residents from the times when Laldhang village was inhabited. Though the animals here are yet weary of humans, in a few years this added zone will prove to be a great buffer between the forest and the villages beyond.

Facing page: During the monsoon season, Peafowl males put up a resplendent show to woo females.

In the newly added Dhela zone, Cheetal (top) on a jungle track; a Wild Boar (above) dashing across the forest road.

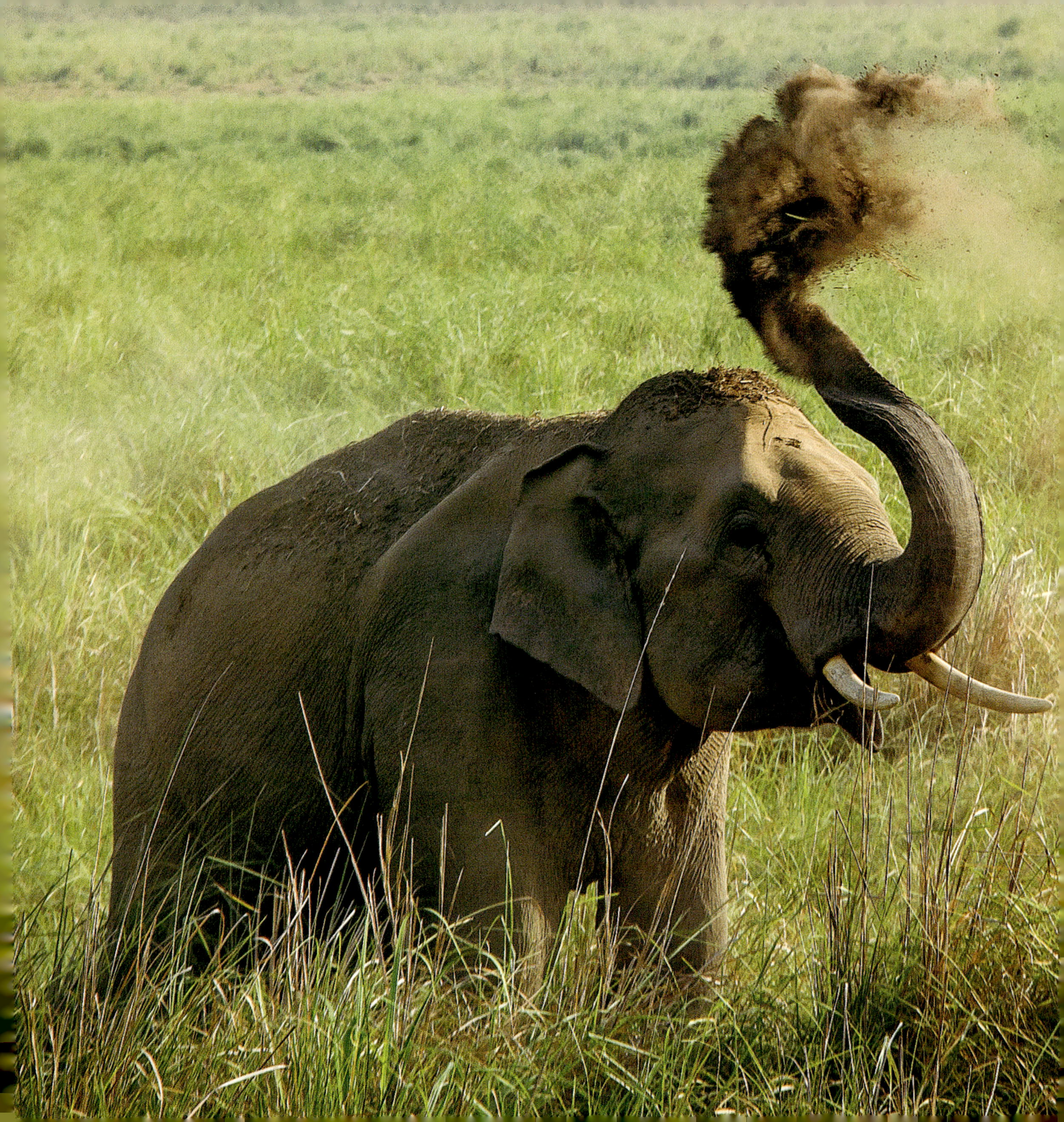

THE MEGA FAUNA OF CORBETT
—*gems of the green vault*

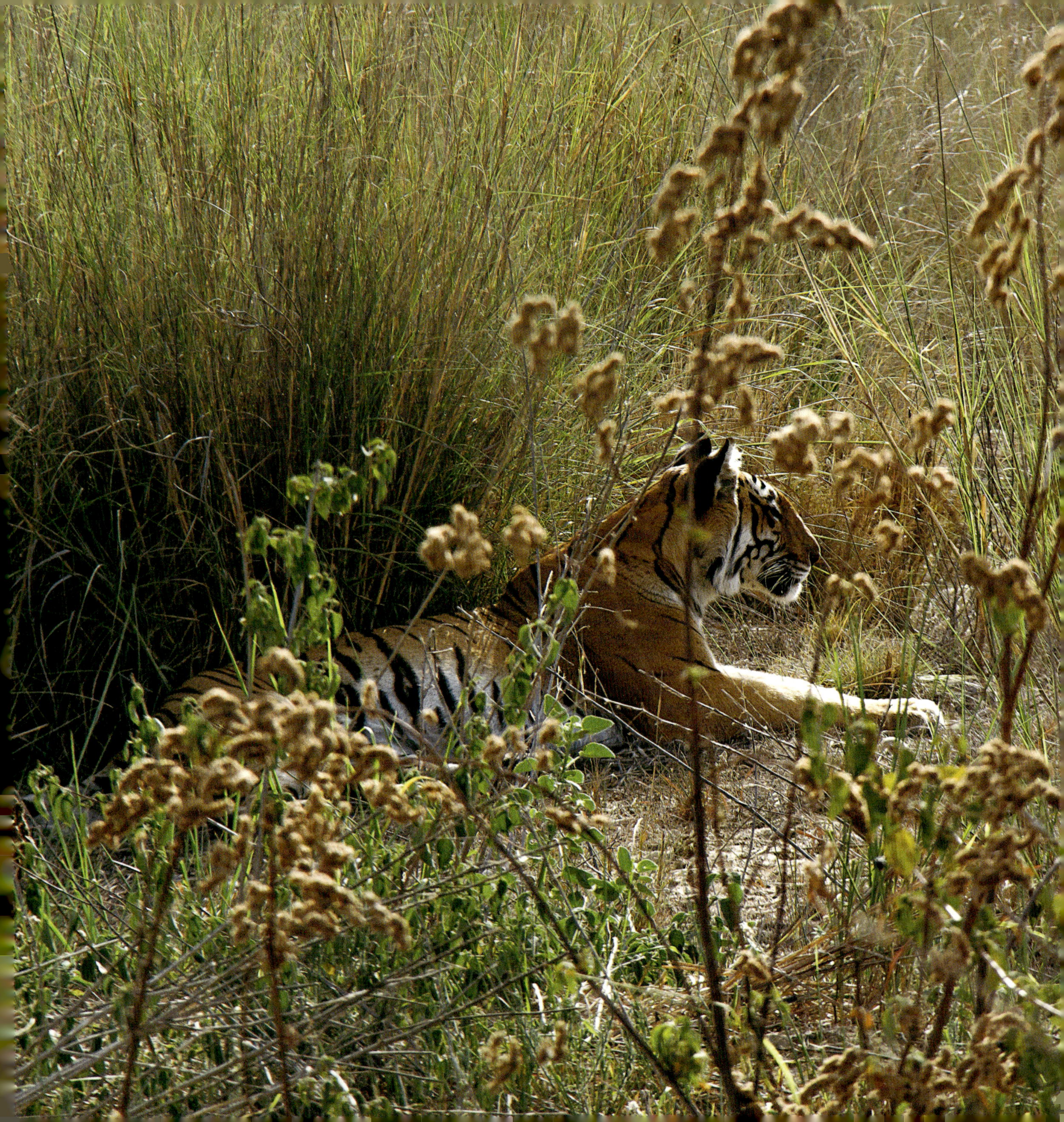

THE MEGA FAUNA OF CORBETT

—gems of the green vault

Corbett National Park is a landscape blessed with wooded hills, closed canopy forests, rich undergrowth, rivers, streams, floodplains and grasslands. Within this protected landscape many species of mega fauna thrive in habitats ideally suited to their existence. The mosaic of Corbett's varied landscape is truly reflected in the kaleidoscope of its dominating species. There are woodland stalkers, mega herbivores, tree dwellers, fresh water giants and critically endangered river residents.

Bengal Tiger (*Panthera tigris tigris*)

At the apex of its faunal pyramid stands the most majestic of all big cats—Bengal Tiger (*Panthera tigris tigris*). Every year thousands of visitors make a bee-line to Corbett to get a glimpse of its 'star with stripes'. The rewarding sighting is never without a thrilling story etched in memory for life.

The Spotted Deer or Cheetal were nervous. Every muscle in their body was taut, necks strained to limit to grasp the slightest of sound or smell that would reveal the predator lurking somewhere nearby. Their alarm calls let us in on the fact that there was indeed a tiger in the vicinity. The tiger was motionless, skillfully camouflaged somewhere in the undergrowth, certainly crouching and waiting for the opportune moment. Then like a flash of lightening he was out of cover and in hot pursuit. There was an instant stampede and within seconds the deer herd dispersed in all directions and each one got away. The tiger stood straining from the exertion for a moment and then silently walked away, a shadow that melted back into the jungle.

Solitary by nature, tigers stalk and ambush prey. They can move very quietly and their stripes help them to remain unseen to a great extent. They usually target

Previous double-spread: A young tusker in the Dhikala grassland enjoying a sand-bath.

Facing page: A well camouflaged tigress relaxes in the shade of tall grass. Resident tigers are well versed with the topography of their home range and use the landscape to their advantage while hunting.

Facing page: Tigers love water and during summers spend a lot of time in the shallow pools and streams to cool off. This tigress with her coat still glistening wet, had just emerged from a dip in the water.

Below: An artist's impression of Panthera zdanskyi, *based on skull fragments of an extinct relative of modern day tiger. These oldest remains were found in northwest China, suggesting the origins of the tiger lineage in that region.*

the weak or an older member of the prey group; there is little chance that the targeted animal will outrun them. Although tigers can produce a short burst of great speed, they cannot sustain it for long because their body temperatures rise alarmingly. It is for this reason that a tiger tries to get as close to the prey as possible before making a dash for it.

There is no way that we can peep into the mind of a tiger when he decides to make a kill but observations suggest that they use a lot of intelligence and strategy in arriving at a decision. Hunting behaviour also varies from individual to individual. There have been cases when a particular tiger chooses a place which provides little escape route to the prey. In some cases tigers have also been known to use a water-body to cut off or slow down the escape. But broad estimates suggest that in spite of all the strength, speed and planning, the success rate of a tiger making a kill varies between five and ten percent of all attempts. Let us not forget that resident tigers are very well versed with the topography of their home range and use the landscape to their advantage. The transient, usually young males in search of new territories do not have this edge when they roam into domains of others.

Tiger trail

It is now well established that modern tigers (*Panthera tigris*) share a common ancestry with long extinct Sabre-tooth Tigers. But where exactly did the big cats of our times evolve, remains a topic of debate among the scientists.

Believers of the Siberian theory feel that tigers evolved some 2.4 million years ago on the fringes of Arctic in Siberia or Northern Asia. With the advancing ice sheet they moved southward into modern Manchuria and China and while moving further split into different groups moving into India, South-East Asia, Malaysia, Burma, Indonesia or Java, Sumatra and Bali.

The advocates of the Asian theory feel that the big cat evolved in eastern Asia and Chinese tiger is its original form. It has a more primitive skull shape than the other subspecies and has continued living in its area of origin. Modern Chinese tiger's shortened cranium and particularly noticeable close-set forward-facing eyes are proof of its primitive lineage. These scientists believe about 2 million years ago tigers split into two groups. The first proceeded towards northerly direction to south-west Asia and further up to Russia and the modern Siberian tiger is the offshoot of this stock. The second group moved in south-easterly direction up to India and Indonesia and their further westward movement was halted by the Caspian Sea.

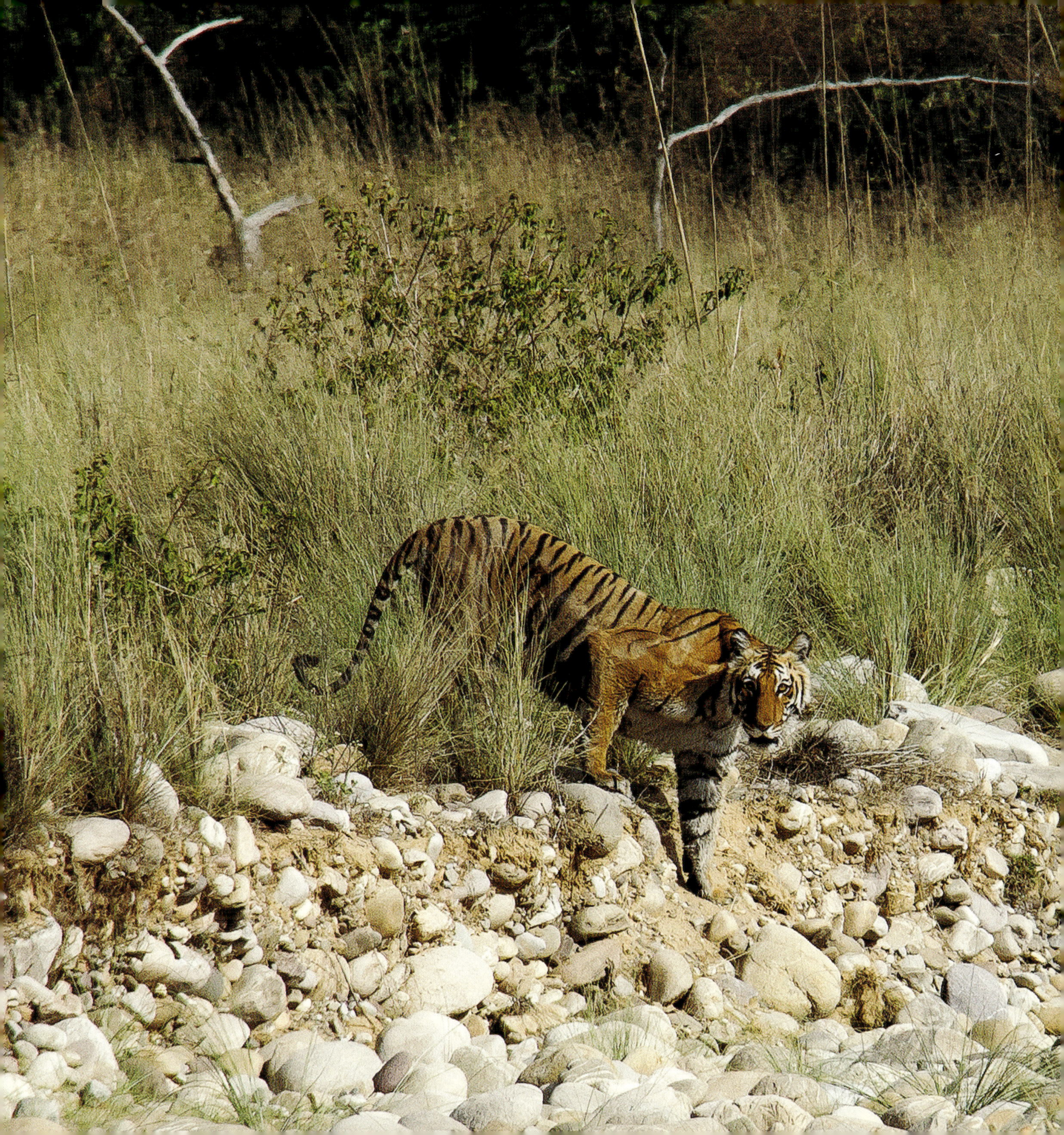

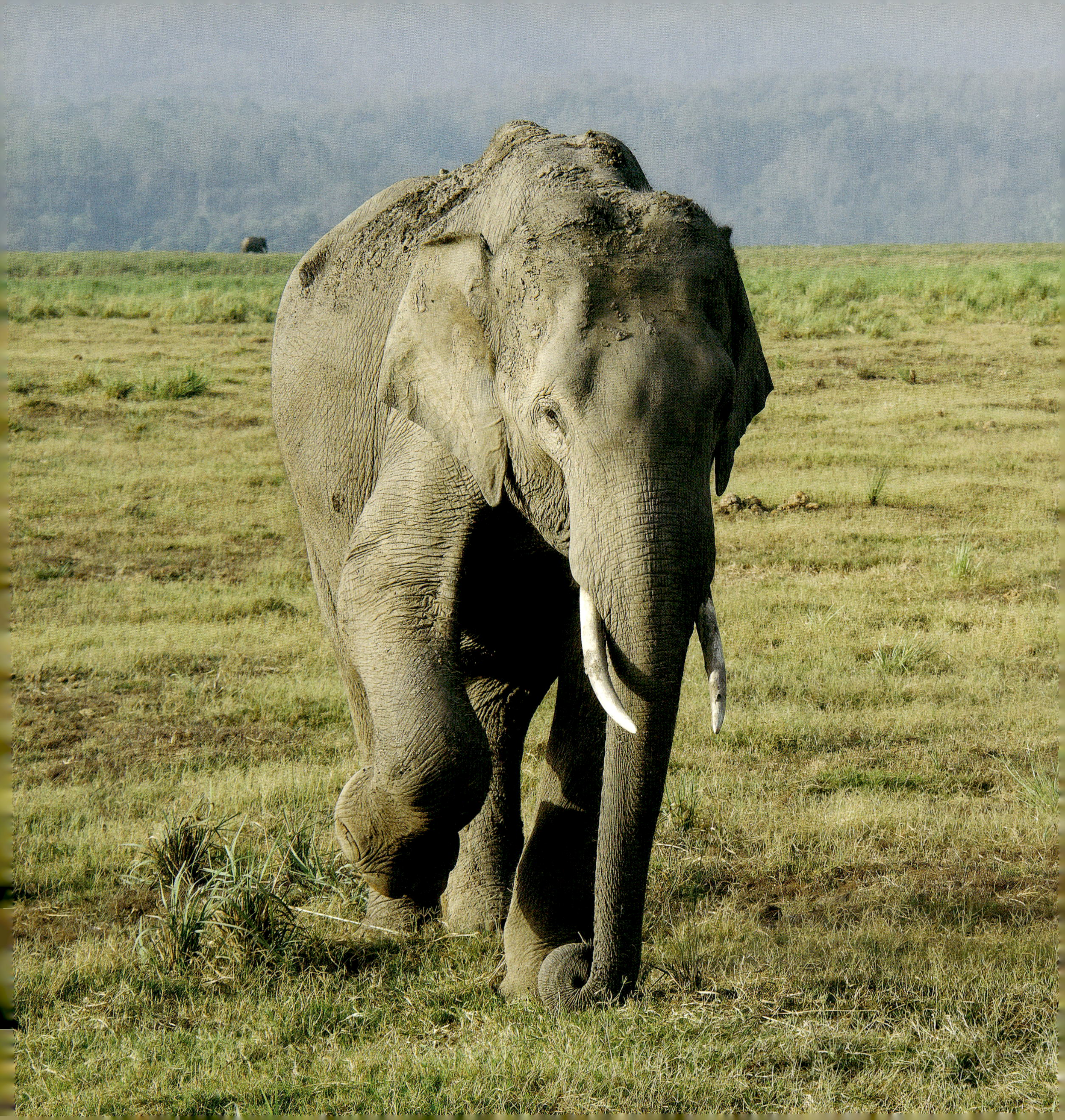

Sambar and Cheetal form their main prey base, but tigers are not averse to taking down Wild Boar and even young elephants, of course not without caution. Wild Boars are tough animals with thick layers of fat and not easy to bring down. The males have sharp tusks and can cause much injury to the predator. Younger members of the elephant herd are fiercely protected by the elders.

It is well known that although one of the most difficult animals to deal with, porcupines do tempt big cats. An encounter with the prickly mass can be a pretty nasty one as they reverse and present their hind to the predator and a bite is bound to embed their quills in the animal of threat. Yet many a tiger have been seen to make the extra effort to kill one. There is always a risk of injury involved as their quills often get embedded in the paws and mouth area of the tigers. The odds make one wonder why tigers put themselves in harm's way for a measly snack. The answer probably lies in the fact that Porcupine meat is rather tasty and hard to resist.

The stripes of a tiger are as individualistic as our finger prints, no two are the same. Corbett is one of the last few havens for this National Animal of India— a heritage we inherited and must preserve for future generations.

Asian Elephant (*Elephas maximus*)

Fossil evidence suggests that the predecessor of modern day elephants appeared on the face of the earth at the same time as the mammoths. The African Elephant (*Loxodonta*), Asian Elephants and the mammoths all originated in Africa about 3-5 million years ago. Fossil remains signal a period of time when mammalian dispersal between Africa and Eurasia remained less restricted than today. *Loxodonta* remained in Africa, *Elephas Maximus* moved into Asia and Europe.

Observing groups of elephants on the Dhikala *chaur* in their natural habitat is always a privilege. Elephants are highly social animals and have strong familial ties not very different from ours. Sitting in a jeep, a short distance from a herd of elephants at the Dhikala *chaur*, one calf in particular in that group caught my eye. I was highly amused to see his antics as he teasingly bullied another adolescent elephant who patiently let him have his way. It was just like a little boy troubling his older sibling in whose care he had been left. Elephant females are very protective of their young, whether their own or belonging to other females of the herd. Aunts, nieces and older cousins all pitch in to take care of the very young.

The Asian Elephant *Elephas Maximus* is the largest land animal in India. A large bull may grow as tall as 3 meters at the shoulders (10 feet) and can weigh up

Facing page: Elephants will go about their business of feeding and browsing in the grasslands without paying much attention to human presence. However if they don't fancy your presence, a raised foot and spread out ears are a warning before a charge.

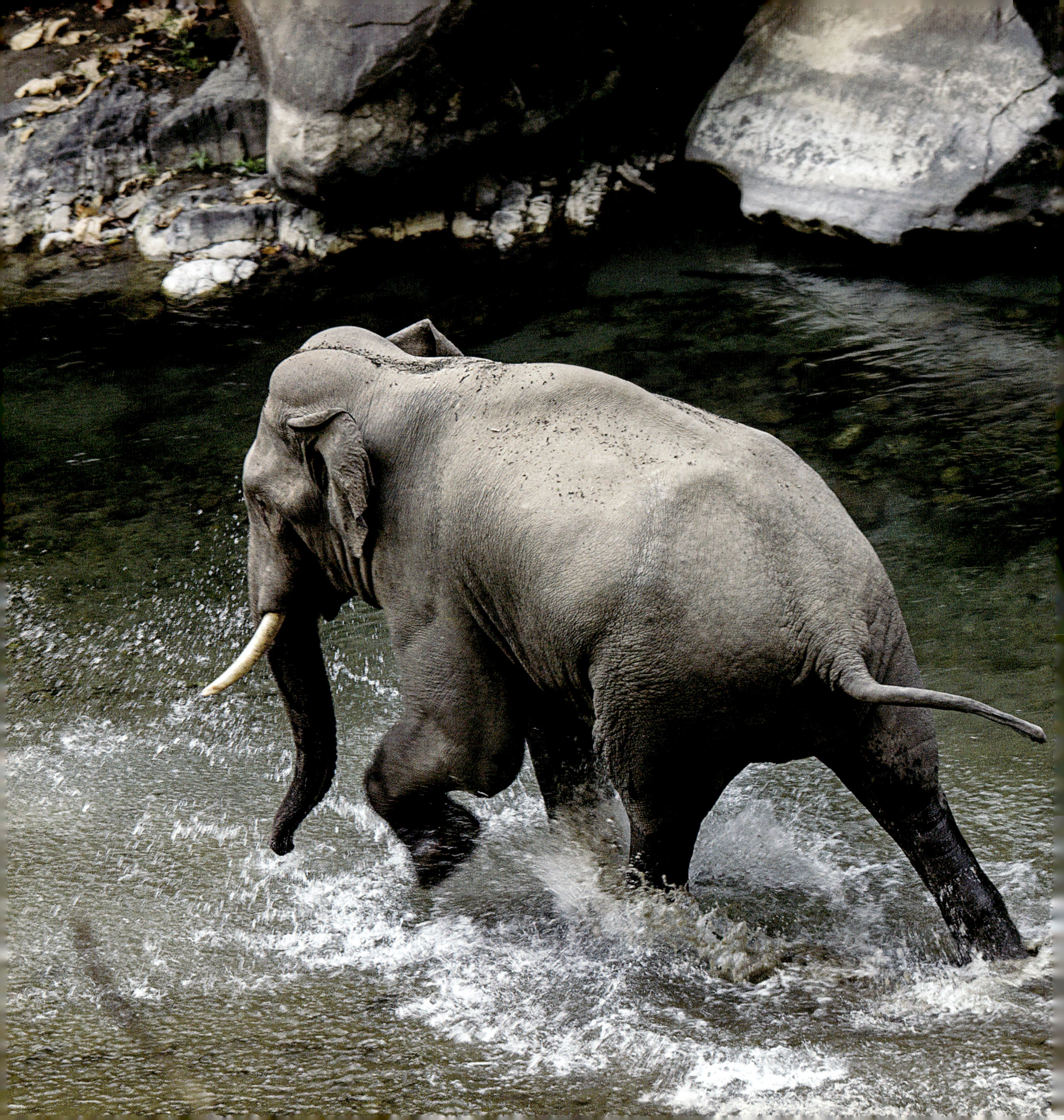

to 5,400 kg. The average adult female is around 2.6 meters (8 feet–8 feet 6 inch) and 3,300 kg in weight. Being large in size, elephants require a large quantity of food on a daily basis. Elephants can eat a varied kind of plant matter like twigs, bark, grass, fruits and roots. Unlike deer, that are partial to fresh grass, elephants can feed on coarse grass as well. Elephants make huge demands on their environment as they eat a lot and feed almost continuously. An adult average size elephant can eat up to 240 kg of fresh plant material over an 18 hour day. For this reason they have to keep moving, migration allows the vegetation to grow back and the habitat to regenerate. Elephants move across traditional tracts or corridors from one habitat to another and return, once the natural cycle has brought back the vegetation.

Elephants are indicators of the health of a habitat; a degraded habitat cannot sustain elephants. Being an apex species the presence of elephants shows a thriving ecosystem where the water is plenty and soil conditions are good. A habitat good for elephants is therefore also good for other grass dependent herbivores.

Elephants are highly intelligent animals and have long term memories, a great indicator of that is their seasonal migration from one habitat to another along the same routes. Captive elephants have been known to recognize and follow up to 40 commands. Elephants have strong family bonds and are known to exhibit grief, humour, compassion and companionship. When an elephant dies they stay with the deceased for a long time caressing and smelling it with their trunks.

When they leave they do so reluctantly. When different groups meet there is a palpable excitement in the air as they greet each other with entwined trunks; the young are almost playful.

Facing page: This giant tusker was chasing away another male across the river.

Below: Elephants can be very playful and observing them one can almost see a game unfolding like this calf nudging and gently pushing the other adolescent elephant.

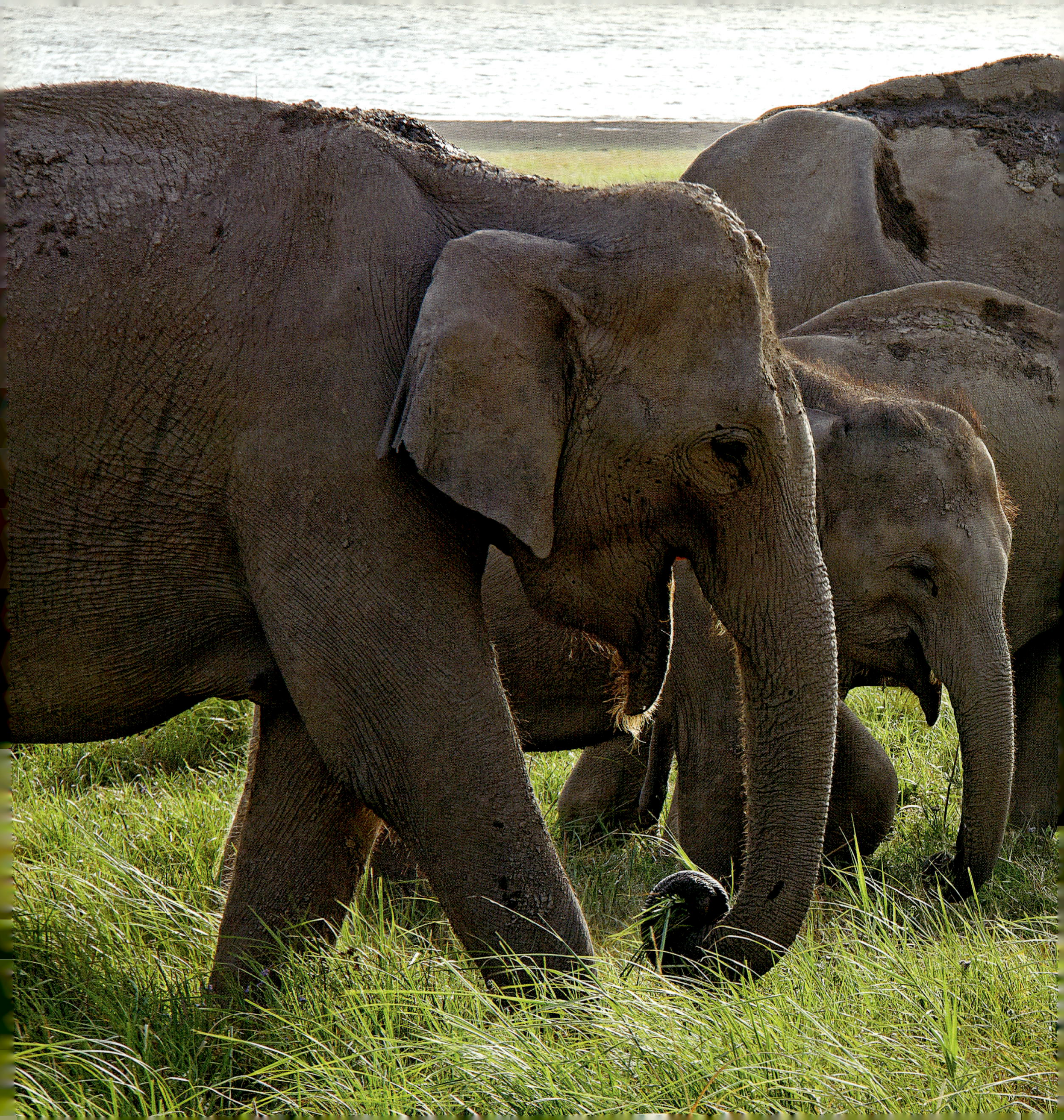

A group of elephants on the Dhikala chaur. Elephants spend a large part of the day eating thus making huge demands on the environment. As a result they need to keep migrating in search of food which also gives a chance to the vegetation to grow back.

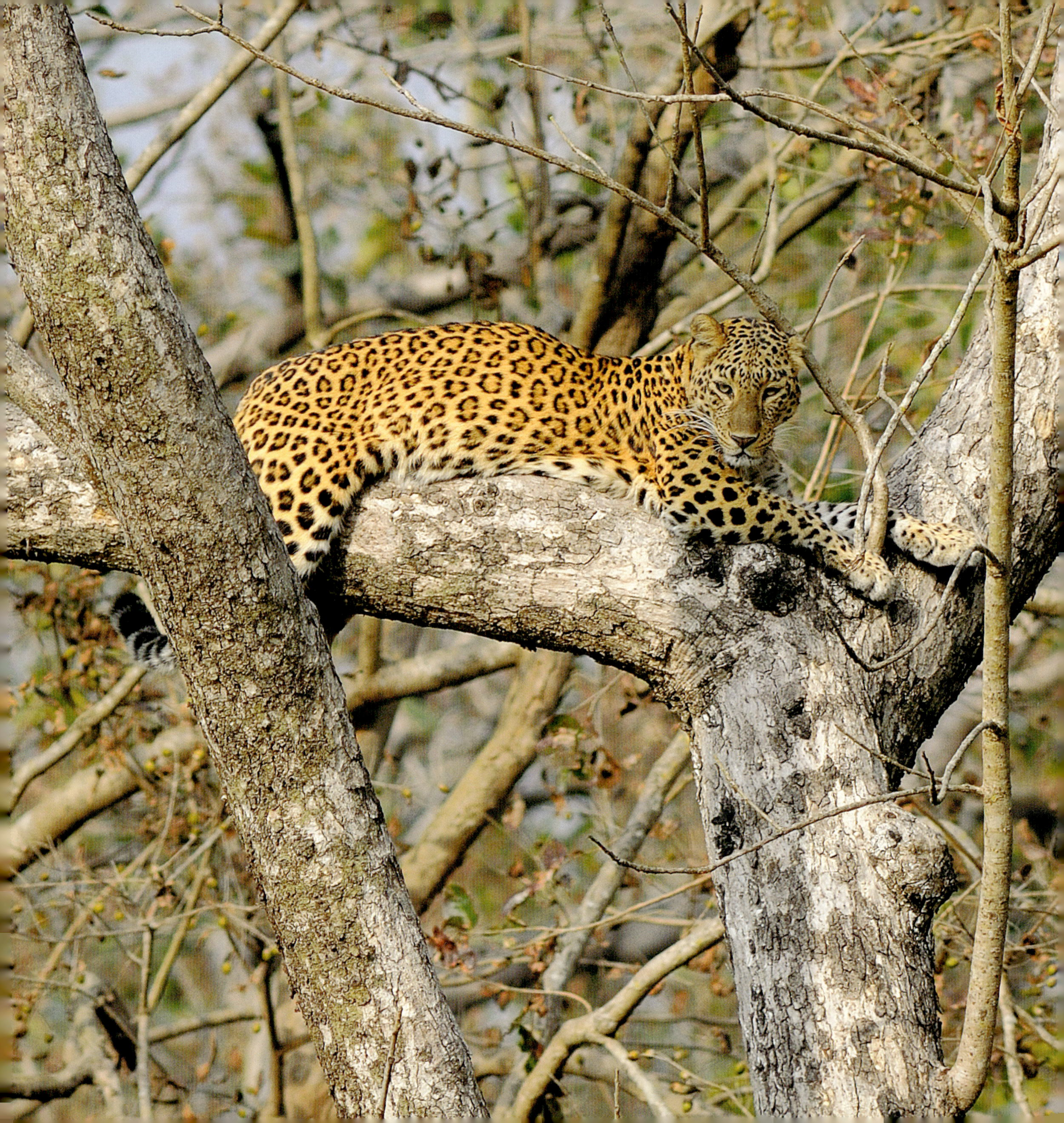

Communication among elephants is as intriguing as the animal itself. Elephants can communicate over long distances with each other through tummy rumbles, roars and loud trumpets. Elephants have also been known to communicate through infrasonic frequencies inaudible to man. Besides this they foot stomp to seismically communicate with each other.

Corbett is a very important breeding habitat for the Asian Elephant. In the months of November to June elephants can be seen in the *chaurs* around the Ramganga valley. As the rains arrive they migrate to the adjoining Sonanadi wildlife sanctuary. However elephants have been observed all year around in Bijrani and Malani.

Indian Leopard (*Panthera pardus fusca*)

An evening drive, along Sambar road, looking through the tree tops hoping to sight the Pallas's Fish Eagle or maybe an owl, what we saw was as unexpected as rare a sighting. On the branch of a tree sat a leopard. We were very pleasantly surprised at this providence. He curiously saw us, and in a matter of seconds gracefully descended into the undergrowth not to be seen again. We considered ourselves blessed to have laid eyes on this shy and elusive of all cats. Smaller than tigers, they are very powerful and more graceful. Leopards avoid confrontations at all costs. More nocturnal and adaptable than tigers they share a common prey base of Cheetal, Barking Deer and Hog Deer. A leopard will also hunt smaller animals like monkeys, hare, peafowl and jungle fowl and even rodents. Leopards are tree dwelling cats and usually carry their kill up a tree in order to protect it from jackals, hyenas and foxes.

Leopards can live in ever green and deciduous forests, scrub jungles, open country and on the fringes of human habitation. They are not averse to carrying away cattle and village dogs are a much favoured meal. This brings them into direct conflict with humans. Apart from humans, the leopard's natural enemies are other carnivores like tigers, wild dogs and hyenas.

The forest between Kanda and Dhikala is an established leopard habitat, however now inaccessible to tourists as the road here has been closed due to massive landslides. Some areas in the Bijrani zone and the periphery of the park are a great place to sight leopards, especially after sunset. Normally leopards stay away from tiger territories but reports of sighting them in the tiger zones are not very unusual.

Leopards usually sit in leafless trees like this one. Sometimes they also carry their kills up into the branches to prevent other animals like jackals from scavenging.
Image courtesy: Gerard David

The spots or rosettes on a leopard's fur are unique to each individual just as stripes are to tigers. Leopards make dedicated caring mothers to one or two cubs that stay in the care of their mothers till the age of 18 to 24 months. The cubs are born with their eyes closed and are highly vulnerable.

An efficient predator and a master of camouflage these elusive cats are the invisible shadows of the jungle. Leopards are as much at threat as the tigers and protection of habitats such as Corbett might just safeguard their future as well.

Golden Mahseer (*Tor putitora*)

Standing at High Bank en route from Dhikala to Sarpduli the mid-morning sun was too high for photography but the river right below looked golden, partly from the light of the sun and partly by the hundreds of mahseer that swam in the waters below.

The Himalayan Mahseer or the Golden Mahseer is the tiger of the river (loosely translated from Hindi *Maha* is big, *Sher* is tiger) fitted with an armour of the largest scales on any fresh water fish. Mahseer can grow up to a length of 2.75 meters and weigh around 54 kg. There are few others to match its speed and agility. Mahseer thrive in the rapid streams and rocky pools of the Ramganga, they feed

Mahseer, shimmering gold in the water of the Ramganga. Mahseer thrive in the rapid streams and rocky pools of the Ramganga river.

on crustaceans, insect larvae, frogs and smaller fish, they even forage on seeds and algae. However this is an endangered species brought to the brink of extinction due to habitat loss, pollution and over fishing. Outside the park Mahseer have been subjected to extermination by dynamite, industrial chemicals and fine mesh fishing nets.

A game fish, the Mahseer is much sought after by anglers. However, it is the anglers that are proving to be key river conservationists. Around Corbett several people keen on angling have taken it upon them to protect the riverine habitat of the region. They function on the principal of catch and release, and have involved villagers and communities living near Corbett to manage their rivers and the sport, thereby gaining economic benefits. Due to this vested interest, the mahseer and its river habitat get protected.

The Crocodilians

Where there is prey there will be a predator. The pristine waters of the Ramganga with its thriving Mahseer and Goonch fish population make it an ideal habitat for the last of Corbett's mega fauna. To my mind there are two contenders—both crocodilians, both residents of the mighty Ramganga in Corbett and both threatened in the past from unregulated hunting and loss of habitat. These are the Gharial (*Gavialis gangeticus*) and the Mugger or Marsh Crocodile (*Crocodylus palustris*)

The Gharial gets its name from the *ghara* or hump at the tip of the male's snout which resembles an earthen water pot or *ghara* in Hindi. Interestingly this feature is completely absent in the male hatchlings but develops as the reptile advances in age; older males have distinctly larger humps. This sign of maturity that begins to grow after ten years is used by the Gharials as a sound resonator to attract a mate.

Gharials are longer in length than Muggers. They are long snouted fish eating reptiles that are more aquatic than other crocodilians. They prefer deep, clear, fast flowing waters and sand banks for basking and nesting. Gharials are fairly fast swimmers but their poorly developed front legs put them at a great disadvantage on land and therefore they do not move far from the water. Unlike Muggers that are known to travel considerable distances over land.

The damming of the Ramganga at Kalagarh led to a huge loss of habitat that adversely affected the Elephants, Cheetal and the Hog Deer which were displaced by the formation of the lake. But a small blessing that came from the creation of

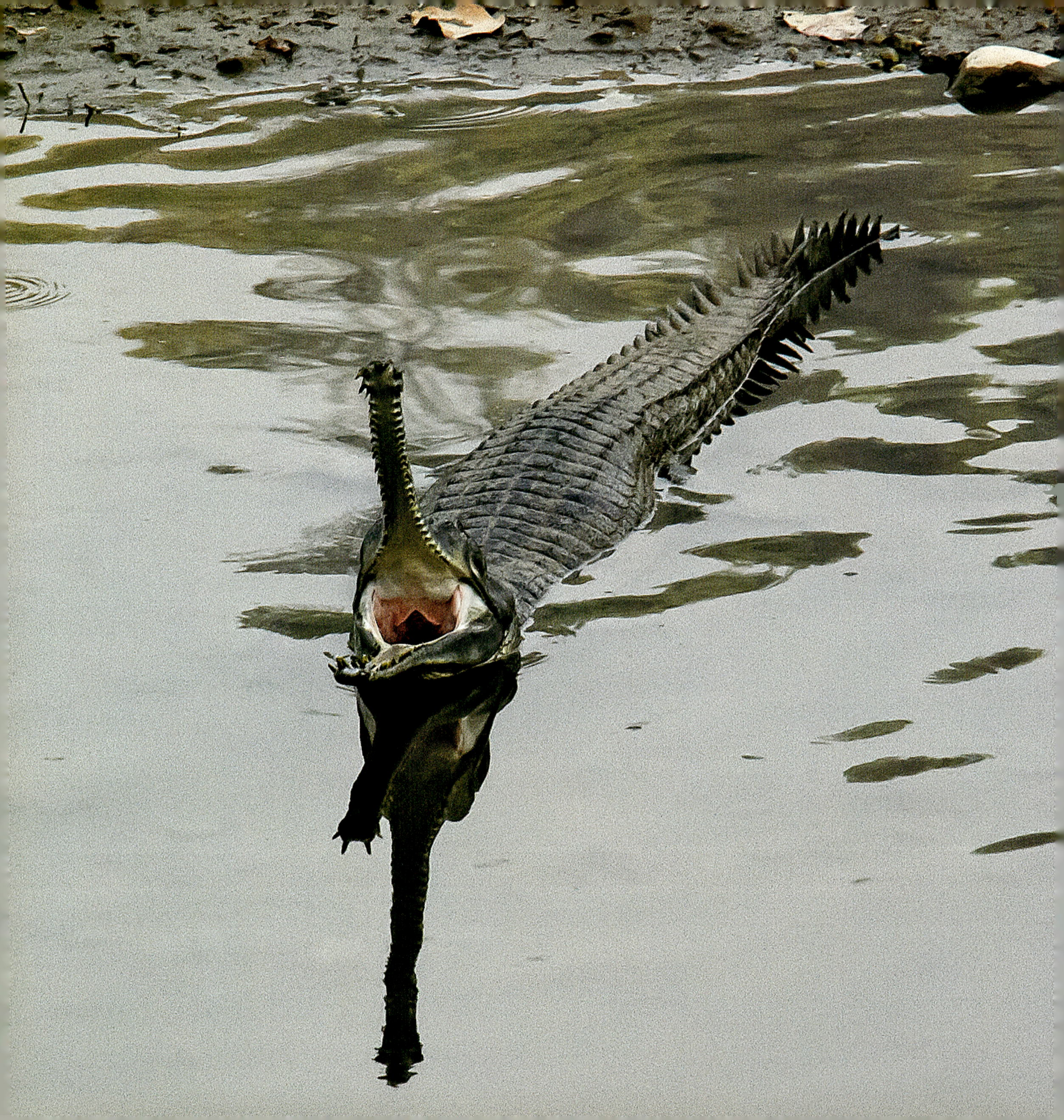

the reservoir is that today it is home to many migratory and resident birds and supports a sizeable number of Gharials and Muggers.

Muggers share habitat with the Gharial but prefer the slow moving shallow parts of the river. They are also known to prey upon larger land animals like Sambar, Cheetal and occasionally monkeys when they come to the waterfront for a drink. Their typical hunting technique is to breech from underwater near the shore, grab the prey and drag their victim in to the water and cause death by drowning.

While Gharials usually remain confined to the park and can be spotted from high bank at the far end of the river, Marsh Crocodiles are more enterprising in exploring up stream areas of Corbett landscape. A drive towards Marchula just before the suspension bridge on the periphery of the park is a good place to look for crocodiles. The vantage point from the road provides a good opportunity to photograph crocodiles basking on the river bank or lazily swimming in the blue waters of the Ramganga here.

Facing page: A Gharial lazying around in Champion's pool.

Left: Crocodiles can spend hours lying motionless in the sun, like this one basking on the soft sandy bank of the Ramganga river.

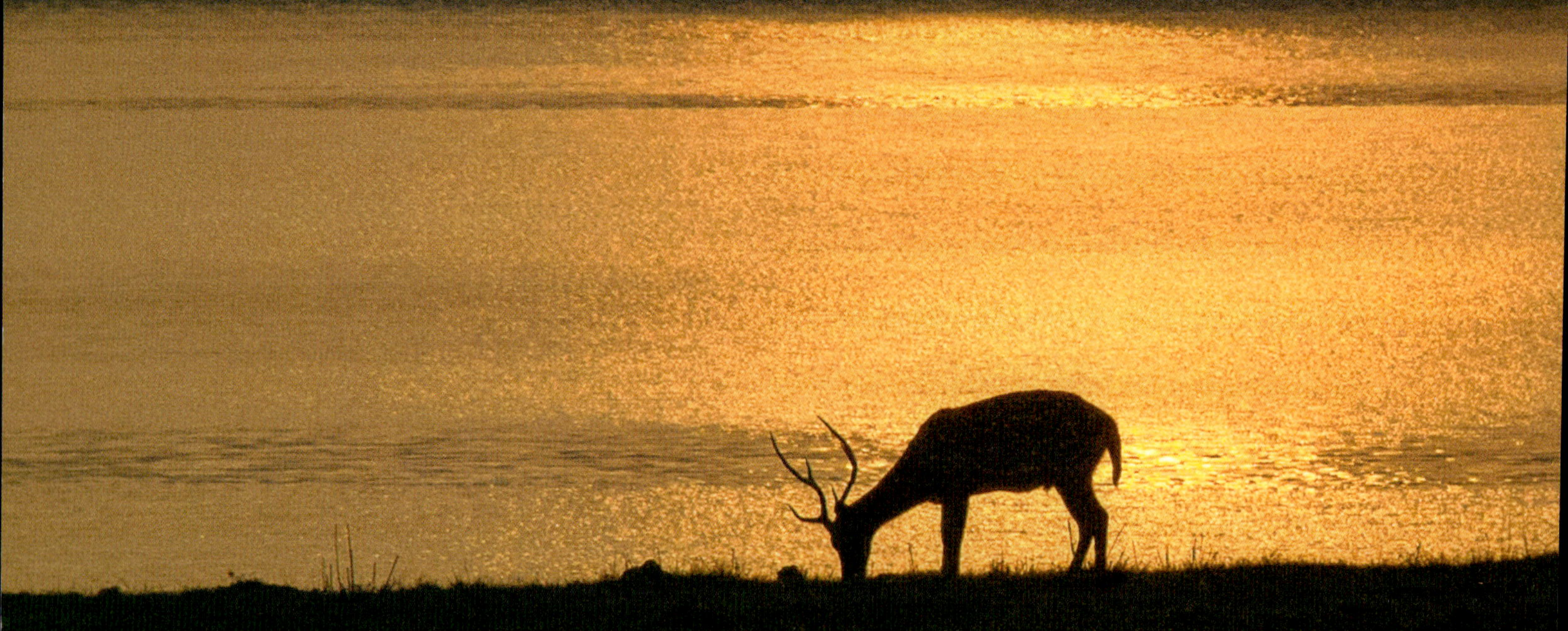

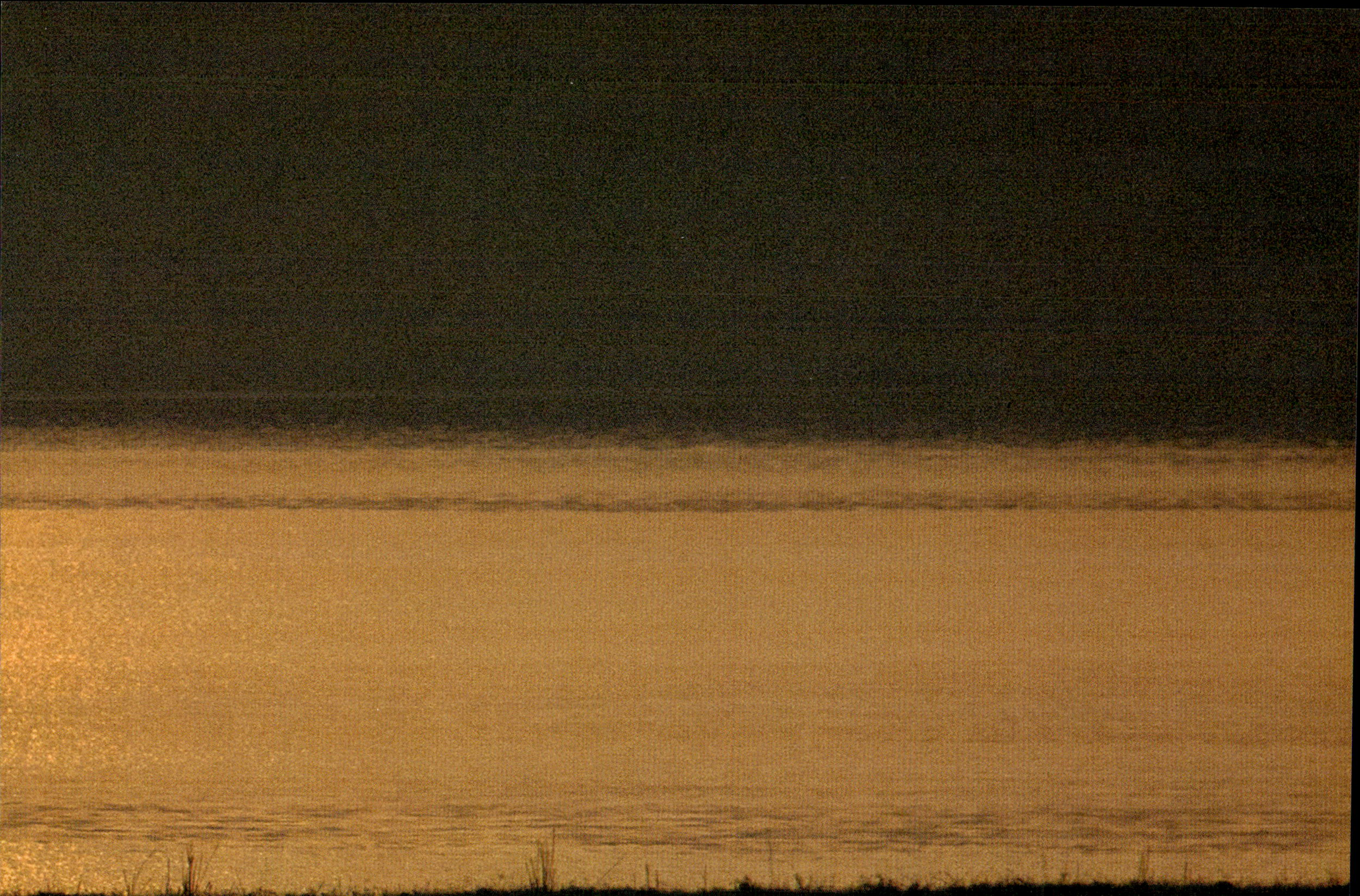

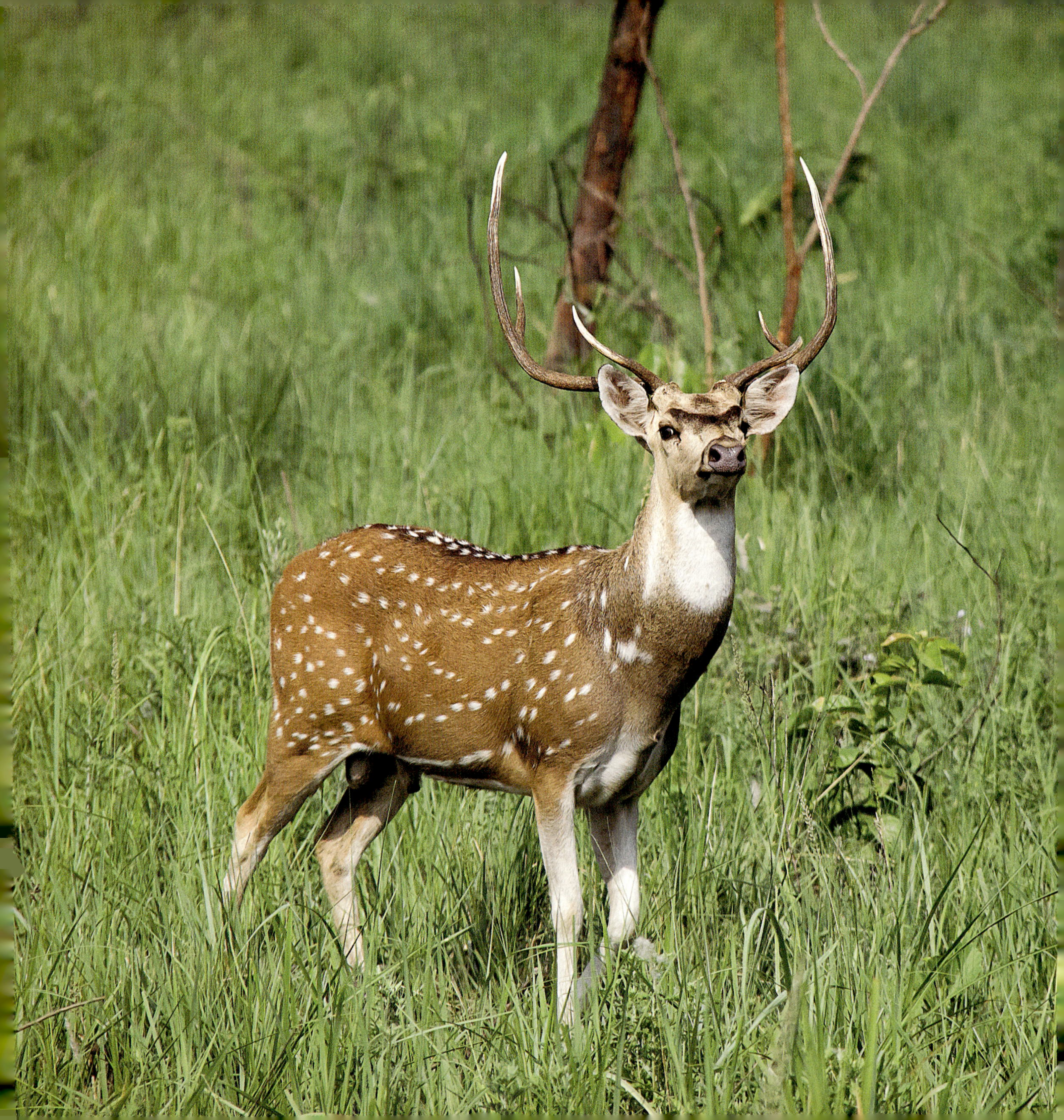

THE OTHER FORMS OF WILDLIFE
—small wonders of nature

Corbett is a small piece of nature still somewhat in its original state. It is wild and unpredictable; that is precisely why no one can guarantee sightings. While the tiger is a must see on every visitor's wish list, but finding one in the jungle can seem like looking for a needle in a haystack. It is all a matter of chance. You might get to see three tigers in a day or not get to see even one during the entire duration of your visit.

The varying habitats of Corbett make for the existence of a great mix of various species of animals besides the mega fauna.

With over 50 species of mammals, 580 species of birds and 25 different species of reptiles, Corbett is truly a wildlife haven, so don't miss out on the smaller wonders of nature.

There are four species of deer that are found here, of which the Cheetal (*Axis axis*) or Spotted Deer is the most beautiful and most abundant. With its delicate features and spots that are present on both sexes, it is certainly one of the most graceful of all antelopes. They are easily sighted as they live in varied

Previous double-spread: A Cheetal stag on the banks of the Ramganga at sunset.

Facing page: Cheetal have a keen sense of smell and hearing and fore warn other animals of the presence of a predator.

In Velvet

Deer and some other members of the Cervidae family like elk, moose and caribou shed their antlers every year and then grow a completely new set. New antlers in their pre-calcified stage of growth are referred to as Velvet antlers. During this period the still developing antler is covered in hair and the tines are rounded. They turn bone-hard and pointed at the ends only when the process of calcification is over.

Velvet antlers are also used in some medicines as (unproven) performance enhancer for athletes, who also believe that it helps in healing cartilage and tendon injuries more quickly and boosts strength and endurance.

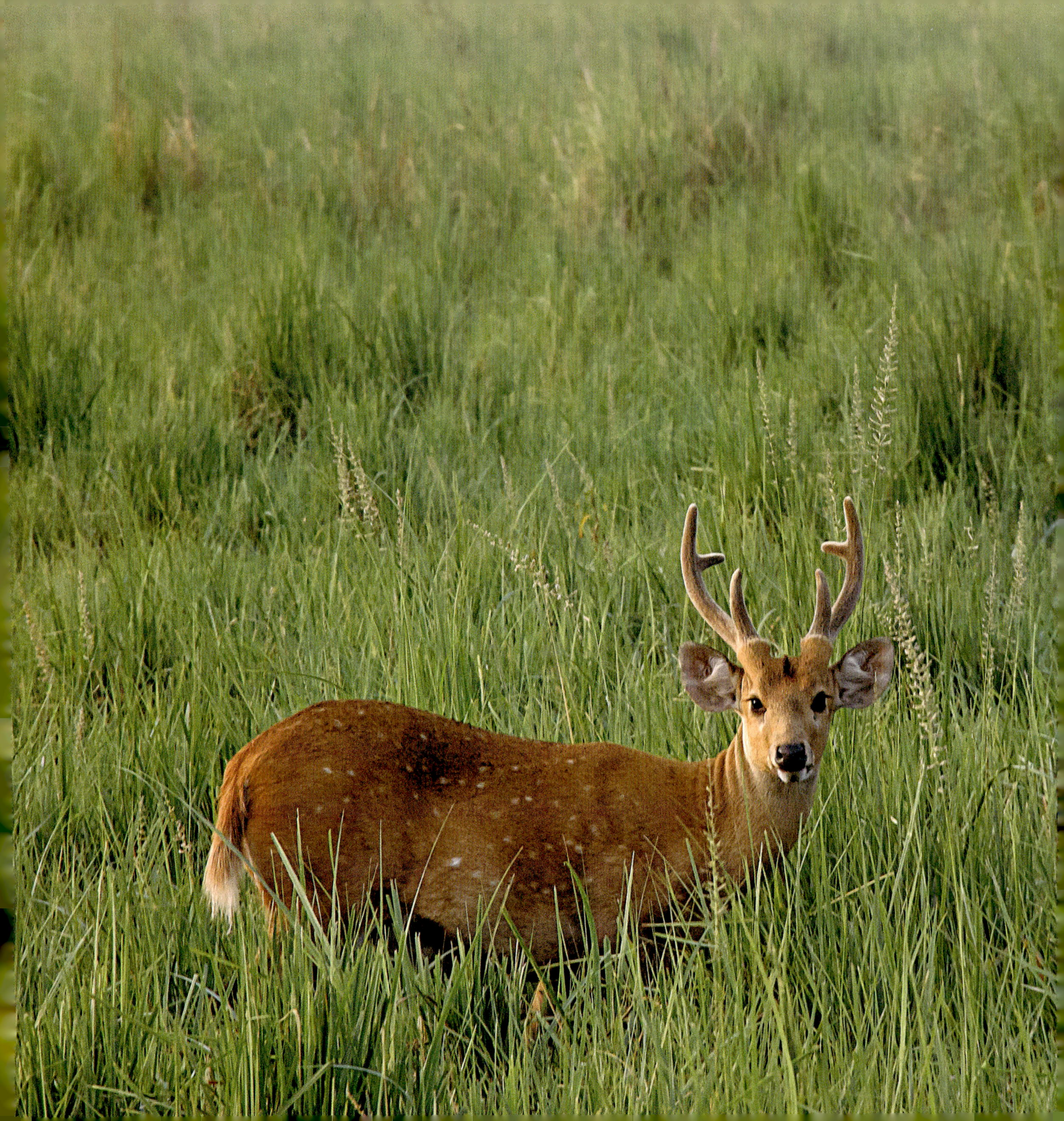

habitats of grassland, deciduous forests, swampy plains, plantations and scrublands. Cheetal seem omnipresent in the Corbett landscape. Large numbers of the species make it the main prey base of the larger carnivores, the tiger and the leopard.

Corbett at one time could boast of a large population of Hog Deer (*Axis porcinus*). Hog Deer are stouter and have shorter legs than cheetal. This gives the deer a pig-like appearance. Old records tell of herds of 100 or more individuals seen on the Phulai and Dhikala *chaurs*. However the submergence of large tracts of the forest by the reservoir of the Kalagarh dam caused a loss of large numbers of the species. Hog Deer, a medium-sized grass-dependent antelope could not adapt to such drastic habitat changes. Today, Hog Deer can be seen only in much smaller numbers, usually at the Dhikala *chaur*.

Facing page: Corbett at one time had a large Hog Deer population, however today one can spot them only in small numbers on the Dhikala chaur.

Salt licks

Salt licks are exposed salty mineral deposits at certain places in the forest. Elephants like many other herbivores seek out regions of natural mineral licks where the soil has a concentration of minerals like sodium, calcium, iron, phosphorus and zinc. Many animals make regular visits to consume the soil rich in nutrients and minerals to supplement their diets.

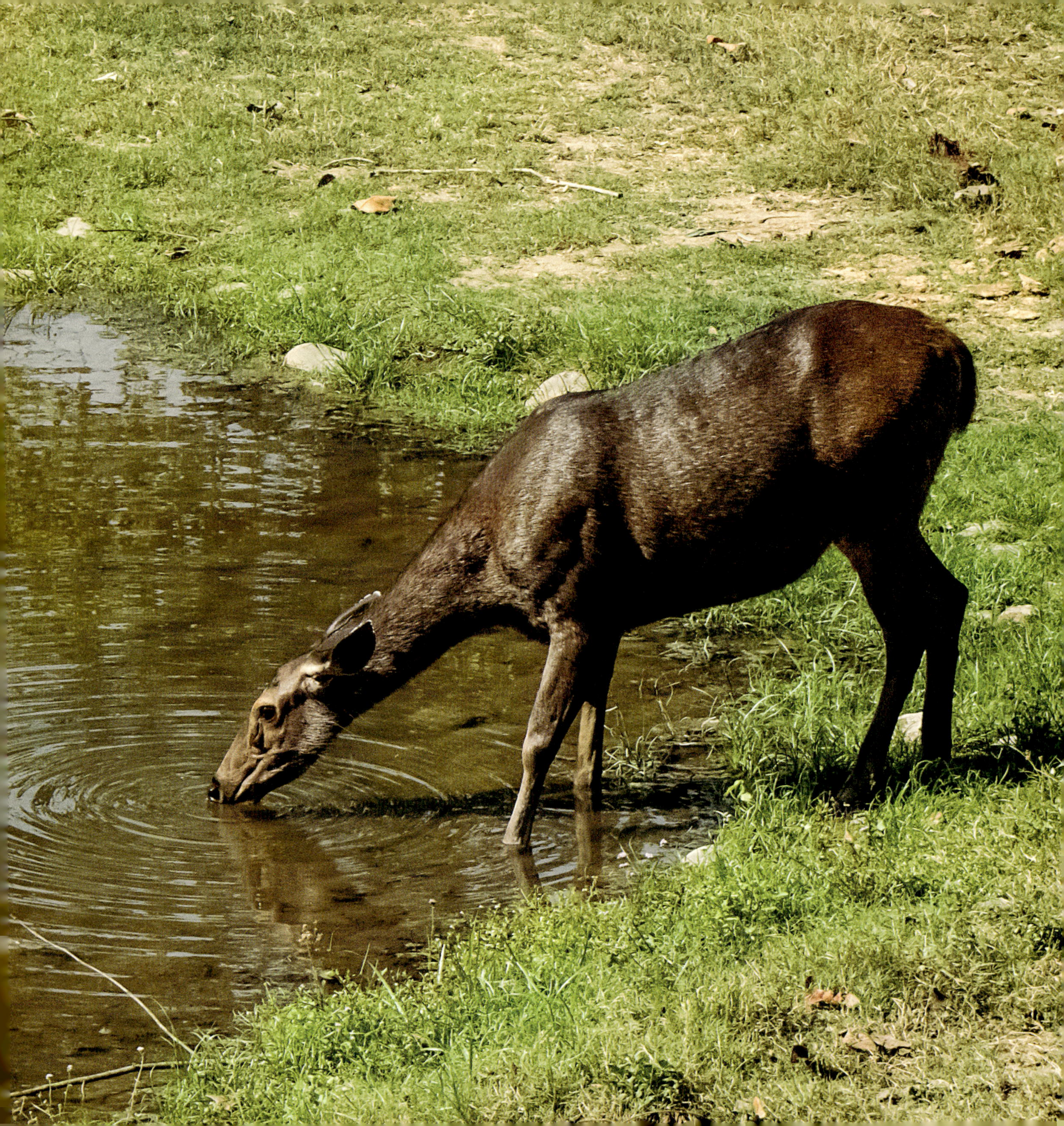

Sambar (*Rusa unicolor*), the largest of Asiatic deer, is easily spotted. Basically a forest deer, it has a shaggy dark brown coat and large spreading antlers. Its sheer size makes it much sought after by tigers.

The Barking Deer (*Muntiacus muntjac*), also known locally as Kakkar, is the smallest of the four. Its short antlers and tusks (downward pointing canine teeth) give it a queer look. It prefers the hilly and moist areas but is highly adaptable and can be found in grasslands as well. It is also a part of the alarm system of the forest. The moment it senses the presence of a tiger it gives out an alarm call that sounds like a dog's bark. This it does even when the tiger is about a kilometer away, thus warning all other animals of impending danger. I am sure this must be much to the consternation of the tiger who knows he has been detected and his chances of making a kill are now dismal.

The Ghoral (*Nemorhaedus goral*), a goat antelope, is found on the hill slopes around Kanda. But it is not easily spotted because of its colour that gives it the perfect camouflage. In the visitors log at Kanda, guests have noted sighting six to eight Ghoral together on the hill slopes before the rest house.

Facing page: A Sambar female stops over at a waterhole for a quick and cautious drink of water.

Above: A full-grown Sambar male with his majestic headgear.

Left: An alert Barking Deer before lowering his head for a drink.

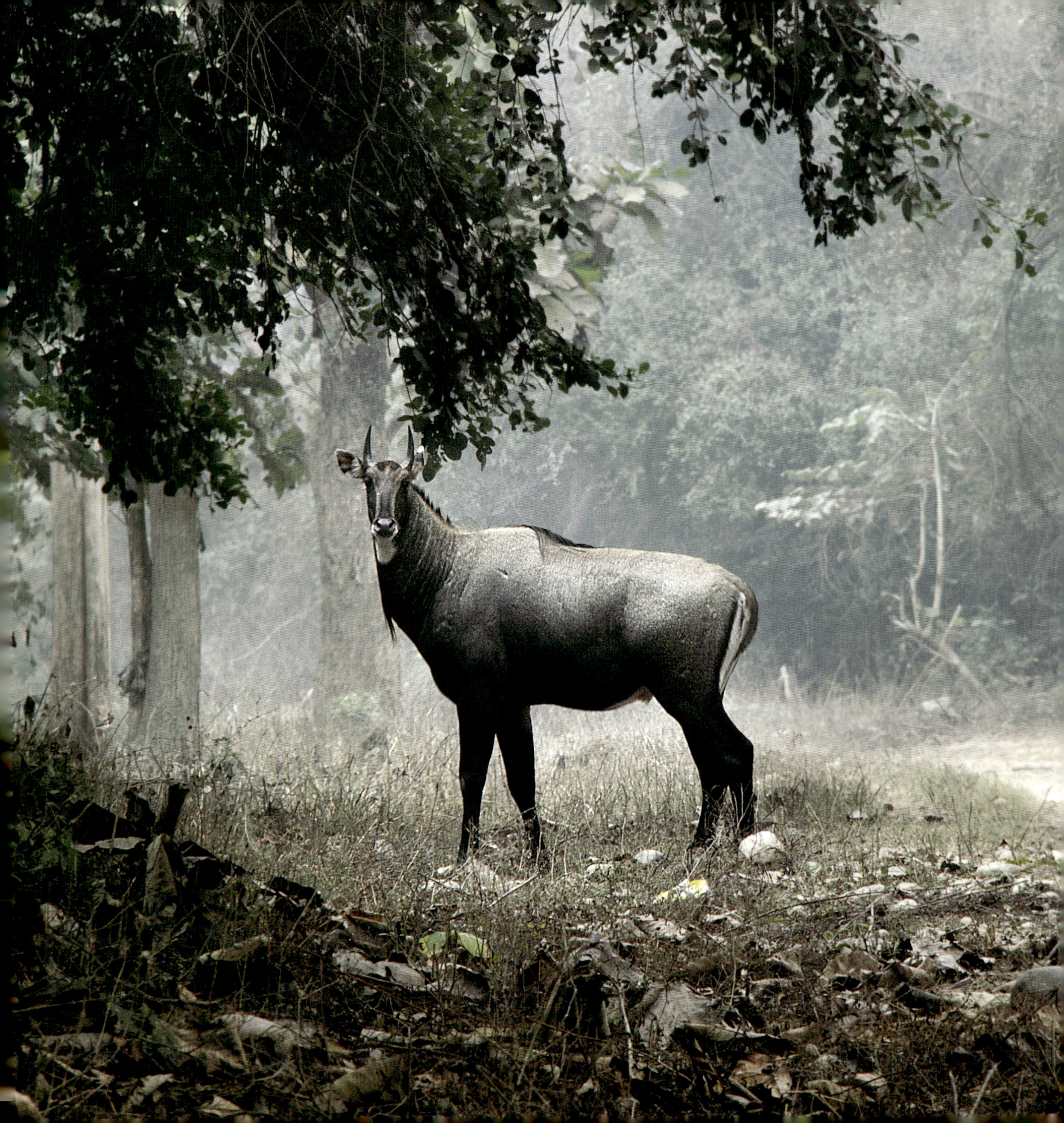

Another large antelope, the Nilgai (*Boselaphus tragocamelus*) or Blue Bull can be easily seen in the periphery of the park, especially if you drive from Kalagarh to Jhirna. The male is a handsome specimen of strength and speed. An easy way to tell a deer apart from an antelope besides the fact that they belong to different family groups is to take a look at the head gear of the animal. Nilgai are more closely related to cows and goats. They have a set of horns that adorn the heads of both the male and females while only male deer have branched antlers. Matured Nilgai male are iron- blue or light grey in colour while the calves and females are sandy brown.

Corbett is home to a number of smaller cats too. The Jungle Cat (*Felis chaus*), the Leopard Cat (*Prionailurus bengalensis*) and the rare Fishing Cat (*Prionailurus viverrinus*) are found here. Being nocturnal they are not easily spotted. However, there is always a slim possibility to spot the Jungle Cat. Highly adaptable, it is sometimes found in close proximity to the resorts and villages in the buffer zones.

Jackals (*Canis aureus*) are easy to sight in Corbett. Successful hunters of rodents and small birds, jackals are very adaptable and can be seen in the grasslands and sometimes even venturing out into the fields close to human habitation on the fringes of the park.

Facing page: A handsome male Nilgai. Usually not found in the park proper, they can be easily seen in the periphery of the park towards Kalagarh.

Left: Jackals are very adaptable and wide-spread throughout the Corbett landscape. They can be seen in the protected area as well as in the fields close to human habitation.

There are four different kinds of Civets found in Corbett. Distinguishable from the yellow throated martens by their markings, are the Small and Large Indian Civet, the Common Palm Civet and the Himalayan Palm Civet. Being mostly arboreal and nocturnal they are very hard to spot.

A most common sight in Corbett, for no other reason but the antics put up by the members of the species are the Langurs (*Semnopethicus entellus*). Widely distributed in the park, these primates can be found in the *chaurs*, forests and on the hill slopes. The most vocal in their alarm system against predators, these monkeys perched on trees have a height advantage over other animals and can spot predators from great distances. Their alarm calls warn other animals if a tiger happens to be in the vicinity.

The Rhesus Macaque (*Macaca mulatta*) on the other hand can adapt well to living in close proximity to humans and can be seen within the forest rest house boundaries. We have made a nuisance of the species by giving it easy access to food and garbage which makes them a constant feature near human habitation. However, in the forest, their behavior is entirely different. There they are shy, cautious and very wary of humans.

Above: A Rhesus Macaque. The behavior of monkeys that live in the forest is very different from those living near humans. Here in the jungle they are weary of humans unlike their counterparts in the cities where they are fearless and often aggressive.

Right: Langurs along with macaques and deer are the alarm system against the predators.

Corbett is also home to the Sloth Bear and the Himalayan Black Bear. Both are hard to see. One sometimes does come across foot-prints left behind in the soft sands by a bear that might have just passed that way. The Sloth Bear (*Melursus ursinus*), so named because of its shaggy lumbering gait, is found more towards Bijrani-Malani areas in the dry deciduous type of forests, scrublands and grasslands. They are known to be attracted to termite mounds, bee-hives and the sweet flowers of Mahua trees.

The Himalayan Black Bears (*Ursus thibetanus*) have only been seen on footage from the camera-traps put up by the forest department. The other animal to be wary of in the forest, whose presence is not taken lightly even by the tiger, is the Wild Boar or Wild Pig (*Sus scrofa*). Normally they keep busy foraging the ground for roots and other delicacies. They are usually seen in sounders of 4 to 10 or more individuals but solitary males are also a common sight. Wild boars are by and large a docile animal by nature, but when an angry male or mother with piglets charge, it can lead to a serious situation as they rarely abandon the attack.

A solitary male Wild Boar (left) in the sal forest and (above) a group of three juveniles foraging in the Dhikala grassland.

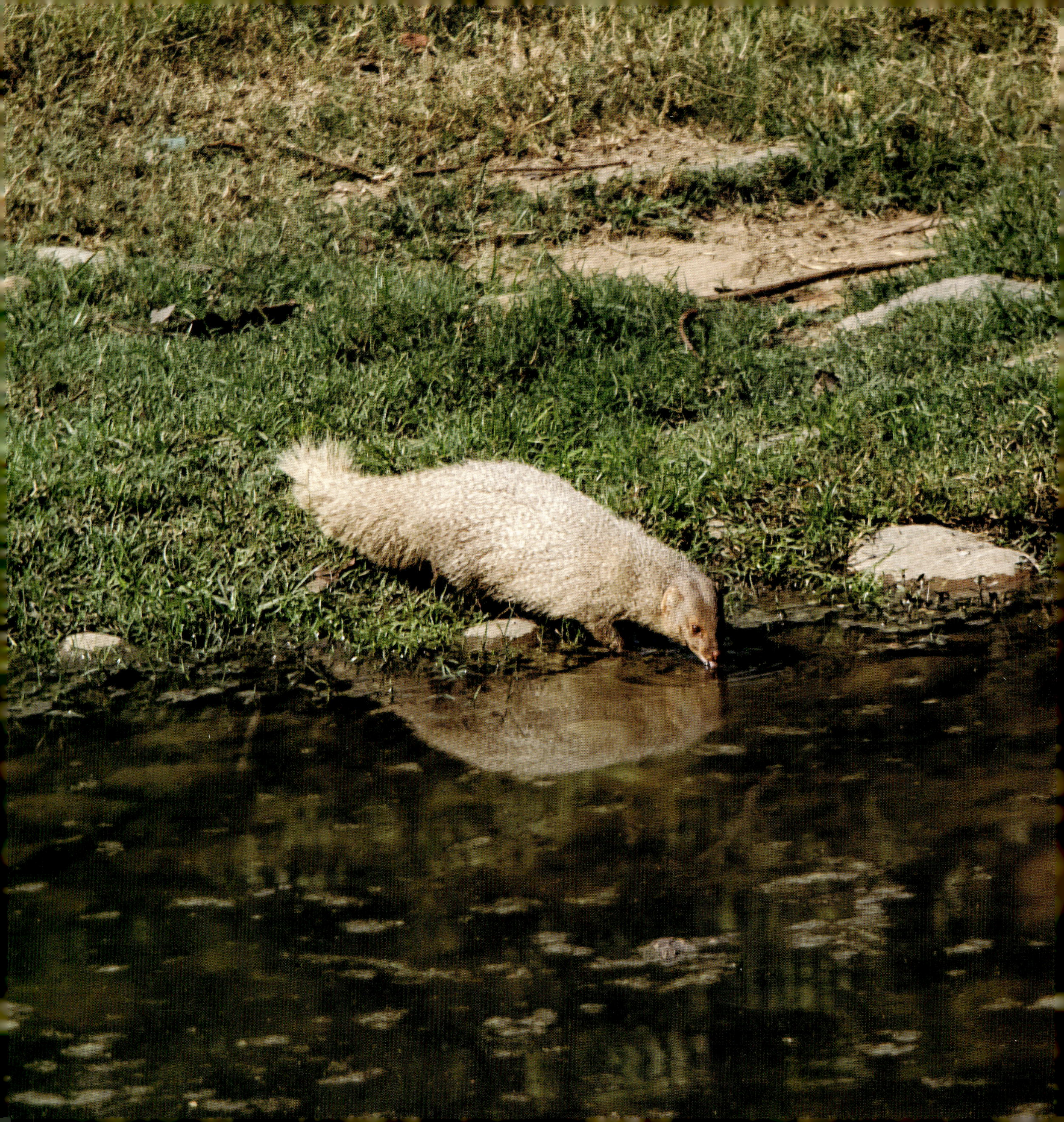

The Grey Mongoose (*Herpestes edwardsii*) can be seen sometimes scurrying along jungle paths or at water holes. Traditionally the sworn enemy of snakes, mongoose can be omnivorous. Otters in small family groups can be seen rolling around grassy banks of rivers and streams with adequate cover. Spotting the Yellow Throated Martins (*Martes flavigula*) can be a bit of a challenge.

Left: A group of Otters frolicking in and around the waters of Ramganga river.

Left below: A Smooth Indian Otter emerging out of water.

Facing page: Mongoose are fairly common and can be seen scurrying along jungle tracks or at water holes. Well known for not backing down in the presence of venomous snakes, mongooses are omnivores.

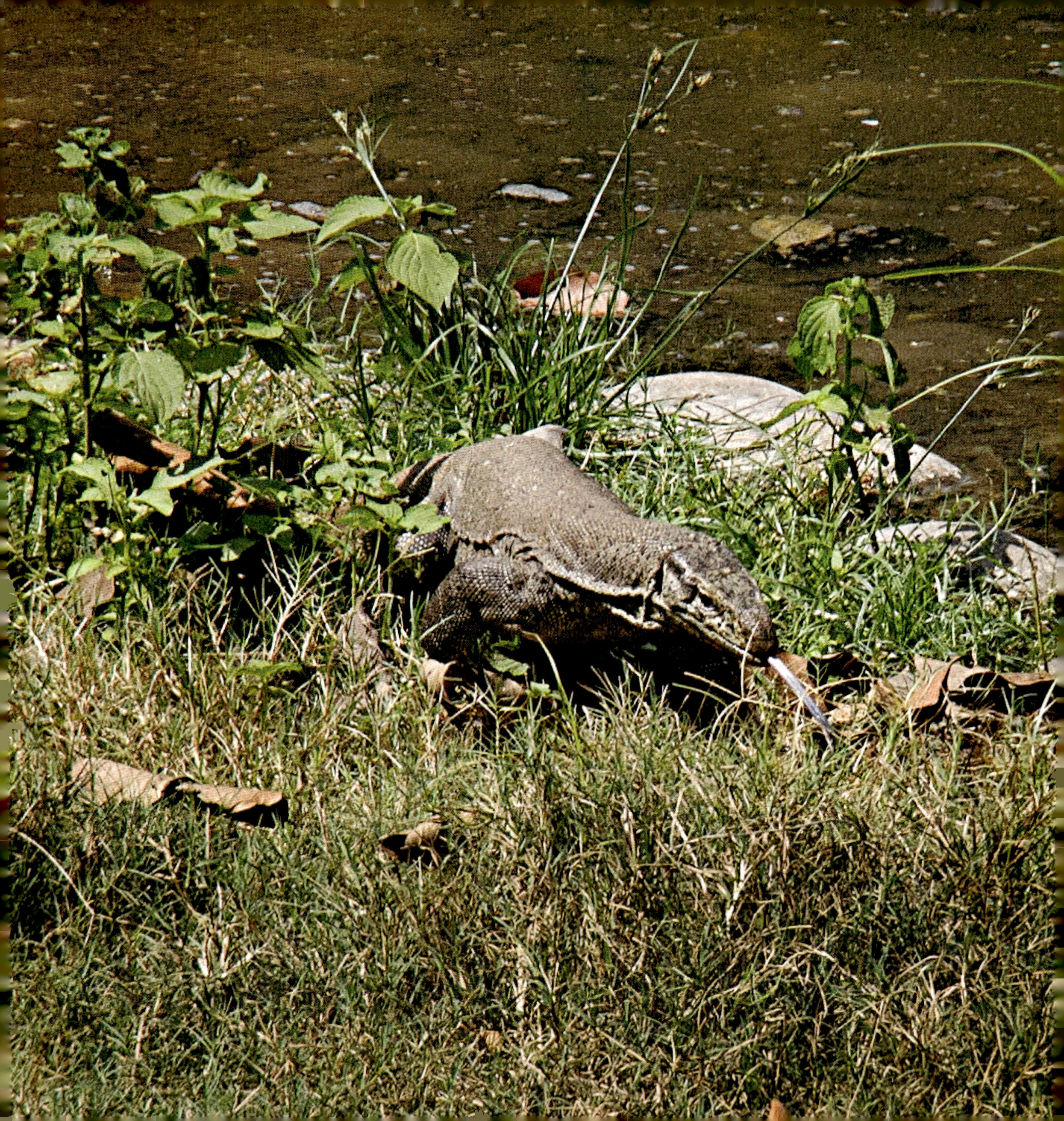

The Shivaliks have a milder climate compared to the Himalayas and that makes for optimum conditions to support a large number of reptiles including snakes like Banded Kraits, Spectacled Cobras and Pythons to name a few. Besides the more visible Gharials and Muggers, there are also Monitor Lizards (*Varanus indicus*). They are probably named so because of their ability to stand on their hind legs to monitor their surroundings to see approaching predators. Monitors are found throughout the park and are often seen crossing the road between Dhikuli and Mohan on the periphery.

Facing page: A large Bengal Monitor Lizard on the water bank and another one (above) basking in the sun on a warm boulder.

Left: A Burmese Python on a termite infested tree stump. Pythons are capable of swallowing fairly large prey and will eat mammals, birds and even other reptiles.

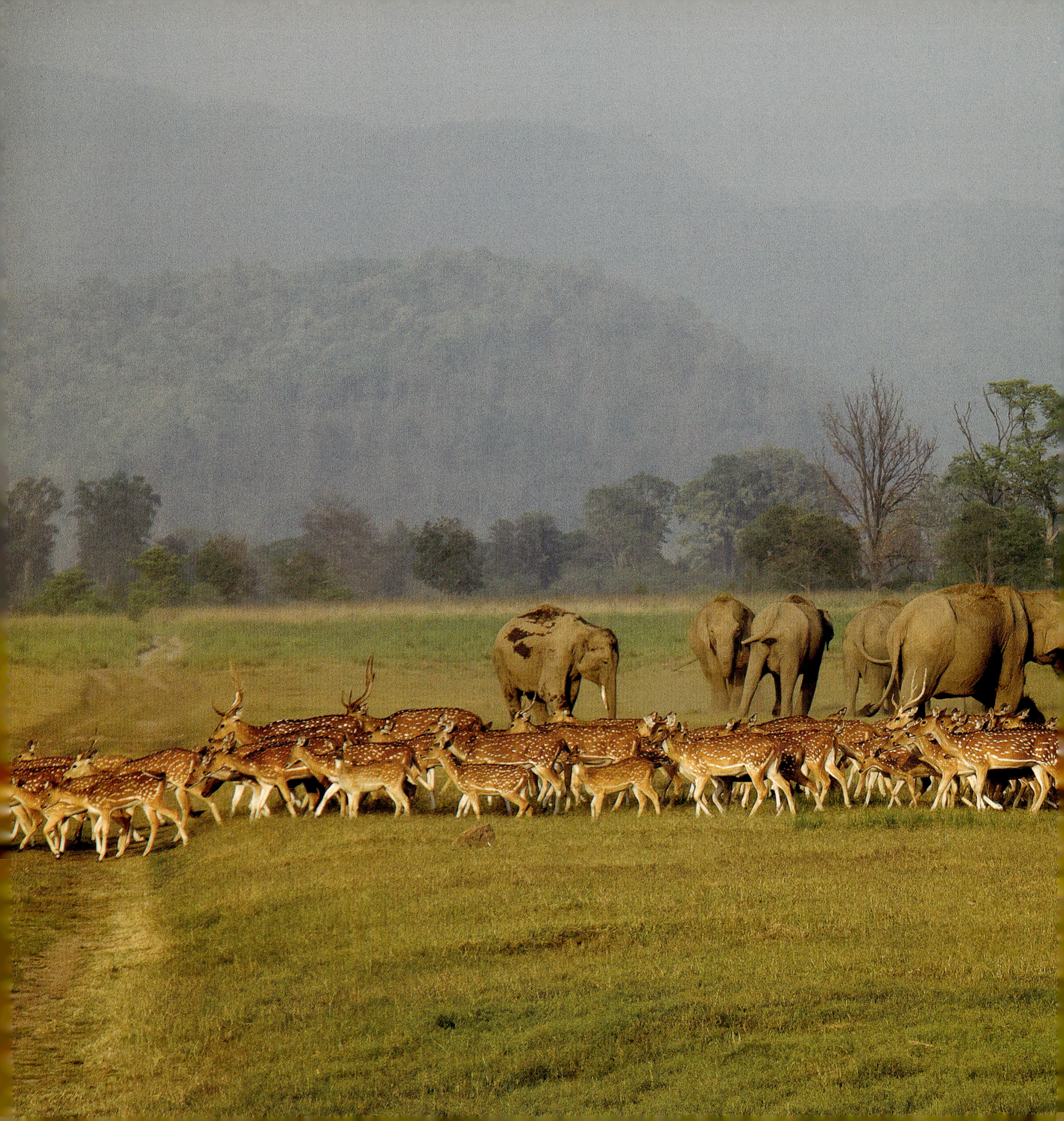

WAYS OF THE WILD
—*a civilized world*

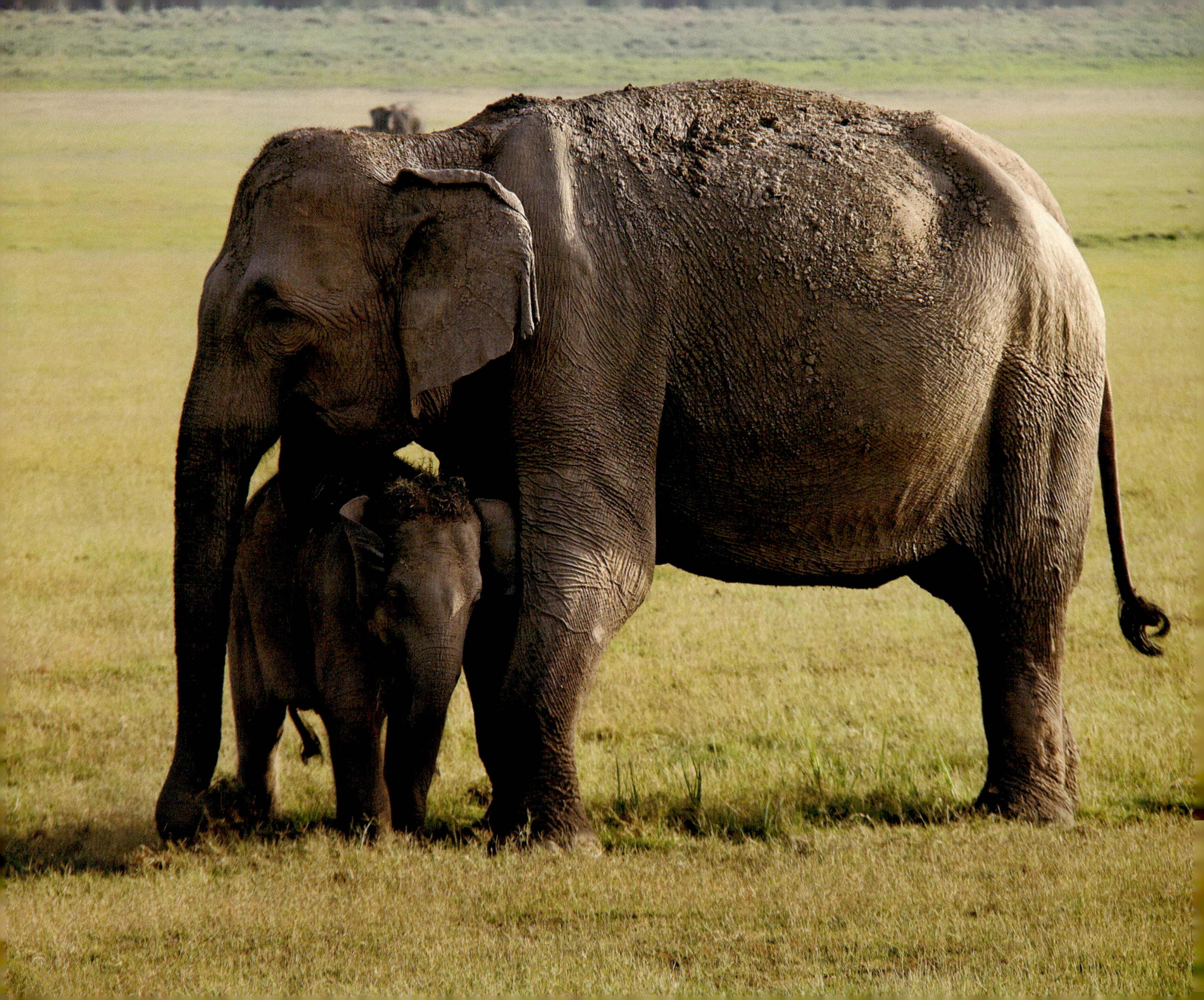

WAYS OF THE WILD

—a civilized world

The word 'wild' brings to mind meanings like brute, savage, unruly, unlawful and uncivilized. The animal world contrary to human belief is more civilized than most humans believe it to be. There is perfect order. Roles are well defined and a fixed social hierarchy with rules exists. There is obedience amongst the members of the same species and cooperation and co-dependence among various species for mutual benefit.

Prey-predator relationship is not the only relationship that exists in the wild. Various species depend on each other for survival and food. In the forest a closer observation makes this apparent. The Cheetal and the primates have a symbiotic unspoken alliance of mutual understanding that benefits both. The primates feeding from their vantage points in the trees can detect a predator from a distance. The Cheetal, always alert, must lower their guard to feed making them vulnerable at that point hence they depend on Langurs and monkeys that give out warning calls that are responded by the deer, and thus imminent danger is detected. The Cheetal also benefit from the wasteful feeding of the Langurs that drop leaves and fruit to the ground. This relationship is truly not one way as the monkeys and Langurs also benefit by having the deer around. They sometimes have to descend from trees. It is at times like this that they depend on the keen hearing and sense of smell of the deer to forewarn them of danger when on the ground; hence a well-tuned relationship for mutual advantage has developed between two species.

Though the different species appear to be randomly scattered in the forest in a disorderly manner, in reality there is perfect order. Territories are well defined and the animals respect the demarcations. Tigers live solitary lives, each tiger reigning over a large area, to live and hunt in. The size of territories varies drastically according to habitat available and density of predator and

Previous double-spread: A large herd of Cheetal crossing the grassland almost in a line while a group of elephants mind their own business. Even in the wild rules exist and animals don't break them for their very survival depends on it.

Above: Cheetal in the grass land and primates on the tree-tops have a great symbiotic relationship where each benefits from the presence of the other.

Facing page: It is a delight to see elephant young under the protection of their mothers.

133

prey population. Although territories are well defined and marked, sometimes they may overlap on the fringes. A male tiger's territory normally overlaps with that of multiple females. In ideal conditions an adult male tiger's territory may spread over sixty to a hundred sq km. A tiger cannot all the time be present in his entire territory and hence leaves behind scent markings and scratches on trees as markers of his ownership. Urinating is an olfactory signpost left by the owner to ward off trespassers. Depending on the height at which it has been sprayed these markings also tell the intruder the size of the resident owner. In case of females it is also a signal to prospective mates if she is ovulating and possibly ready to mate. Similarly scratch marks left by tigers are for cleaning nails as well as to display size and high reach of the individual. These signs are well respected by other tigers and act as a deterrent to intruders.

Fights sometimes arise between individuals to protect territories. Tigers avoid serious injury and accept dominance well in time because injury in the wild is certain death. The dominant individual establishes his right in victory and the loser leaves. In a good habitat where space is not a problem the animal moves elsewhere to form his own territory. When a male loses his vigour he is ousted by another male. This social hierarchy ensures that only the strongest and healthy males have the right to mate and propagate.

Some animals like elephants exhibit complex social structures to ensure survival of the species. While in most species it is the male that is dominant, in elephants it is a matriarchal society. Elephants live in nurturing groups made of

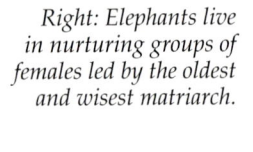

Right: Elephants live in nurturing groups of females led by the oldest and wisest matriarch.

related females and their young. The head of a group is usually the oldest and the wisest matriarch. These units are also called family groups. A group can comprise of 8-10 elephants that include mature cows, sub adult elephants and suckling young calves. The young are lovingly protected by the group as a whole. Females live with their mothers group for life. Adolescent males leave the group and temporarily form bachelor herds. Eventually all male elephants go on to lead a solitary life. This probably happens to prevent inbreeding. Several family groups make a herd, especially when elephants are migrating from one area to another through the elephant corridors. Adult males go in to a herd when a female is in Oestrus, a period when ovulation occurs and copulation can take place. The logic of packs and herds only goes to prove that there is strength in numbers.

Parenting by no means is an easy feat. Birds do a dedicated job at bringing up the next generation. Finding a viable mate and locating a perfect nest site and building a nest. The task is endless as they have to not only brood the eggs but also feed, protect and teach the fledglings how to fly. Hornbills display extraordinary trust in each other during the breeding season. The female builds a nest in the hollow of a tree and seals herself in it for the entire nesting period. During this time she relies solely on her mate to bring her food. The food is fed to her by the male through a slit in the seal. When the chicks hatch they remain inside with the female and only when they get too big to fit with the mother does she break open the seal. Both parents then take on the task of feeding the chicks.

There are also others who as they go about their life cycles generation after generation do a great service to other animals and the health of the forest. Bees,

Above: Bracket Fungi or Shelf Fungus are a large family of common arboreal fungi. They grow on both living and dead trees.

Far left: A colony of beehives on a tree near Dhela. As one of the most important pollinators, bees play a very important role in our ecosystem.

Left: Green algae on a water body in Bijrani zone. Algae is a critical component of almost all aquatic ecosystems. This photosynthetic organism is an important source of oxygen and food for many other forms of life.

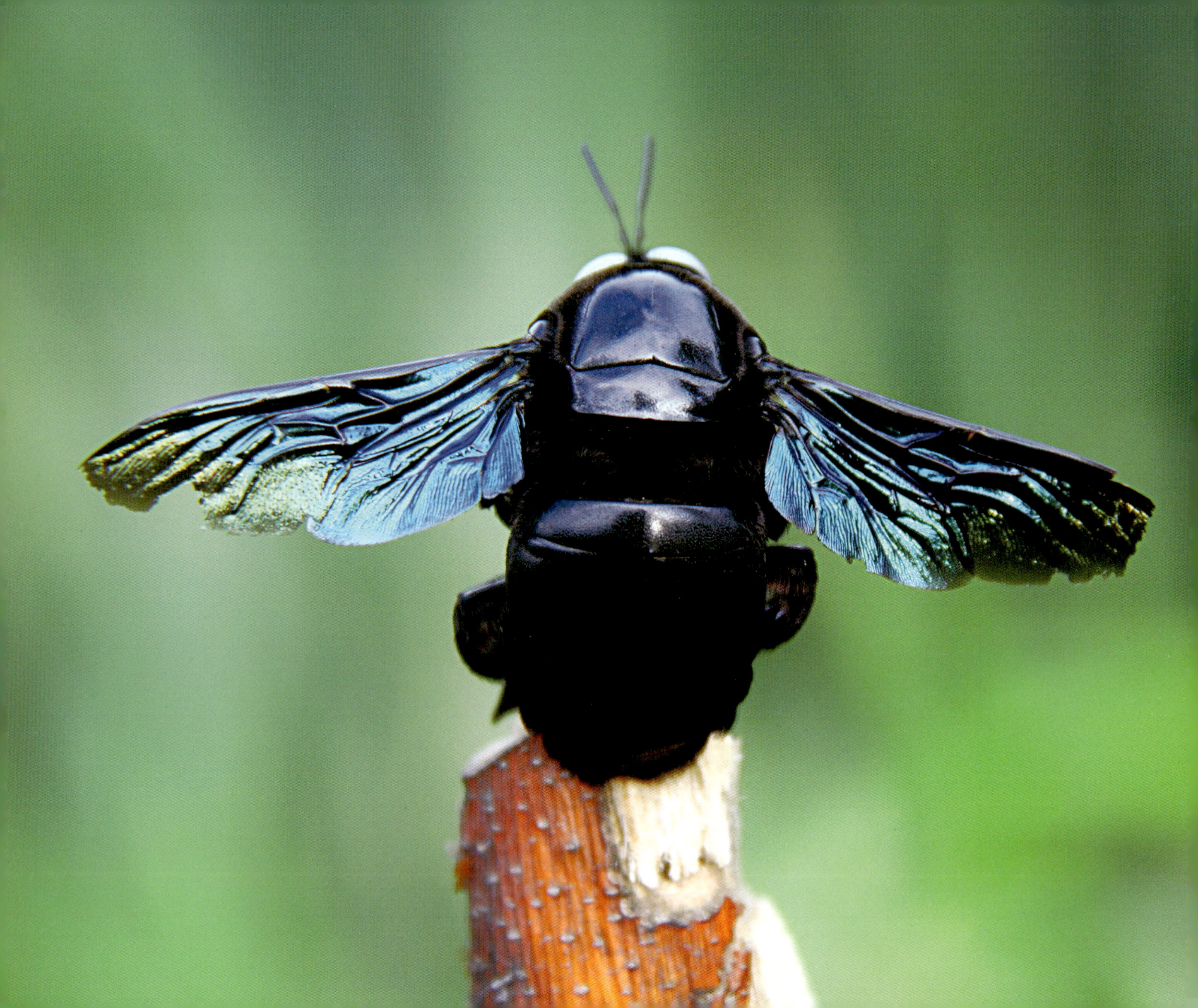

beetles, butterflies, moths, ants, various other insects and termites are bestowed with the task of pollination, cleaning up and maintaining a forest ecosystem. Hence each one of them is also an integral part of the larger food chain.

These insects, the unsung heroes of forests play an important role in plant reproduction, soil fertility, and decomposition of plant and animal remains. They maintain forest health and diversity. Nothing goes waste in an undisturbed ecosystem.

A small example of the importance of insects and earthworms is that a large number of them appear from underground during the rainy season. Each one of them leaving a fine capillary in the ground that it makes as a path for his exit. These countless tiny capillaries make the ground porous and act as water inlets to re-charge the ground water during the rains. They also break the flow of water and prevent soil erosion in the process. The high population of insects during the rainy season is welcomed by the birds that go on a feeding frenzy in those days for building fat, preparing for the food scarcity months of winter. The insects and moths have a short life span and after performing their role as pollinators and instruments of water harvesting become part of the food chain. Nature works in perfect harmony. But for insects our water tables would deplete and but for birds, insect populations would explode to alarming proportions and harm our crops.

Facing page: A Large Carpenter Bee. These high temperature tolerant insects have a long season of activity which makes them important agricultural pollinators.

Top: Spiders play an important role in the ecosystem by controlling insect populations.

Above: Handy work of friendly ants. Holes in the ground like this one are capillaries that drain rainwater into the earth to recharge the water-table.

Left: Mud-puddling by butterflies is a common behavior of these beautiful pollinators. In this activity of flocking over the wet soil, dung or carrion they obtain important nutrients such as salts and amino acids.

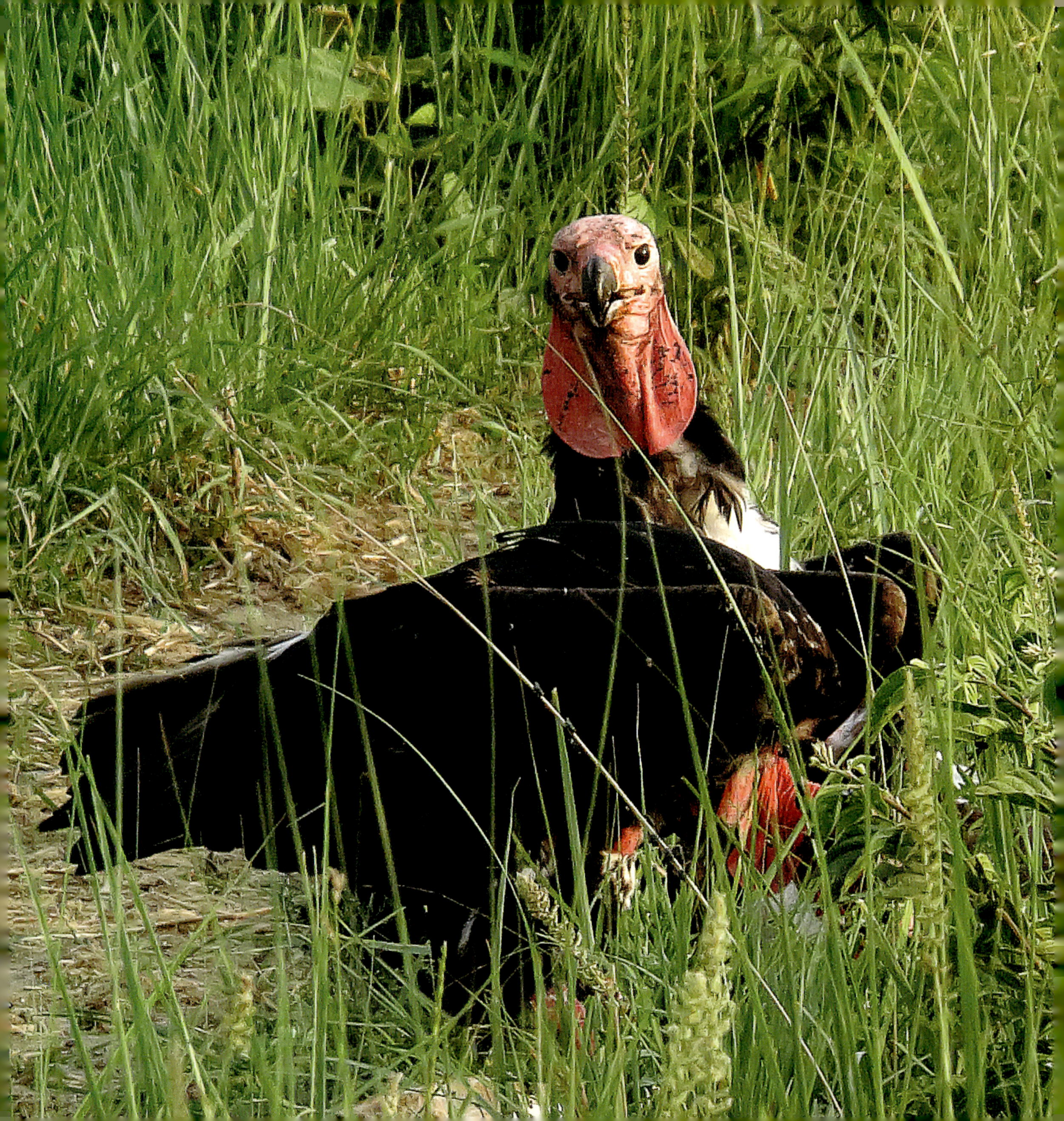

BIRD LIFE OF CORBETT
—*wildlife on wings*

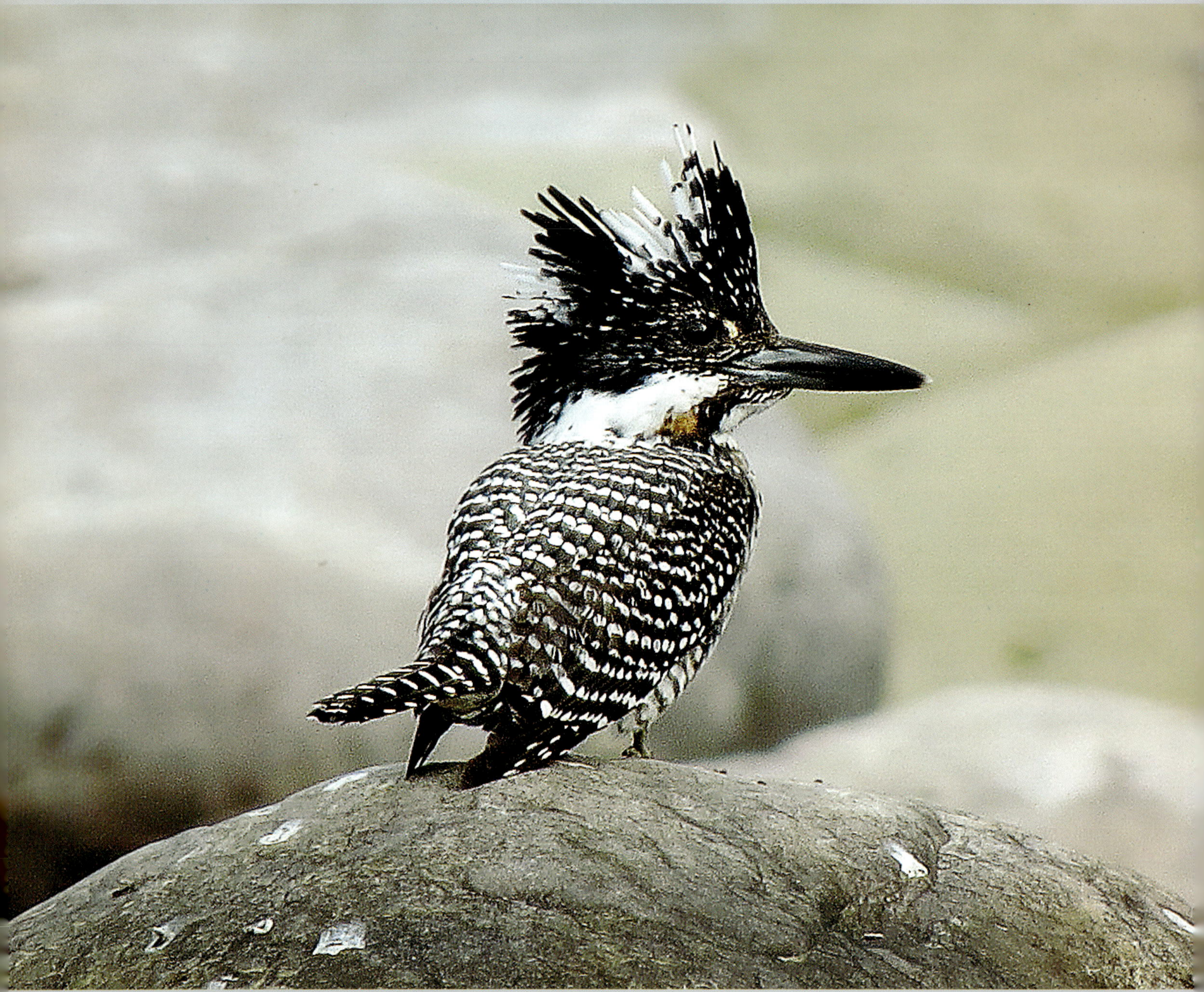

BIRD LIFE OF CORBETT

—wildlife on wings

Within few minutes of our entering Corbett National Park from Dhangarhi gate, we were greeted by that unmistakable loud call that the ornithologists refer to as the 'bark of the Great Hornbill'. About half a dozen of these magnificent birds were hopping from tree-to-tree in short flights as if leading us into this birder's paradise. These birds have a meter and a half wing span with heavy casks over their massive bills and are usually associated with South-east Asia. In India they are synonymous with the north-east and the south-west coastal states. Other than that, the only place where there is a resident breeding population of these 'near threatened' birds is Corbett. If I was ever asked to name one bird that is the pride of Corbett, my answer certainly would be, the Great Hornbill.

If Corbett was not famous for its star attraction—the tiger, it would still have its place of pride on the map of Indian wildlife for its abundance of avian-fauna. More than one third of all the birds found in the Indian subcontinent can be seen here. Corbett's grasslands, riverine landscape, thickly wooded forests and Himalayan foot-hills make

Previous double-spread: Red-headed Vulture seen here in the Dhikala zone, is also known as the Asian King Vulture. It is a threatened species listed by the IUCN as critically endangered.

Facing page: A Crested Kingfisher

Left: A pair of Ruddy Shelducks who are winter migrants to the Corbett landscape.

Above: An Oriental Pied Hornbill and a Great Hornbill (far above) in flight.

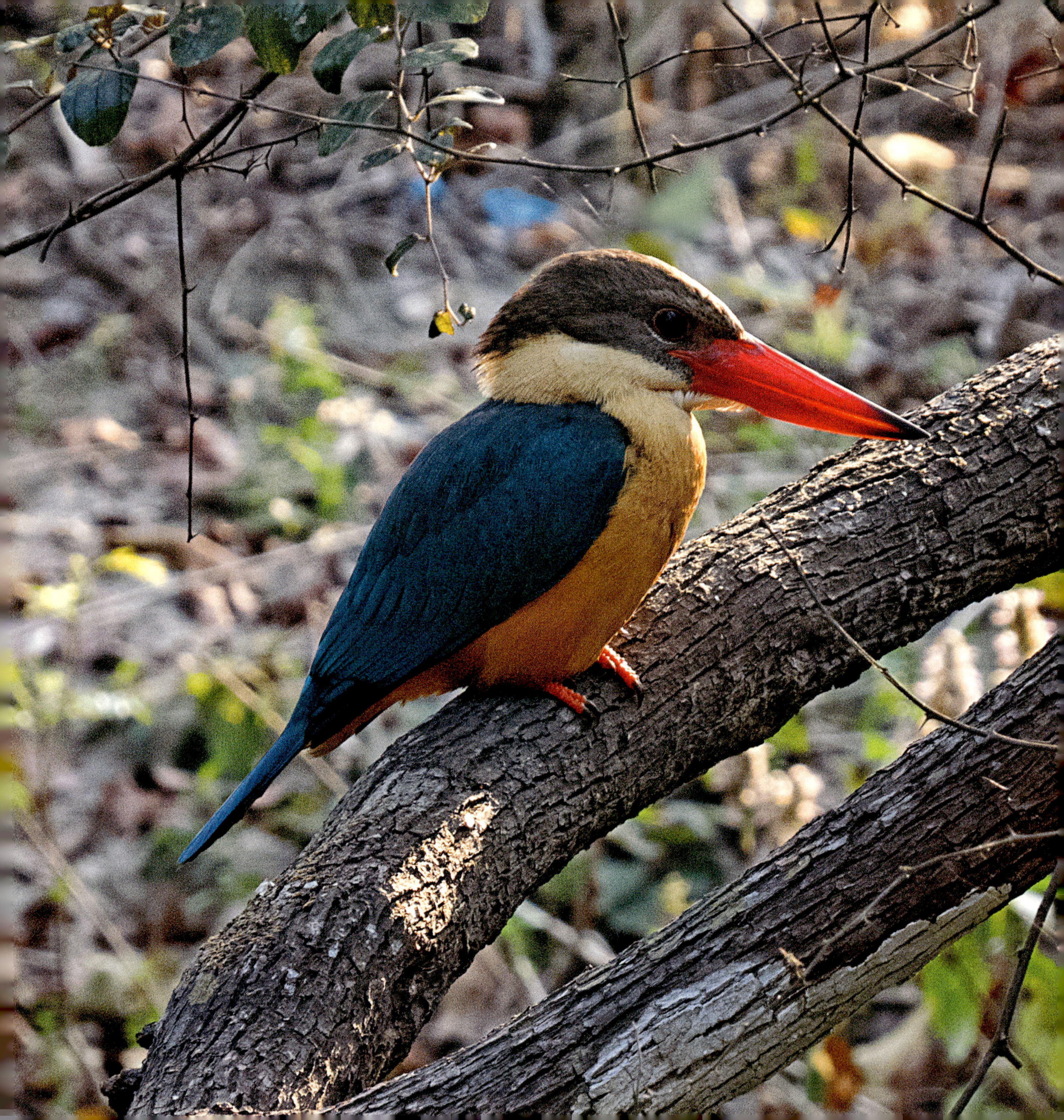

it an ideal habitat not only for a number of resident species but also for those who migrate from the plains of south and the higher reaches of north. Be it rivers, water-front, forest floor, tree trunks, foliage, forest canopy or even the sky above; you can find birds everywhere in Corbett.

During the winter months, its rivers, well-stocked with aquatic life, come alive with the calls of many species of ducks, grebes, storks, bitterns, herons, cormorants, egrets, crakes, coots, stilts, snipes, jacana, teals and many other species that come from far off places to spend winter here. With Kosi river forming its eastern boundary and Ramganga running through it, this entire area is feasting ground for fish eating birds. The calls of various kingfishers are a constant component of the Corbett symphony. From the tiny Common Kingfisher to the giant Crested Kingfisher its waterways are home to a total of five species. Its river sides are also ideal for spotting various redstarts; White-capped, Plumbeous and Blue-capped being common sightings. Among the lapwings Red-wattled, Yellow-wattled and River Lapwings are common, while critically endangered Sociable Lapwings can also be seen sometimes.

Facing page: A Stork-billed Kingfisher

A White-capped Redstart (left), a White-throated Kingfisher (above), a River Lapwing (far above) and a Common Kingfisher (below).

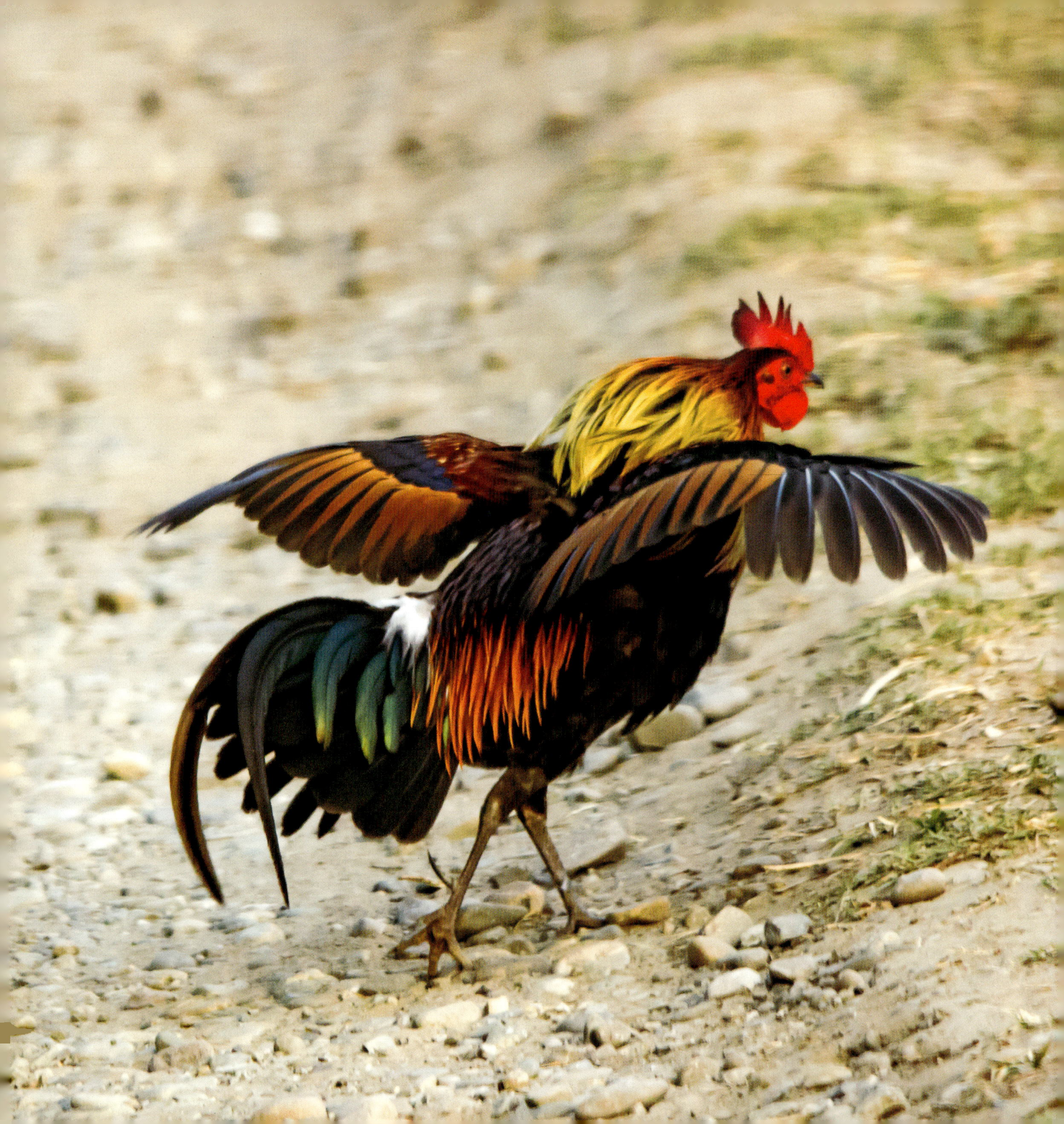

Foraging through its forest floor you'll find many pheasants. Indian Peafowl, the largest of all birds found in India, are common. During the rainy season the males are at their best, with full-grown tail streamers. It is a wonderful sight to find them displaying to woo the females around. As you travel around the park, some Red Junglefowls and Kalij Pheasants are also sure to cross your path. During the summer months a sizeable number of Indian Pitta also descends on the Corbett landscape from their winter home in southern parts of India. And if you are lucky you might even see an occasional Hooded Pitta. At times you can also chance upon a Grey Francolin darting across the dirt track, with a number of young ones in tow. Common Quail, Jungle Bush Quail, Common Buttonquail and Barred Buttonquail are usually so well camouflaged that nothing but their own movement can give away their presence.

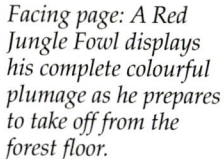

Facing page: A Red Jungle Fowl displays his complete colourful plumage as he prepares to take off from the forest floor.

Above: Red Jungle Fowl —male and a female.

Left: An Indian Pitta

Below far left: A Kalij Pheasant, male and (below centre) a female.

Below: A Hooded Pitta

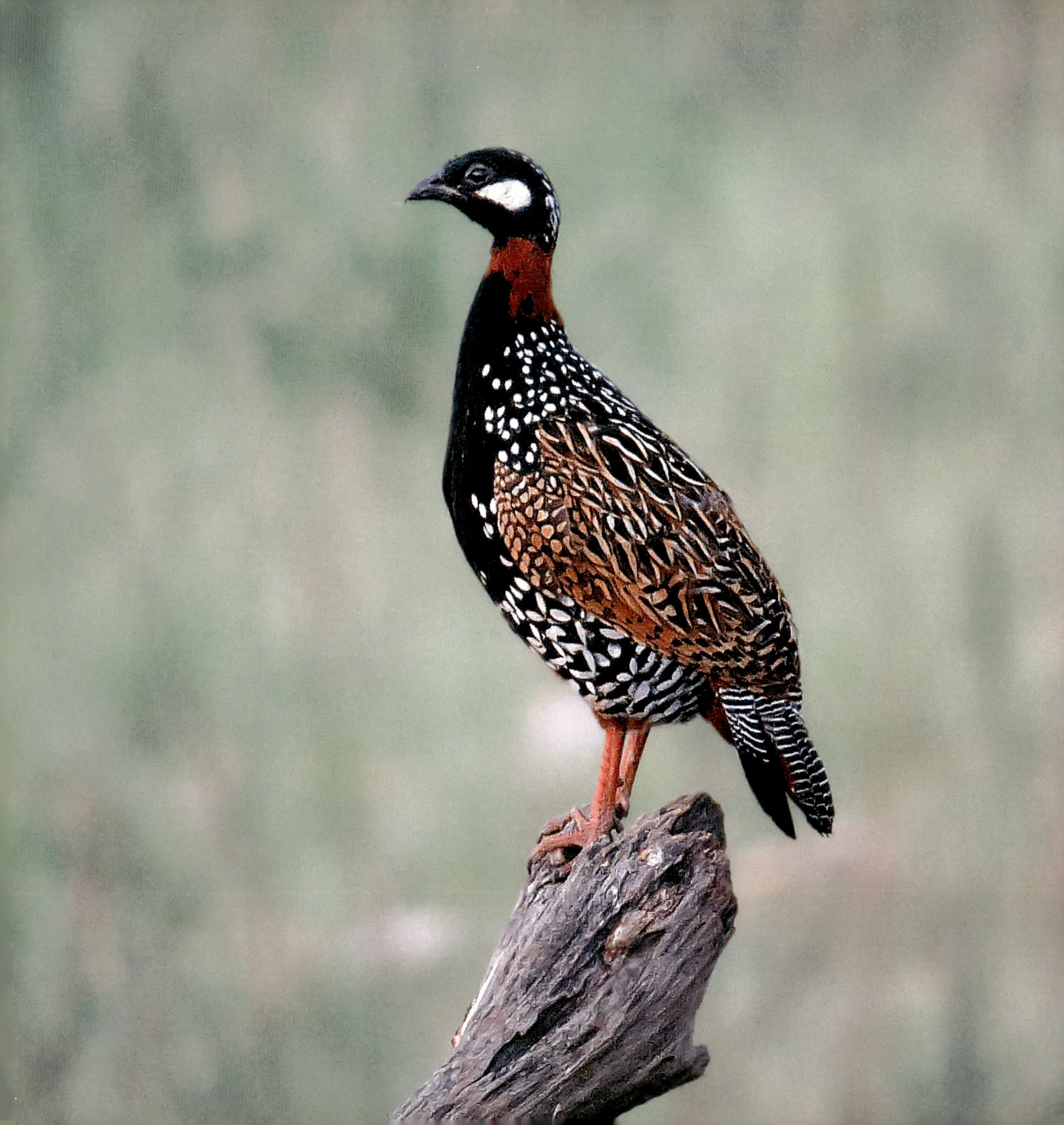

Grasslands of Dhikala *chaur* are permanent habitat of Black Francolin, and it is a common sight to see them perched on termite-hills and tree stumps. Here you can also see a number of munias, sparrows, buntings, larks, prinias, bee-eaters and many other grassland birds. On certain trees within the grassland there are also colonies of baya weavers.

Tree trunks are an ideal place to look for tree creepers and nuthatch, and you can find them clinging to them looking for insects hidden in the bark crevices. Giving them company as insect hunters are the woodpeckers. Corbett is particularly rich in woodpecker species and as many as sixteen different variety have been sighted here, including the largest of them all—the Great Slaty Woodpecker.

Facing page: A Black Francolin perched on a tree stump in Dhikala grassland provides an uncluttered clear shot opportunity.

Left: A Greater Flemback (female) also known as Large Golden-backed Woodpecker and (above) A Brown-capped Pygmy Woodpecker

147

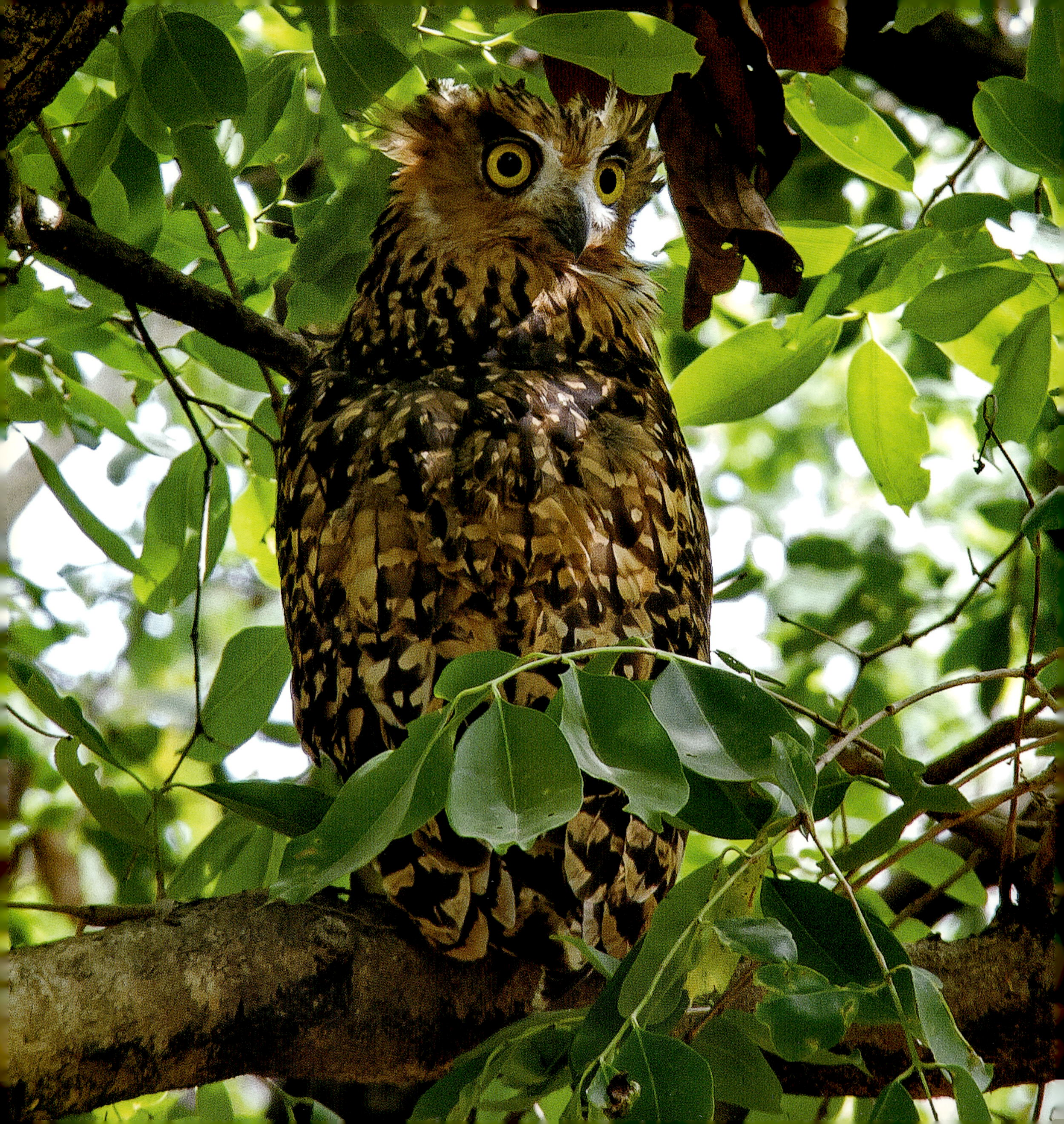

Foliage and the canopy of Corbett woodlands are home to an amazing variety of woodland birds. Various species of bulbul, parakeet, pigeon, dove, cuckoo, barbet, minivet, drongo, magpie, jay and bunting are visible throughout in good numbers. The forest is also home to a number of colourful fly-catchers, sunbirds, flowerpeckers, tits, warblers and babbler species. Indian roller and dollar bird are also common here.

No visitor to the Corbett landscape can miss that it is a raptor rich country. Over thirty species of eagles, harriers, kites, hawks, buzzards and other members of the *Accipitridae* family can be found here, many of them critically endangered worldwide. Sightings are easy, as they usually prefer to perch on leaf-less dry trees. Corbett is also the favoured home to over a dozen species of owls and owlets. Brown Fish Owl and Tawny Fish Owl are particularly a common sighting during a drive from Dhangarhi gate to Dhikala campus. For others one has to be a little lucky as they prefer to spend the day hiding in thick foliage.

Facing page: A Tawny Fish Owl

Yellow-footed Green Pigeon (left) Dollar Bird (above) and a Spot-bellied Eagle Owl (far above)

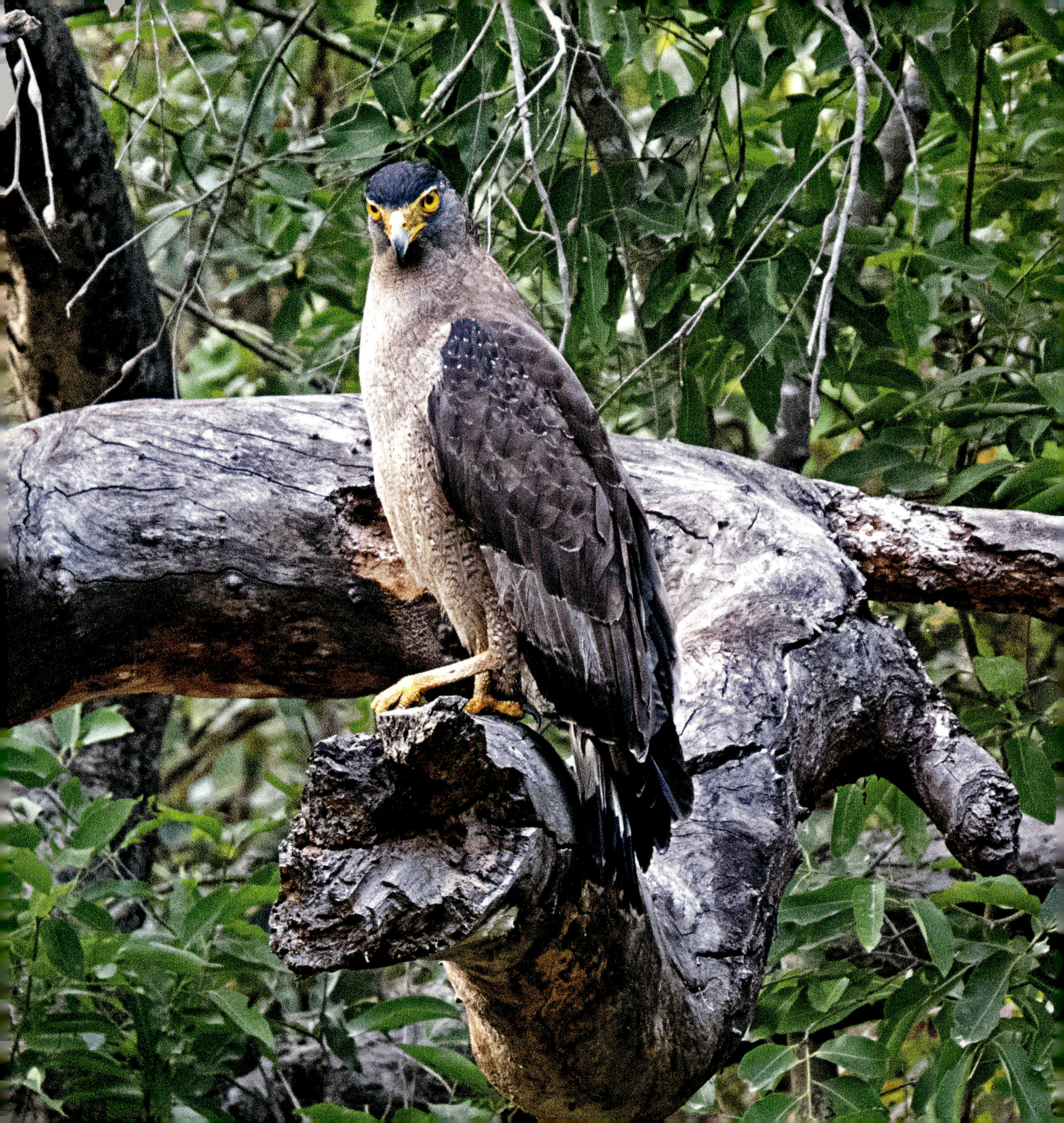

Vultures are an important part of our overall ecosystem. They are nature's most efficient cleaners. Unfortunately, in the past decade and a half their population is estimated to have declined by over 98 per cent due to the use of Diclofenac, an anti-inflammatory drug given to livestock. The residual remains of the medicine in dead animals cause kidney failure and ultimately death in many species of vultures. Fortunately it was only in protected areas like Corbett, where vultures were not feeding on carcasses of domestic animals that these species managed to survive in small numbers. Of the eight species of vultures found in Corbett all but the Griffon Vulture are at various levels of threat; with Red-headed Vulture, White-rumped Vulture and Slender-billed Vulture listed as critically endangered. On one of our trips to Dhikala we were particularly lucky to spot six red-headed vultures that had settled to feed on the carcass of a male spotted deer. The unfortunate animal had managed to get away from the jaws of a tiger but had succumbed to its injuries in the grassland near the Forest Rest House campus.

Although walking is the best way for bird-watching and one does not have that privilege in Corbett National Park, yet a lot of avian life is visible even while travelling in a vehicle. The other option is to spend the day sitting on the machan and see the birds coming for a drink to the water hole or perched all around you at eye-level in the forest canopy.

Facing page: A very handsome Crested Serpent Eagle obligingly poses for the camera.

Left: An Oriental Honey Buzzard having a drink.

Above: Red-headed Vultures on the carcass of a male Spotted Deer in Dhikala zone.

Far above: A Himalayan Griffon at their nesting site in Jhirna zone.

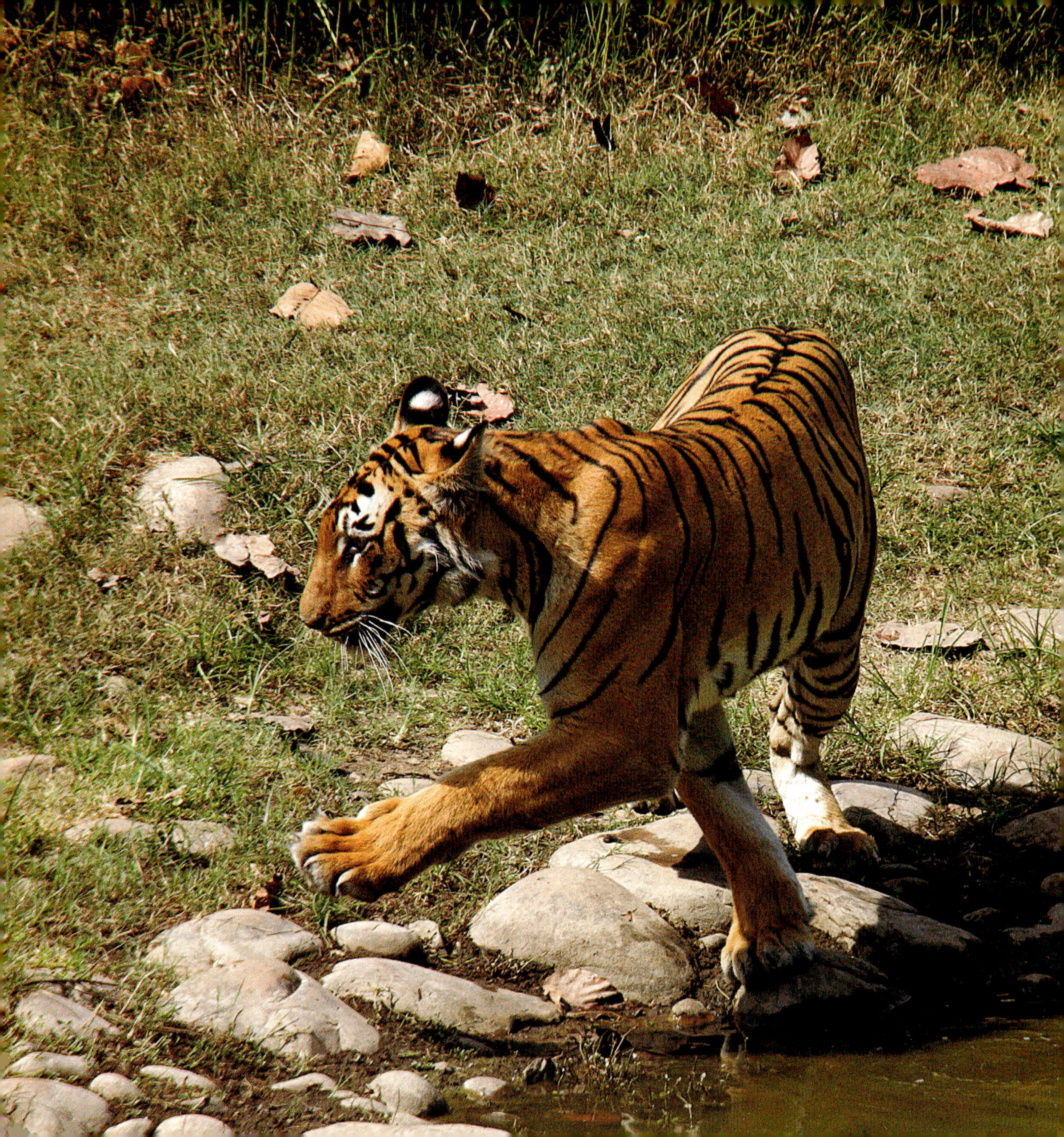

HIGH UP IN A MACHAN
—view from the top

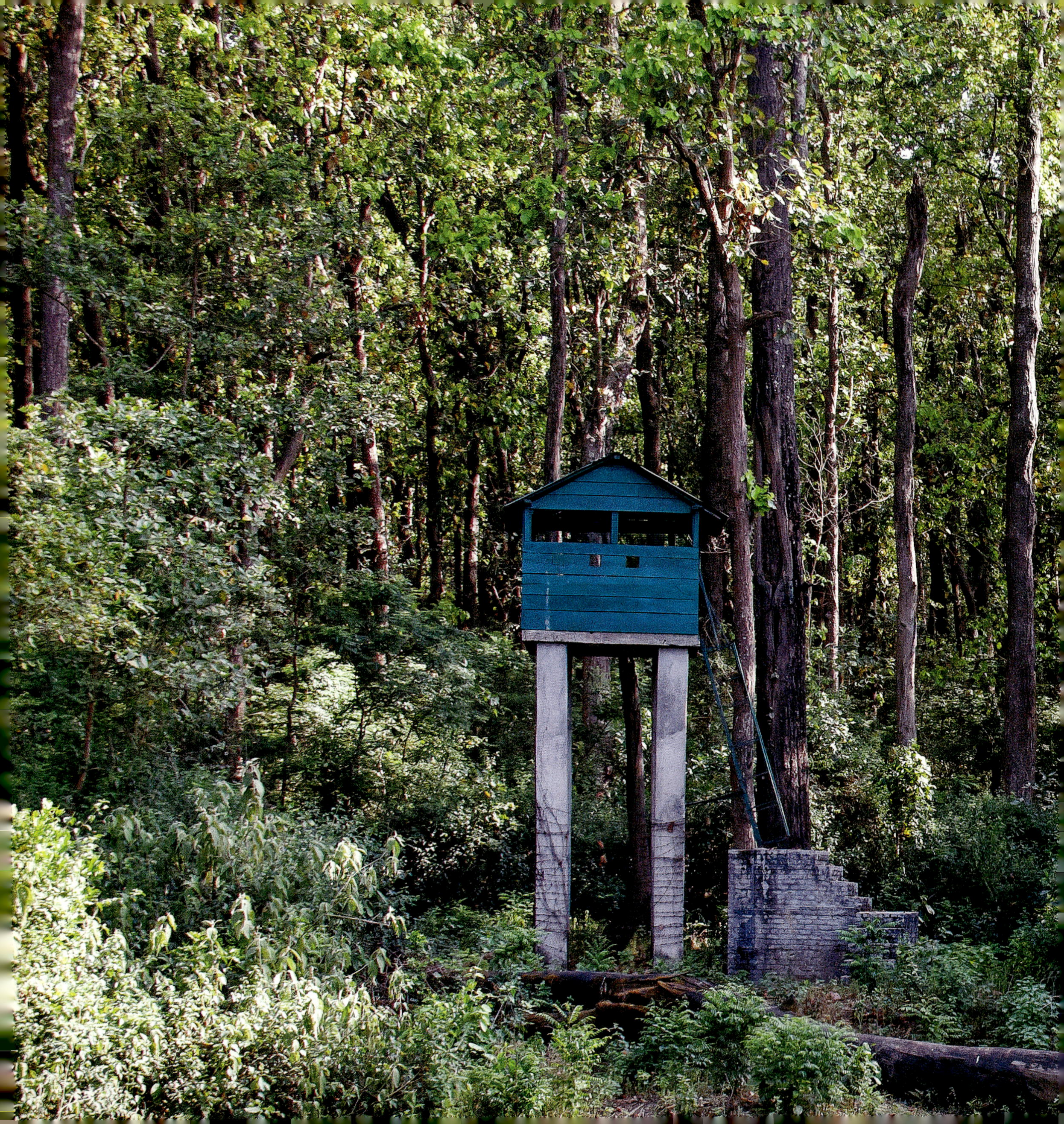

HIGH UP IN A MACHAN

—view from the top

There are many ways to experience Corbett. Other than the usual safari option, with a little effort, one can convince the forest officials to grant permission for spending the day at the strategically built machans in the forest. These watch towers are built in close proximity to water holes and offer a commanding view of the happenings at the centre of activity, particularly in the summer months when most of the water-bodies in the forest dry up. Spending a day at the watch tower is a trial of patience and endurance. Once you are lodged there, there is no going back before the appointed time when your transport will come to pick you up. During the summer months the temperature inside the tin roofed box-in-the-air can soar to a sizzling 40+! It is a must that to sustain through the day one carries plenty of water and some snacks that don't make crunchy sounds.

In June 2014, when we embarked on our 'Mission Machan', the sweltering heat of the north Indian summer was at its worst. Sitting motionless and quiet with eyes focused on the little hub of activity in front was like seeing a power point presentation by Mother Nature. The 360° view around us was the forest canopy, which from our high perch provided a rare opportunity to look at the birds from eye level. The jungle symphony was the rustle of leaves and constant chirping of birds seen and unseen.

Previous double-spread: This tiger had a quick drink and turned around and vanished into the foliage.

Left: Machan—our high perch in the forest.

Left: A Spangled Drongo on the trees around and a Common Green Magpie (above) having a bath at the waterhole.

A couple of Indian Paradise Flycatchers were putting up quite a show as they swooped in the water and flew to a nearby perch. The male of the species who have a black head and crest with white or rufous upperparts and long tail streamers were exhibiting exquisite agility, followed by the females in their attempt at catching some flying insects. In the far corner a turtle had taken possession of the shallow as he cooled off and an assortment of bulbuls were making a din at the edge as if squabbling over first right.

Above: A Shikra looking for respite from the summer heat rests in a little puddle of water.

Right: An Indian Paradise Flycatcher caught during his antics over the waterhole.

By mid-morning a light breeze had picked up. A Black-hooded Oriole merrily hopped around on a tree near the machan. This magnificently brilliant coloured male has a black head contrasting with a golden-yellow body and is a resident of the wooded areas of Corbett. An Oriental Magpie Robin was showing off its various whistling songs. In the afternoon, when all was at its stillest and sleepiest best, a Crested Serpent Eagle came in for a drink of water. After scanning the area for a long time, he finally flew down to quench his thirst. A mongoose lumbered in an hour later but no big cat.

On the day before, there had been a sighting of a female tigress with her three cubs, around a year old. They had been frequently seen on the Dhikala *chaur*. A female with three cubs was a matter of much excitement for the staff and the guides as more often than not all the cubs in a litter do not make it to maturity due to a high rate of mortality. By evening we had a female Sambar gingerly approach the water and after satisfying herself of her safety, drank and left quickly.

We decided to try our luck the next day at a different waterhole. The waterhole perpendicular to the machan is surrounded by a thick growth of Lantana and weed. One look at the place and I felt as though today we would see a tiger. It was exceptionally quiet and soon the heat started to take a toll on the senses. In the lull, my mind almost drifted into dreams. Suddenly a Wild Boar dashed across the view and I knew that a tiger was certainly somewhere close by. I looked through the peep hole and there he was, looking straight at me. He had walked through the narrow clearing between the bushes and stood looking at us as if aware of our presence. With dappled light playing a light and shade dance, fiery eyes blazing with no fear, stood a handsome male tiger. He gently walked to the water hole and took a few quick laps of water. I was transfixed, unable to move a muscle or even pick up my camera. I just looked at him in awe. But all this while my colleague, a seasoned wildlife photographer, was focused and shooting. His camera whizzing like a machine gun at seven frames per second captured every single twist and turn of the big cat before he gently walked away.

This was not the first time I had seen a tiger but I still felt blessed to once again have set my sight on this magnificent creation of God.

Above: This Wild Boar had sensed the presence of the tiger near the waterhole and bolted from the scene without stopping for a drink and this tiger (left) emerged from the bushes just a few moments later.

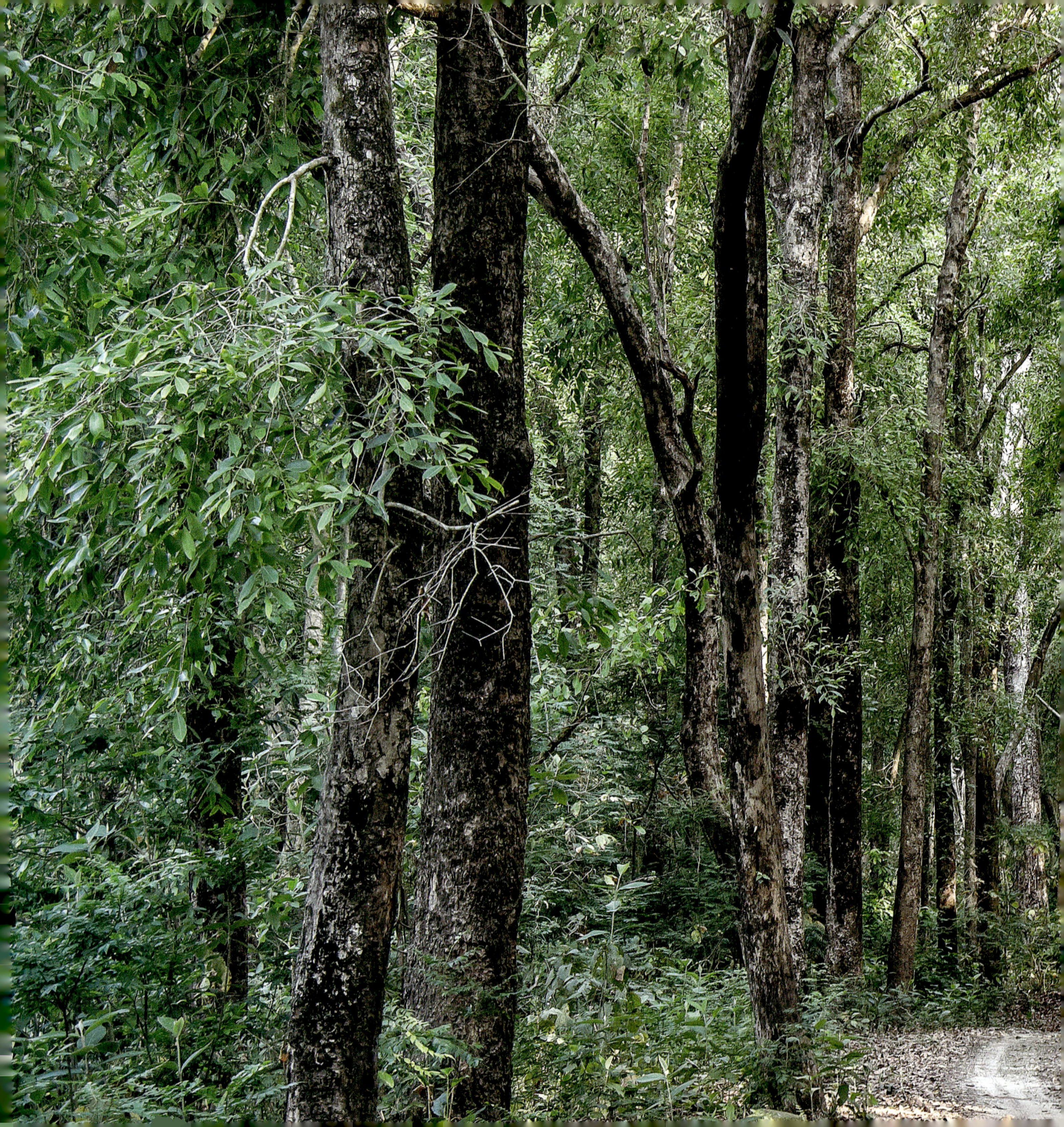

FORESTS
—lungs of our environment

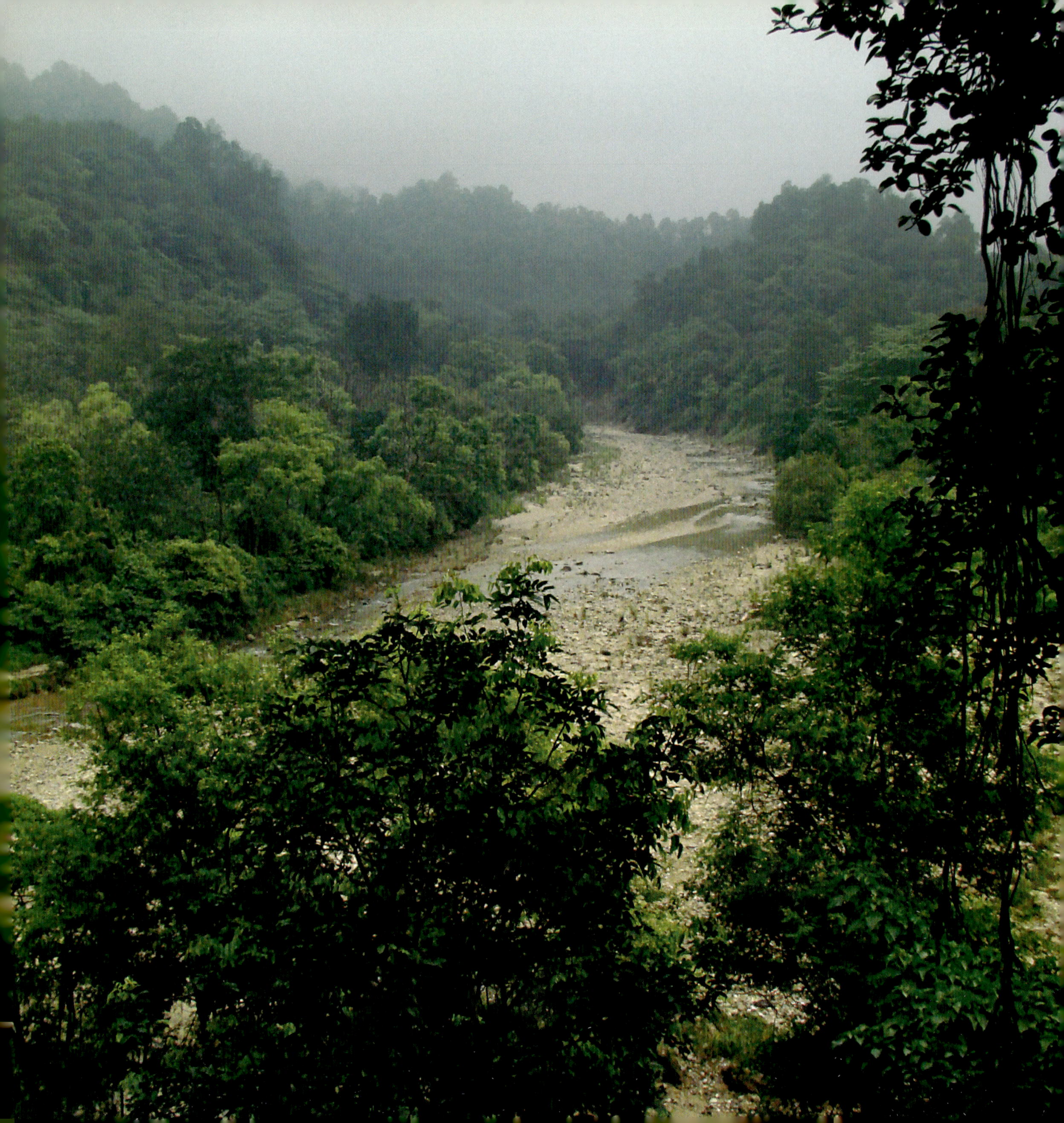

FORESTS

—lungs of our environment

Forests are literally the lungs of our earth. We owe our survival to them. Just as we take in oxygen and exhale carbon dioxide, trees take carbon dioxide from the air and restore oxygen to the atmosphere for us to breathe again. Forests like Corbett National Park are a valuable resource not only because it provides a home for the tiger and a host of other species, but also because without them our own survival would be threatened. With tigers at the apex of wildlife, humans and forests are links of the same chain. Presence of tiger population in a forest is a sign of an intact habitat—a forest that is viable and healthy. If we look carefully at the shrinking tiger landscape of India in historical perspective, it becomes clear that the disappearance of tigers has almost always spelled disaster for the forest too. The erstwhile tiger areas slowly get depleted, deforested and encroached, adding to the ecological disaster in a significant manner. Our remaining forests are there because there is the tiger in those forests in the first place. The presence of one is vital to the other. Deforestation is an open invitation to global warming and the monster of greenhouse effect.

As a natural phenomenon greenhouse effect is what makes life possible on earth and gives us the warmth to survive and grow food. Without it, scientists estimate that the average temperature on Earth would be colder by approximately 30 degrees Celsius, far too cold to sustain our current ecosystem. But the same phenomenon which makes life on Earth possible, when stretched beyond natural limits by spewing excessive quantities of greenhouse gases into the atmosphere, contributes to global climate change. It melts polar ice deposits, shrinks glaciers, brings torrential rains, droughts and wreaks worldwide havoc. To maintain the balance between too little and too much warming of our planet, nature provided us with the most effective carbon absorption system—the trees.

Trees not only replenish oxygen but also cool and moisten the air. They break wind speed, anchor soil, shade land from sun, prevent surface moisture evaporation, slow the movement of water, prevent land erosion, provide food, fuel, medicines and shelter countless species. They are the largest living organisms of our earth and they have almost 350 million years' experience in doing their job of sequestering carbon. Half of a tree by weight is stored carbon. With their unique ability to lock up large amounts of carbon in

Previous double-spread: A forest drive under the green canopy of a mix forest in the Dhikala zone.

Facing page: A seasonal stream surrounded by a lush green forest. A view from the Jhirna zone.

161

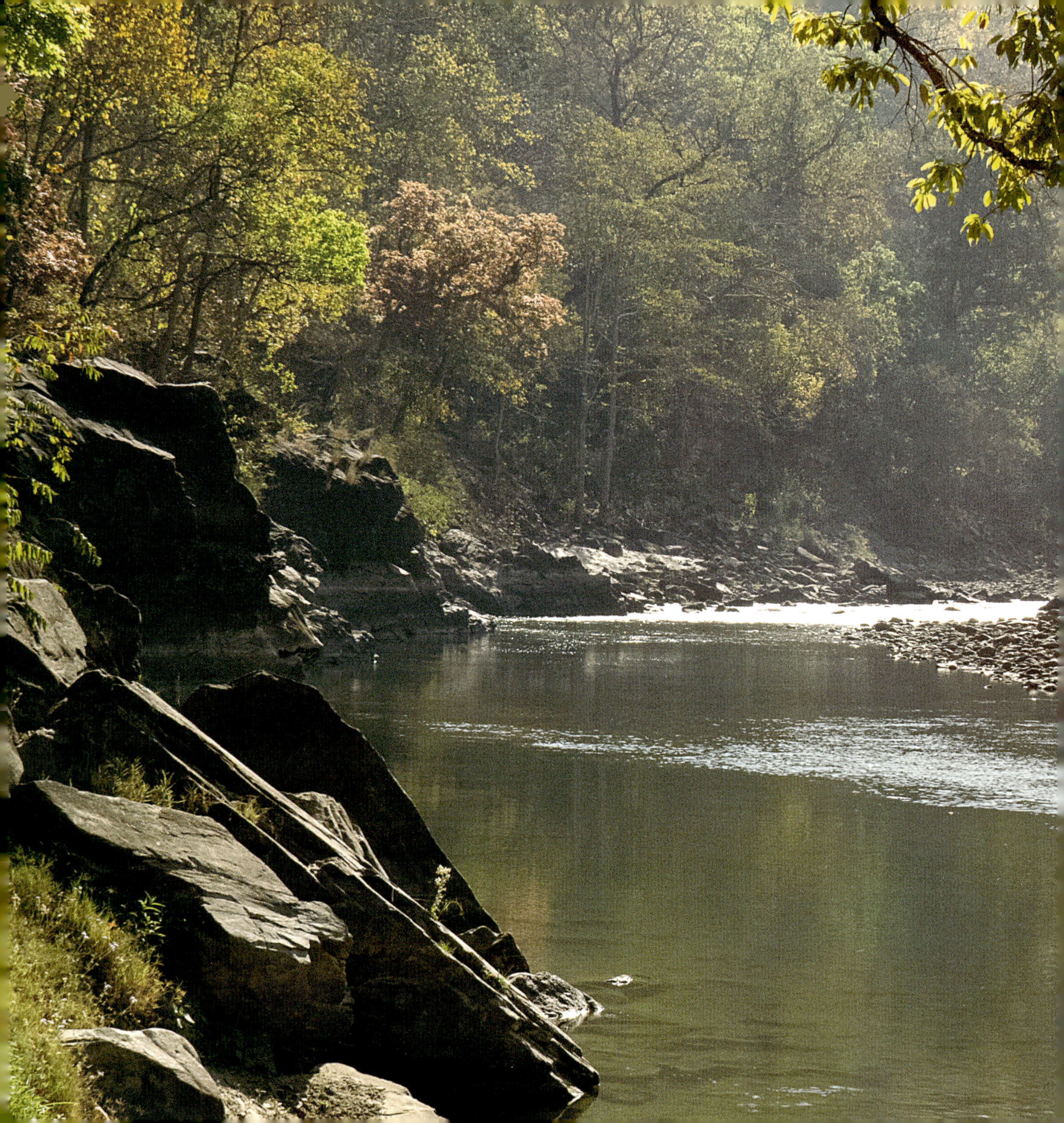

their biomass, they are the world's greatest carbon vaults. If ever a question was to surface in any human mind as to why we need the forests, the answer will be simple—we need them for life on earth to survive.

Today we are at a stage where human activities, especially those of burning fossil fuels and land clearing, has led to an all-time increase in the concentrations of greenhouse gases which is contributing to the warming of the earth. These excess carbon emissions are leading to alarming climate change and global warming. Earth's air is thick with extra emissions. We have to safeguard our remaining forests as that's our only chance to fight global warming. All plants require carbon dioxide for photosynthesis and produce oxygen in the process. More forests would mean more absorption of CO_2 that fuels global warming.

Large forests can influence regional weather patterns, creating their own microclimates. Forests also act as an efficient flood control system by acting like giant sponges that catch the run off. Roots of the trees can absorb a lot of water during a flash flood and reduce soil loss and damage. Forests help stabilize the soil and thus prevent erosion by wind and water. If we look at some of the recent natural disasters like flash floods and mud-slides, it is evident that the loss of life and property would have been far less if forest cover of those areas was left intact to soften the fury of nature.

A green landscape complete with tree canopy, creepers and undergrowth, thriving with birds animals and insects is not only a source of clean air and water, if managed well; it is also a great resource with tremendous economic potential. Forests, mountains and rivers have always been a great getaway for the tired mind and soul. It is in the lap of nature that man returns time and again to rest and rejuvenate. Sustainable tourism is an important economic activity that can flourish in the shadow of healthy environment. It can provide jobs to sons of the soil who have traditionally lived in harmony with nature. Local employment can prevent migration to the already over-burdened cities. More forests would mean more wildlife, more visitors to admire it, more trekking, camping, birding and more professionals to guide the visitors. Tourism—the industry without a chimney, can certainly grow in harmony with nature.

Above: A road block that no one will ever complain about. In the Bijrani zone, a tigress decides to have a siesta on the soft sand of the forest road in the shade of a wayside tree. Such god-sent situations provide a great photo opportunity for the visitors.

Facing page: Pristine beauty of undisturbed nature. A gently flowing Ramganga river framed by the rocky riverside and the forest dressed in a colourful spring attire.

In praise of Termites

According to David Bignell, a termite expert and emeritus professor of zoology at Queen Mary University of London, 'They're the ultimate soil engineers.'

The holes that they dig through the ground serve as macro-pores to soak the rainwater deep into the ground preventing otherwise a run-off with topsoil. Their art full recipe of mixing inorganic materials like clay, granules of stones and sand with organic bits of leaf litter, discarded shells, other dead remains of insects and even pieces of furs and feathers, creates a unique blend that helps the soil retain nutrients and resist erosion.

Over all, termites are a blessing for the soil, and isn't that what our earth is made of?

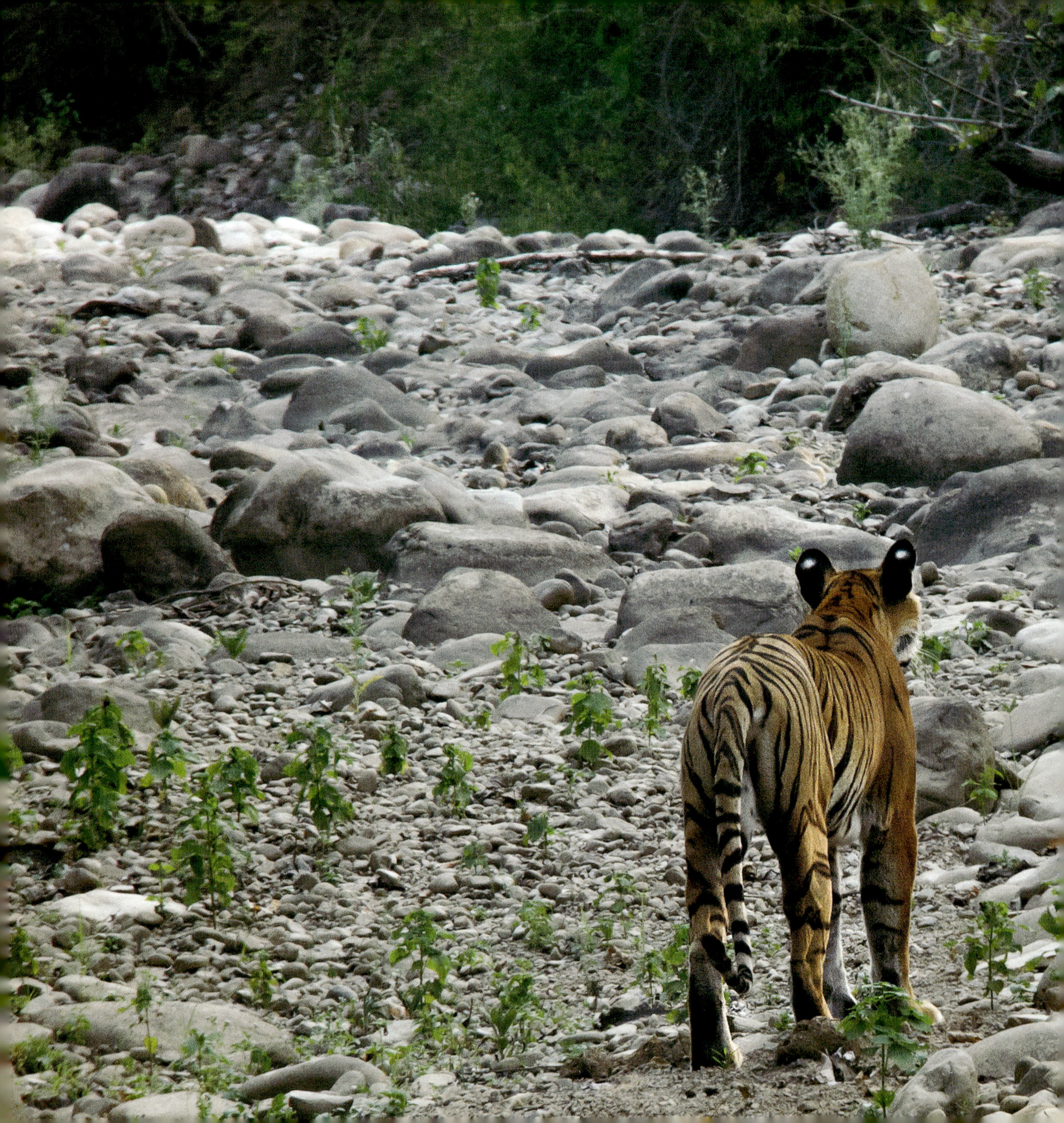

THREATS TO WILDLIFE
fighting for survival

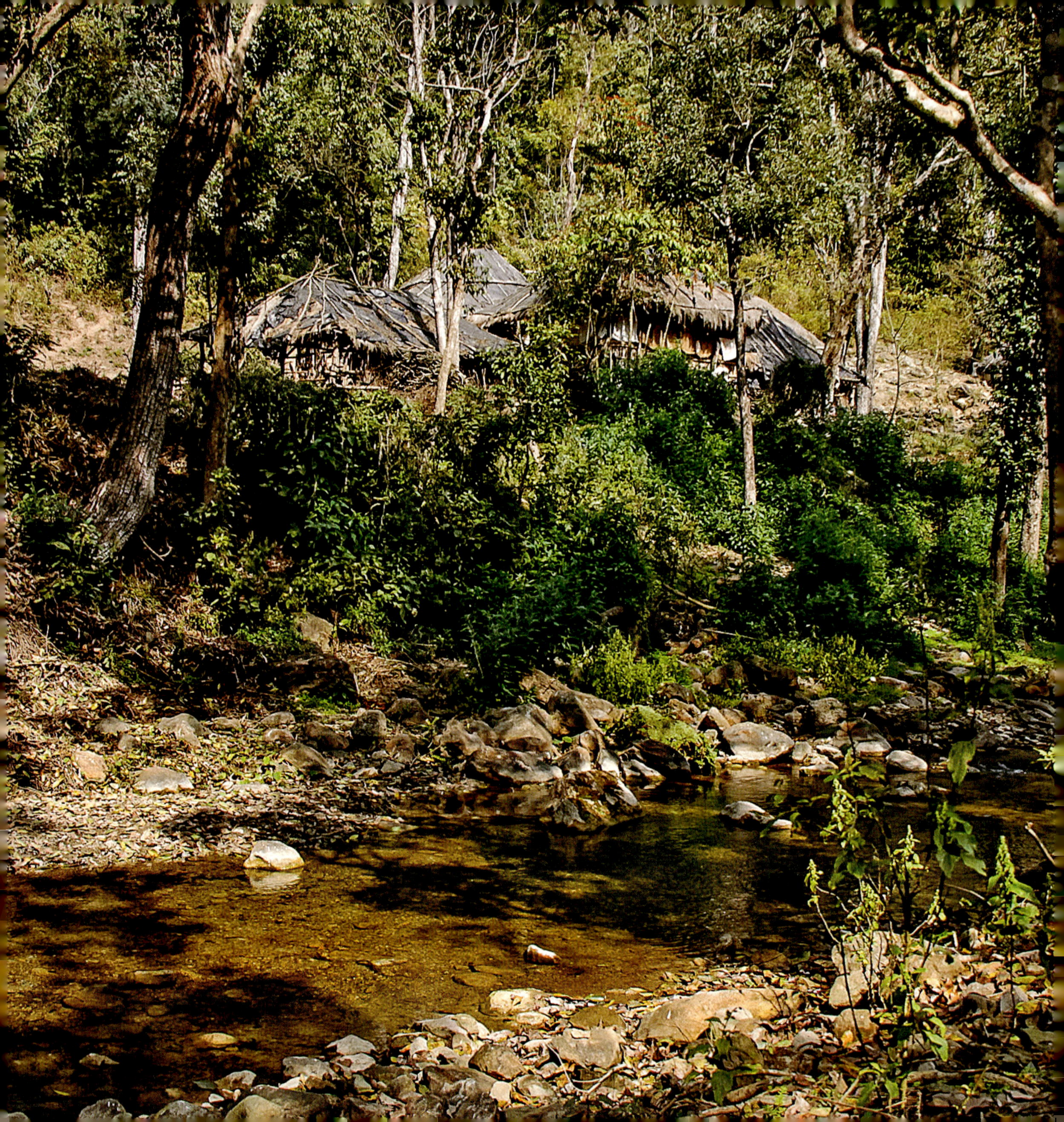

THREATS TO WILDLIFE
—*fighting for survival*

In nature there is a great bond between the habitat and its inhabitants. The survival of one is dependent on the other. If the habitat is disturbed the effect on wildlife is almost instant. By experience we know that the disappearance of wildlife results in certain depletion of forest too. In both cases, loss of habitat and poaching, the reason can always be traced to direct human actions. As we all know, mindless *shikar*, poaching and loss of habitat had brought tiger numbers to an alarming low level by the first decade of the twentieth century.

Shrinking protected areas push wildlife into direct conflict with humans, a threat even greater than the menace of poaching. As per data available more tigers and elephants have died in man-animal conflict than the numbers that fell to poachers. As many as 176 elephants and 110 tigers perished in the wildlife conflict zones between 2012 and 2014; while 20 elephants and 52 tigers were lost due to poaching in the corresponding period.

Tigers have remained at the apex of faunal pyramid for ages. They are prolific breeders. Tiger numbers boom when given the right kind of habitat and protection. A breeding tigress in a span of ten years can produce over a dozen cubs; if circumstances allow at least half that number can reach maturity.

Protection and awareness are two established key factors in tiger conservation. It is amply evident from the fact that tiger numbers increased from 1,706 in 2011 to 2,226 in 2014. During the same period tiger population in Uttarakhand has doubled and now stands at 340. Only Karnataka has more tigers at 408. Uttarakhand has achieved this success from 178 tigers in 2006 to 340 in 2014 by providing better protection to its tigers and safeguarding its habitat from poachers and encroachment. Now, we also have more accurate and scientific methods of survey. The earlier method of pug-mark identification to estimate tiger numbers was always open to doubts. The new system of census by camera trap images is certainly a more accurate method.

Tigers are fiercely territorial animals. A male tiger has a large territory that is interspersed by the territories of up to five females. The size of a male's territory may vary depending on the availability of food. In a healthy habitat with an abundance of prey a tiger's home range or territory may be as small as 7-10 sq km. In areas where there is less prey the territory can be as big as 60-100 sq km. A well protected area like a reserve that

Previous double-spread: At the end of the day this tiger on the dry riverbed seemed to be looking into an uncertain future.

Facing page: A human settlement in the domain of the wild. Dwellings like these of the Van Gujjars *or traditional cattle herders of the forest, are now gradually being relocated outside the wildlife areas.*

has an abundance of large prey will have a surplus of tigers that roam from place to place because they have not been able to find a vacant territory. They are called transients that are always on the lookout for a territory of their own. Transients may challenge a resident tiger or oust an aging or weaker tiger from its territory. However, when all territories in a reserve are occupied, these tigers may get pushed towards the edges of the forests.

With the number of tigers on the rise, there is one more question which is now staring us in the face. Where will all these increasing number of tigers go? The growing numbers will lead to tiger population spilling out of the protected areas, and an increase in conflict with humans. Young adults will need to move outwards in search of new territory to mate and hunt. Shrinking green boundaries bring them in direct conflict with human habitation and hamper their free movement. This enhances the need for contiguous forests through wildlife corridors. The survival of any population depends on its ability to sustain a viable gene pool. A Tiger Reserve with more than twenty adult tigresses can sustain a good population on its own because of genetic viability.

Though Corbett sits secure with its 150 plus tigers, young adults need to disperse outward to look for their own territories. According to a study by WWF, Ramnagar Forest Division with over 15 tigers per 100 sq km has the highest density of tigers outside a Protected Area anywhere in India and perhaps the world. In fact this density is higher than that of many well-known Tiger Reserves of India.

A solitary male in musth busy feeding himself. Elephants spend a large part of the day consuming fodder.

During the county-wide tiger estimation conducted in 2014 it came to light that around 35 to 40 per cent of India's tigers are today living outside protected areas. This scenario makes the importance of restoring wildlife corridors more urgent than ever before. It is only these corridors that can help wild cats find safe homes in nearby protected areas. With these figures glaring in our face, connectivity of forests through wildlife corridors cannot be under estimated any more. In the Corbett landscape the Kosi river corridor lies in the Nainital and Almora districts. Beautiful and mighty Kosi, towards the end of its journey in Uttarakhand, flows down the Himalayan foothills. Kosi does not enter the park but forms the eastern boundary of Corbett National Park as it flows from Mohan through Dhikuli towards Ramnagar. A drive along the river through that length makes it evident that this is an important wildlife corridor that connects the forests of Corbett Tiger Reserve with the forests of Ramnagar Forest Division on the other side. The connectivity between the two areas is vital for the free movement of wildlife, especially tigers.

Connectivity through this corridor is, however, threatened by the unchecked development along the Ramnagar-Ranikhet highway along the banks of the river. A wide road built through the Bangajhala valley has further cut off elephant migratory routes. This kind of rapid change and fragmentation to the habitat can isolate the source population as has been seen towards the Chilla-Motichur corridor.

Wildlife corridors are important to prevent inbreeding by allowing a viable exchange of genes. Elephants need to migrate in their search for large amounts of food and water. Sunderkhal, an illegal human habitation, sits in the middle of a vital elephant corridor and has seen various incidents of conflict with wild animals.

Garjia temple is an interesting structure built on a rock in the middle of Kosi river. It is dedicated to goddess Girija, believed to be the daughter of the Himalayas and consort of lord Shiva the preserver of the universe.

Poaching

Poaching continues to be a big threat to wildlife. Tigers are poached for their skin and parts which are sold in the illegal market. It is believed that components of a single tiger can fetch hundreds of thousands of dollars in the international market. Although this international trade in tiger and tiger parts is banned under the Convention of International Trade in Endangered Species (CITES), in reality it continues unabated due to the unending demand from China, Taiwan, Japan and South Korea. The Indian sub-continent, which is home to nearly 60 per cent of the global wild population of tigers is naturally always under threat from poachers and smugglers of this lucrative illegal contraband. Almost all poached tigers reach China through the porous 1,751 km border India shares with Nepal. Tigers are poached mainly for their skin and bones that are used to make tiger bone wine and various traditional Chinese medicines. The use of tiger parts in Chinese medicines is nothing new but in recent times their demand has increased manifold due to an increase in the standards of living in South East Asia. Today a larger number of neo-rich see these expensive endangered tiger products as a symbol of status to show-off their wealth.

Unless China embarks on a policy of running an environment-friendly awareness campaign to highlight the impending danger to global tiger population, the majestic big cat will remain in the cross-hairs of poachers' guns.

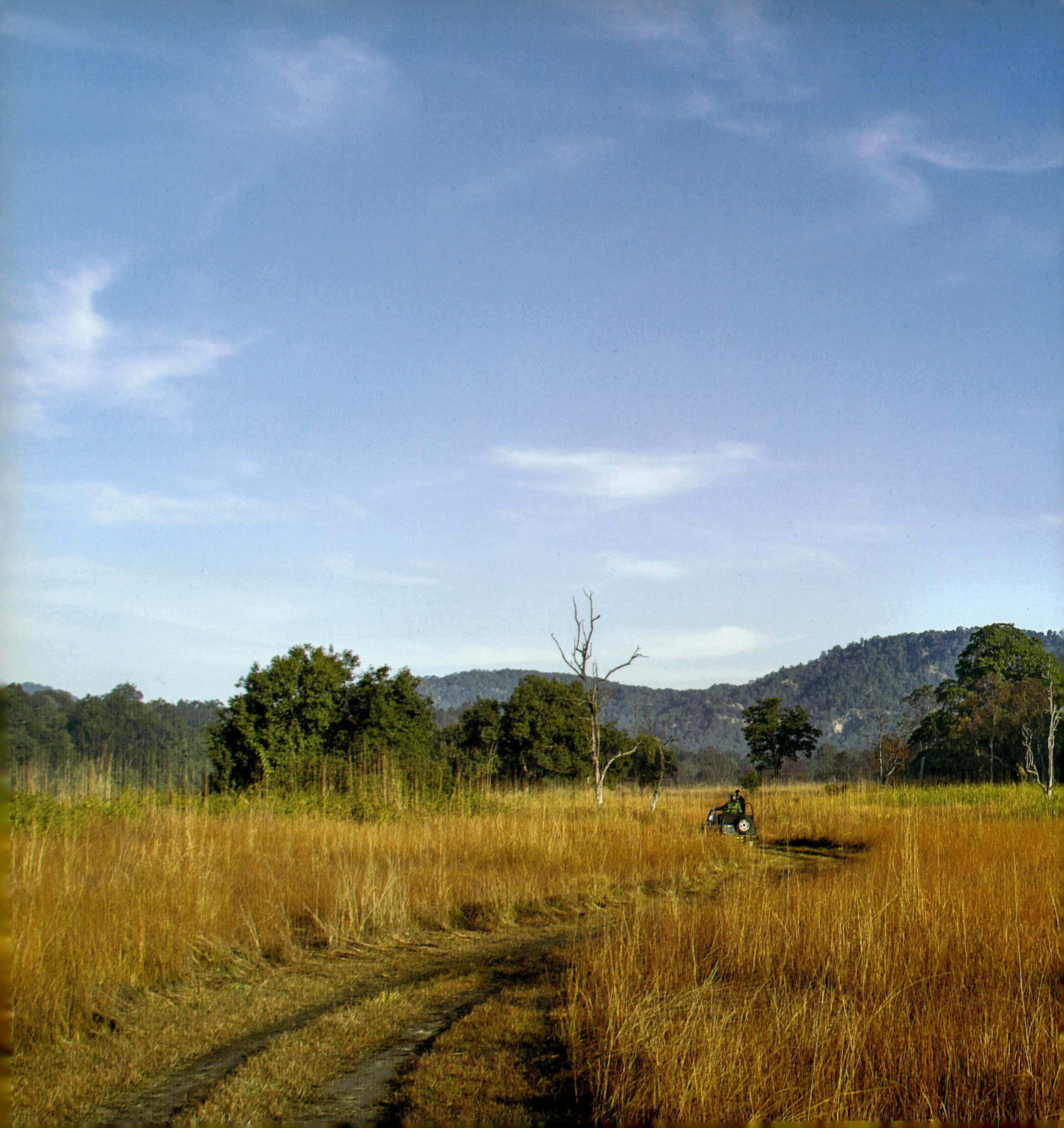

DEVELOPMENT VERSUS CONSERVATION
—in search of a balance

DEVELOPMENT VERSUS CONSERVATION

—in search of a balance

In the Indian way of thinking, Earth, Sky, Air, Fire and Water (*Bhumi, Gagan, Vayu, Agni* and *Neer*) are the five fundamental constituents of nature. '*Bhagwan*'—the generic term for 'God' in Hindi is nothing but an abbreviation of these five words (Bh+Ga+Wa+Aa+Na) which simply means that according to the ancient Indian wisdom, 'Nature is God'.

We have traditionally referred to earth and rivers as mother, called sky, air and fire *Devtas* or Gods, worshiped trees and revered mountains as abode of the divine. Aquatic, amphibian and land animals feature as incarnations of God in Indian mythology. A very large number of reptiles, rodents, mammals and birds are associated with the Indian pantheon and command great respect. Living in harmony with nature has always been a way of life in India. Great sages of the past always lived in the lap of nature, retreating to forests and mountains as sanctuary for meditation and contemplation. Even today, if you explore any forest, you will find an ancient temple or a site associated with a great sage, somewhere deep in its green folds. Man derived sustenance from nature and in return revered and protected his environment.

Our survival as a species is linked to our environment. But with the pressure of population and development today, our environment is depleting at a fast pace. If we do not wake up to this changing scenario, the very survival of not only many plant and animal species but also of us humans will be threatened. The results of dwindling green cover and flow of human and industrial waste into rivers is visible all around. Polluted urban air and contaminated rivers are already a cause of great concern as respiratory diseases and water born maladies are visibly on the increase. On our path to progress we are drawing a lot more from nature than its capacity to recover and regenerate. The equation has gone out of balance. Our environment and we humans, both are today standing at the threshold of a disaster.

India of course needs to develop. According to the 2012 report by the Planning Commission of India (Tendulkar Committee), 21.9 % population of India lives below the international poverty line of US$ 1.25 per day. Over the past decade, poverty in India has consistently been on the decline, and now the number of poor is estimated at 250 million. Today poverty decline in India is one of the fastest in the world.

Below: Blending with its environment, Vanghat—an eco-friendly resort on the periphery of Corbett.

It is not a coincidence that over the same past decade our environment has also deteriorated to alarming levels. Two of our rivers, one of them the Holy Ganga, are among the world's most polluted rivers. 13 of the world's most polluted 20 cities of the world are in India, with Delhi—the capital, ranking at number one position on the shameful chart.

The connection between an estimated daily loss of over three hundred acres of forest cover worldwide, and deteriorating environment is not an alarmist hypothesis any more. It is an established fact that merits serious thought to balance the equation between development and environment. We have now reached that critical point where if we have to keep our earth fit for humans to live, the environment cannot be ignored any more. The government must formulate policies and grant sanctions to development projects keeping in mind their environmental cost.

As a global citizen, India has a great responsibility that it cannot escape. We are not only the custodians of the world's largest population of tigers and one-horned rhinos in the wild, India is also home for the 132 species of plants and animals listed as 'Critically Endangered' worldwide.

We have to ensure that the juggernaut of development does not trample over the environmental heritage which is ours only for safekeeping. We have to pass it on to the future generations.

Previous double-spread: a view of the sprawling grassland in Bijrani zone.

Below: Spring is a celebration of the next generation. Colourful new leaves herald the beginning of a new cycle in nature.

CHECKLISTS OF CORBETT NATIONAL PARK

BIRDS

ORDER: STRIGIFORMES

Family: *Tytonidae*

Barn Owl *Tyto alba*
Grass Owl *Tyto capensis*

Family: *Strigidae*

Mountain Scops Owl *Otus spilocephalus*
Oriental Scops Owl *Otus sunia*
Collared Scops Owl *Otus bakkamoena*
Eurasian Eagle Owl *Bubo bubo*
Spot-bellied Eagle Owl *Bubo nipalensis*
Brown Fish Owl *ketupa zeylonensis*
Tawny Fish Owl *Ketupa flavipes*
Brown Wood Owl *Strix leptogrammica*
Collared Owlet *Glaucidium brodiei*
Asian Barred Owl *Glaucidium cuculoides*
Jungle Owlet *Glaucidium radiatum*
Spotted Owlet *Athene brama*
Brown Hawk Owl *Ninox scutulata*
Long-eared Owl *Asio otus*
Short-eared Owl *Asio flammeus*

Family: *Caprimulgidae*

Grey Nightjar *Caprimulgus indicus*
Large-tailed Nightjar *Caprimulgus macrurus*
Indian Nightjar *Caprimulgus asiaticus*
Savanna Nightjar *Caprimulgus affinis*

ORDER: GALLIFORMES

Family: *Phasianidae*

Black Francolin *Francolinus francolinus*
Grey Francolin *Francolinus pondiceriannus*
Common Quail *Coturnix coturnix*
Rain Quail *Coturnix coromandelica*
Blue-breasted Quail *Coturnix chinensis*
Jungle Bush Quail *Perdicula asiatica*
Rock Bush Quail *Perdicula argoondah*
Hill Partridge *Arborophila torqueola*
Red Junglefowl *Gallus gallus*
Kalij Pheasant *Lophura leucomelanos*
Indian Peafowl *Pavo cristatus*

ORDER: ANSERIFORMES

Family: *Dendrocygnidae*

Lesser Whistling-Duck *Dendrocygna javanica*

Family: *Anatidae*

Greylag Goose *Anser anser*
Bar-headed Goose *Anser indicus*
Ruddy Shelduck *Tadorna ferruginea*
Common Shelduck *Tadorna tadorna*
Comb Duck *Sarkidiornis melanotos*
Cotton Pygmy-goose *Nettapus coromandelianus*
Gadwall *Anas strepera*
Eurasian Wigeon *Anas penelope*
Mallard *Anas platyrhynchos*
Spot-billed Duck *Anas poecilorhyncha*
Northern Shoveler *Anas clypeata*
Northern Pintail *Anas acuta*
Garganey *Anas querquedula*
Common Teal *Anas crecca*
Red-crested Pochard *Rhodonessa rufina*
Common Pochard *Aythya ferina*
Ferruginous Pochard *Aythya nyroca*
Tufted Duck *Aythya fuligula*
Common Merganser *Mergus merganser*

Family: *Turnicidae*

Small Buttonquail *Turnix sylvatica*
Yellow-legged Buttonquail *Turnix tanki*
Barred Buttonquail *Turnix suscitator*

ORDER: PICIFORMES

Family: *Picidae*

Eurasian Wryneck *Jynx torquilla*
Speckled Piculet *Picumnus innominatus*
Brown-capped Pygmy Woodpecker *Dendrocopos nanus*
Grey-capped Pygmy Woodpecker *Dendrocopos canicapillus*
Brown-fronted Woodpecker *Dendrocopos auriceps*
Fulvous-breasted Woodpecker *Dendrocopos macei*
Yellow-crowned Woodpecker *Dendrocopos mahrattensis*
Rufous Woodpecker *Celeus brachyurus*
Lesser Yellownape *Picus chlorolophus*
Greater Yellownape *Picus flavinucha*
Streak-throated Woodpecker *Picus xanthopygaeus*
Scaly-bellied Woodpecker *Picus squamatus*
Grey-headed Woodpecker *Picus canus*
Himalayan Flameback *Dinopium shorii*
Black-rumped Flameback *Dinopium benghalense*
Greater Flameback *Chrysocolaptes lucidus*
White-naped Woodpecker *Chrysocolaptes festivus*
Great Slaty Woodpecker *Mulleripicus pulverulentus*

Family: *Megalaimidae*

Great Barbet *Megalaima virens*
Brown-headed Barbet *Megalaima zeylanica*
Lineated Barbet *Megalaima lineata*
Blue-throated Barbet *Megalaima asiatica*
Coppersmith Barbet *Megalaima haemacephala*

ORDER: CORACIIFORMES

Family: *Bucerotidae*

Indian Grey Hornbill *Ocyceros birostris*
Great Hornbill *Buceros bicornis*
Oriental Pied Hornbill *Anthracoceros albirostris*

Family: *Coraciidae*

Indian Roller *Coracias benghalensis*
Dollarbird *Eurystomus orientalis*

Family: *Upupidae*

Common Hoopoe *Upupa epops*

Family: *Alcedinidae*

Common Kingfisher *Alcedo atthis*

Family: *Halcyonidae*

Stork-billed Kingfisher *Halcyon capensis*
White-throated Kingfisher *Halcyon smyrnensis*

Family: *Cerylidae*

Crested Kingfisher *Megaceryle lugubris*
Pied Kingfisher *Ceryle rudis*

Family: *Meropidae*

Blue-bearded Bee-eater *Nyctyornis athertoni*
Green Bee-eater *Merops orientalis*
Blue-tailed Bee-eater *Merops philippinus*
Chestnut-headed Bee-eater Merops *leschenaulti*

ORDER: CUCULIFORMES

Family: *Cuculidae*

Pied Cuckoo *Clamator jacobinus*
Chestnut-winged Cuckoo *Clamator coromandus*
Large Hawk Cuckoo *Hierococcyx sparverioides*
Common Hawk Cuckoo *Hierococcyx varius*
Indian Cuckoo *Cuculus micropterus*
Eurasian Cuckoo *Cuculus canorus*
Oriental Cuckoo *Cuculus saturatus*
Banded Bay Cuckoo *Cacomantis sonneratii*
Grey-bellied Cuckoo *Cacomantis passerinus*
Drongo Cuckoo *Surniculus lugubris*
Asian Koel *Eudynamys scolopacea*
Green-billed Malkoha *Phaenicophaeus tristis*
Sirkeer Malkoha *Phaenicophaeus leschenaultii*

Family: *Centropodidae*

Greater Coucal *Centropus sinensis*
Lesser Coucal *Centropus bengalensis*

ORDER: PSITTACIFORMES

Family: *Psittacidae*

Alexandrine Parakeet *Psittacula eupatria*
Rose-ringed Parakeet *Psittacula krameri*

Slaty-headed Parakeet *Psittacula himalayana*
Plum-headed Parakeet *Psittacula cyanocephala*
Red-breasted Parakeet *Psittacula alexandri*

ORDER: APODIFORMES

Family: *Apodidae*

Himalayan Swiflet *Collocalia brevirostris*
White-rumped Needletail *Zoonavena sylvatica*
Silver-backed Needletail *Hirundapus cochinchinensis*
Asian Palm Swift *Cypsiurus balasiensis*
Alpine Swift *Tachymarptis melba*
Common Swift *Apus apus*
Fork-tailed Swift *Apus pacificus*
House Swift *Apus affinis*

Family: *Hemiprocnidae*

Crested Treeswift *Hemiprocne coronata*

ORDER: COLUMBIFORMES

Family: *Columbidae*

Rock Pigeon *Columba livia*
Hill Pigeon *Columba rupestris*
Oriental Turtle Dove *Streptopelia orientalis*
Laughing Dove *Streptopelia senegalensis*
Spotted Dove *Streptopelia chinensis*
Red Collared Dove *Streptopelia tranquebarica*
Eurasian Collared Dove *Streptopelia decaocto*
Emerald Dove *Chalcophaps indica*
Orange-breasted Green Pigeon *Treron bicincta*
Yellow-footed Green Pigeon *Treron phoenicoptera*
Pin-tailed Green Pigeon *Treron apicauda*
Wedge-tailed Green Pigeon *Treron sphenura*

ORDER: GRUIFORMES

Family: *Gruidae*

Sarus Crane *Grus antigone*
Demoiselle Crane *Grus virgo*
Common Crane *Grus grus*

Family: *Rallidae*

Water Rail *Rallus aquaticus*
Slaty-legged Crake *Rallina eurizonoides*
Brown Crake *Amaurornis akool*
White-breasted Waterhen *Amaurornis phoenicurus*
Ruddy-breasted Crake *Porzana fusca*
Purple Swamphen *Porphyrio porphyrio*
Common Moorhen *Gallinula chloropus*
Common Coot *Fulica atra*

ORDER: CICONIIFORMES

Family: *Scolopacidae*

Eurasian Woodcock *Scolopax rusticola*
Wood Snipe *Gallinago nemoricola*
Pintail Snipe *Gallinago Stenura*
Common Snipe *Gallinago gallinago*
Jack Snipe *Lymnocryptes minimus*
Black-tailed Godwit *Limosa limosa*
Eurasian Curlew *Numenius arquata*
Common Redshank *Tringa totanus*
Marsh Sandpiper *Tringa stagnatilis*
Common Greenshank *Tringa nebularia*
Green Sandpiper *Tringa ochropus*
Wood Sandpiper *Tringa glareola*
Common Sandpiper *Actitis hypoleucos*
Little Stint *Calidris minuta*
Temminck's Stint *Calidris temminckii*
Long-toed Stint *Calidris subminuta*
Dunlin *Calidris alpina*

Family: *Rostratulidae*

Greater Painted-snipe *Rostratula benghalensis*

Family: *Jacanidae*

Pheasant-tailed Jacana *Hydrophasianus chirurgus*
Bronze-winged Jacana *Metopidius indicus*

Family: *Burhinidae*

Eurasian Thick-knee *Burhinus oedicnemus*
Great Thick-knee *Esacus recurvirostris*

Family: *Charadriidae*

Ibisbill *Ibidorhyncha struthersii*
Black-winged Stilt *Himantopus himantopus*

Pied Avocet *Recurvirostra avosetta*
Long-billed Plover *Charadrius placidus*
Little Ringed Plover *Charadrius dubius*
Kentish Plover *Charadrius alexandrinus*
Lesser Sand Plover *Charadrius mongolus*
Great Sand Plover *Charadrius leschenaultii*
Northern Lapwing *Vanellus vanellus*
Yellow-wattled Lapwing *Vanellus malarbaricus*
River Lapwing *Vanellus duvaucelii*
Red-wattled Lapwing *Vanellus indicus*
Sociable Lapwing *Vanellus gregarius*
White-tailed Lapwing *Vanellus leucurus*
Small Pratincole *Glareola lactea*

Family: *Laridae*

Yellow-legged Gull *Larus cachinnans*
Pallas's Gull *Larus ichthyaetus*
Brown-headed Gull *Larus brunnicephalus*
Black-headed Gull *Larus ridibundus*
Gull-billed Tern *Gelochelidon nilotica*
River Tern *Sterna aurantia*
Black-bellied Tern *Sterna acuticauda*
Whiskered Tern *Chlidonias hybridus*

Family: *Accipitridae*

Osprey *Pandion haliaetus*
Black Baza *Aviceda leuphotes*
Black-shouldered kite *Elanus caeruleus*
Black Kite *Milvus migrans*
Brahminy Kite *Haliastur indus*
Pallas's Fish Eagle *Haliaeetus leucoryphus*
White-tailed Eagle *Haliaeetus albicilla*
Lesser Fish Eagle *Ichthyophaga humilis*
Grey-headed Fish Eagle *Ichthyophaga ichthyaetus*
Lammergeier *Gypaetus barbatus*
Egyptian Vulture *Neophron percnopterus*
White-rumped Vulture *Gyps bengalensis*
Slender-billed Vulture *Gyps tenuirostris*
Himalayan Griffon *Gyps himalayensis*
Eurasian Griffon *Gyps fulvus*
Cinereous Vulture *Aegypius monachus*
Red-Headed Vulture *Sarcogyps calvus*
Short-toed Snake Eagle *Circaetus gallicus*
Crested Serpent Eagle *Spilornis cheela*
Eurasian Marsh Harrier *Circus aeruginosus*
Pied Harrier *Circus melanoleucos*
Hen Harrier *Circus cyaneus*
Pallid Harrier *Circus macrourus*
Shikra *Accipiter badius*
Besra *Accipiter virgatus*
Eurasian Sparrowhawk *Accipiter nisus*
Northern Goshawk *Accipiter gentilis*
Crested Goshawk *Accipiter trivirgatus*
Oriental Honey-Buzzard *Pernis ptilorhyncus*
White-eyed Buzzard *Butastur teesa*
Common Buzzard *Buteo buteo*
Long-legged Buzzard *Buteo rufinus*
Black Eagle *Ictinaetus malayensis*
Indian Spotted Eagle *Aquila hastata*
Greater Spotted Eagle *Aquila clanga*
Tawny Eagle *Aquila rapax*
Steppe Eagle *Aquila nipalensis*
Imperial Eagle *Aquila heliaca*
Bonelli's Eagle *Hieraaetus fasciatus*
Booted Eagle *Hieraaetus pennatus*
Rufous-bellied Eagle *Hieraaetus kienerii*
Changeable Hawk Eagle *Spizaetus cirrhatus*
Mountain Hawk Eagle *Spizaetus nipalensis*

Family: *Falconidae*

Collared Falconet *Microheirax caerulescens*
Common Kestrel *Falco tinnunculus*
Red-necked Falcon *Falco chicquera*
Amur Falcon *Falco amurensis*
Oriental Hobby *Falco severus*
Laggar Falcon *Falco jugger*
Peregrine Falcon *Falco peregrinus*

Family: *Podicipedidae*

Little Grebe *Tachybaptus ruficollis*
Great Crested Grebe *Podiceps cristatus*
Horned Grebe *Podiceps auritus*

Family: *Anhingidae*

Darter *Anhinga melanogaster*

Family: *Phalacrocoracidae*

Little Cormorant *Phalacrocorax niger*
Indian Cormorant *Phalacrocorax fuscicollis*
Great Cormorant *Phalacrocorax carbo*

Family: *Ardeidae*

Little Egret *Egretta garzetta*
Western Reef Egret *Egretta gularis*
Grey Heron *Ardea cinerea*
Purple Heron *Ardea purpurea*
Great Egret *Casmerodius albus*
Intermediate Egret *Mesophoyx intermedia*
Cattle Egret *Bubulcus ibis*
Indian Pond Heron *Ardeola grayii*
Little Heron *Butorides striatus*
Black-crowned Night Heron *Nycticorax nycticorax*
Little Bittern *Ixobrychus minutus*
Yellow Bittern *Ixobrychus sinensis*
Cinnamon Bittern *Ixobrychus cinnamomeus*

Family: *Phoenicopteridae*

Greater Flamingo *Phoenicopterus ruber*

Family: *Threskionithidae*

Glossy Ibis *Plegadis falcinellus*
Black-headed Ibis *Threskiornis melanocephalus*
Black Ibis *Pseudibis papillosa*
Eurasian Spoonbill *Platalea leucorodia*

Family: *Pelecanidae*

Great White Pelican *Pelecanus onocrotalus*
Spot-billed Pelican *Pelecanus philippensis*

Family: *Ciconiidae*

Painted Stork *Mycteria leucocephala*
Asian Openbill *Anastomas oscitans*
Black Stork *Ciconia nigra*
Woolly-necked Stork *Ciconia episcopus*
White Stork *Ciconia ciconia*
Black-necked Stork *Ephippiorhynchus asiaticus*
Lesser Adjutant *Leptoptilos javanicus*

ORDER: PASSERIFORMES

Family: *Pittidae*

Indian Pitta *Pitta brachyura*
Hooded Pitta *Pitta sordida*

Family: *Eurylaimidae*

Long-tailed Broadbill *Psarisomus dalhousiae*

Family: *Irenidae*

Golden-fronted Leafbird *Chloropsis aurifrons*
Orange-bellied Leafbird *Chloropsis hardwickii*

Family: *Laniidae*

Rufous-tailed Shrike *Lanius isabellinus*
Brown Shrike *Lanius cristatus*
Bay-backed Shrike *Lanius vittatus*
Long-tailed Shrike *Lanius schach*
Grey-backed Shrike *Lanius tephronotus*
Southern Grey Shrike *Lanius meridionalis*

Family: *Corvidae*

Eurasian Jay *Garrulus glandarius*
Black-headed Jay *Garrulus lanceolatus*
Red-billed Blue Magpie *Urocissa erythrorhyncha*
Common Green Magpie *Cissa chinensis*
Rufous Treepie *Dendrocitta vagabunda*
Grey Treepie *Dendrocitta formosae*
House Crow *Corvus splendens*
Large-billed Crow *Corvus macrorhynchos*
Ashy Woodswallow *Artamus fuscus*
Eurasian Golden Oriole *Oriolus oriolus*
Black-hooded Oriole *Oriolus xanthornus*
Maroon Oriole *Oriolus traillii*
Large Cuckooshrike *Coracina macei*
Black-winged Cuckooshrike *Coracina melaschistos*
Black-headed Cuckooshrike *Coracina melenoptera*
Rosy Minivet *Pericrocotus roseus*
Small Minivet *Pericrocotus cinnamomeus*
Long-tailed Minivet *Pericrocotus ethologus*
Short-billed Minivet *Pericrocotus brevirostris*
Scarlet Minivet *Pericrocotus flammeus*
Bar-winged Flycatcher-Shrike *Hemipus picatus*

Yellow-bellied Fantail *Rhipidura hypoxantha*
White-throated Fantail *Rhipidura albicollis*
White-browed Fantail *Rhipidura aureola*
Black Drongo *Dicrurus macrocercus*
Ashy Drongo *Dicrurus leucophaeus*
White-bellied Drongo *Dicrurus caerulescens*
Bronzed Drongo *Dicrurus aeneus*
Lesser Racket-tailed Drongo *Dicrurus remifer*
Spangled Drongo *Dicrurus hottentottus*
Greater Racket-tailed Drongo *Dicrurus paradiseus*
Black-naped Monarch *Hypothymis azurea*
Indian Paradise-flycatcher *Terpsiphone paradisi*
Common Iora *Aegithina tiphia*
Large Woodshrike *Tephrodornis gularis*
Common Woodshrike *Tephrodornis pondicerianus*

Family: *Cinclidae*

Brown Dipper *Cinclus pallasii*

Family: *Muscicapidae*

Blue-capped Rock Thrush *Monticola cinclorhynchus*
Chestnut-bellied Rock Thrush *Monticola rufiventris*
Blue Rock Thrush *Monticola solitarius*
Blue Whistling Thrush *Myophonus caeruleus*
Orange-headed Thrush *Zoothera citrina*
Long-tailed Thrush *Zoothera dixoni*
Scaly Thrush *Zoothera dauma*
Long-billed Thrush *Zoothera monticola*
Tickell's Thrush *Turdus unicolor*
White-collared Blackbird *Turdusalbocintus*
Grey-winged Blackbird *Turdus boulboul*
Red-throated Thrush *Turdus ruficollis*
Black-throated Thrush *Turdus atrogularis*
Dark-sided Flycatcher *Muscicapa sibirica*
Asian Brown Flycatcher *Muscicapa dauurica*
Rusty-tailed Flycatcher *Muscicapa ruficauda*
Slaty-backed Flycatcher *Ficedula hodgsonii*
Rufous-gorgeted Flycatcher *Ficedula strophiata*
Red-throated Flycatcher *Ficedula albicilla*
Red-breasted Flycatcher *Ficedula parva*
Snowy-browed Flycatcher *Ficedula hyperythra*

Little Pied Flycatcher *Ficedula westermanni*
Ultramarine Flycatcher *Ficedula superciliaris*
Slaty Blue Flycatcher *Ficedula tricolor*
Verditer Flycatcher *Eumyias thalassina*
Small Niltava *Niltava macgrigoriae*
Rufous-bellied Niltava *Niltava sundara*
Pale-chinned Flycatcher *Cyornis poliogenys*
Blue-throated Flycatcher *Cyornis rubeculoides*
Tickell's Blue Flycatcher *Cyornis tickelliae*
Grey-headed Canary Flycatcher *Culicicapa ceylonensis*
Siberian Rubythroat *Luscinia calliope*
White-tailed Rubythroat *Luscinia pectoralis*
Bluethroat *Luscinia svecica*
Indian Blue Robin *Luscinia brunnea*
Orange-flanked Bush Robin *Tarsiger cyanurus*
Golden Bush Robin *Tarsiger chrysaeus*
Oriental Magpie Robin *Copsychus saularis*
White-rumped Shama *Copsychus malabaricus*
Indian Robin *Saxicoloides fulicata*
Rufous-backed Redstart *Phoenicurus erythronota*
Blue-capped Redstart *Phoenicurus coeruleocephalus*
Black Redstart *Phoenicurus ochruros*
Hodgson's Redstart *Phoenicurus hodgsoni*
Blue-fronted Redstart *Phoenicurus frontalis*
White-capped Water Redstart *Chaimarrornis leucocephalus*
Plumbeous Water Redstart *Rhyacornis fuliginosus*
White-bellied Redstart *Hodgsonius phoenicuroides*
Little Forktail *Enicurus scouleri*
Black-backed Forktail *Enicurus immaculatus*
Slaty-backed Forktail *Enicurus schistaceus*
Spotted Forktail *Enicurus maculatus*
Purple Cochoa *Cochoa purpurea*
Hodgson's Bushchat *Saxicola insignis*
Common Stonechat *Saxicola torquata*
White-tailed Stonechat *Saxicola leucura*
Pied Bushchat *Saxicola caprata*
Grey Bushchat *saxicola ferrea*
Variable Wheatear *Oenanthe picata*
Desert Wheatear *Oenanthe deserti*
Isabelline Wheatear *Oenanthe isabellina*

Brown Rock-chat *Cercomela fusca*

Family: *Sturnidae*

Spot-winged Starling *Saroglossa spiloptera*
Chestnut-tailed Starling *Sturnus malabaricus*
Brahminy Starling *Sturnus pagodarum*
Common Starling *Sturnus vulgaris*
Asian Pied Starling *Sturnus contra*
Common Myna *Acridotheres tristis*
Bank Myna *Acridotheres ginginianus*
Jungle Myna *Acridotheres fuscus*
Northern Hill Myna *Gracula religiosa*

Family: *Sittidae*

Chestnut-bellied Nuthatch *Sitta castanea*
White-tailed Nuthatch *Sitta himalayensis*
Velvet-fronted Nuthatch *Sitta frontalis*
Wallcreeper *Tichodroma muraria*

Family: *Certhiidae*

Bar-tailed Treecreeper *Certhia himalayana*
Winter Wren *Troglodytes troglodytes*

Family: *Paridae*

Fire-capped Tit *Cephalopyrus flammiceps*
Rufous-naped Tit *Parus rufonuchalis*
Spot-winged Tit *Parus melanolophus*
Great Tit *Parus major*
Green-backed Tit *Parus monticolus*
Black-lored Tit *Parus xanthogenys*

Family: *Aegithalidae*

Black-throated Tit *Aegithalos concinnus*

Family: *Hirundinidae*

Sand Martin *Riparia riparia*
Plain Martin *Riparia paludicola*
Eurasian Crag Martin *Hirundo rupestris*
Dusky Crag Martin *Hirundo concolor*
Barn Swallow *Hirundo rustica*
Wire-tailed Swallow *Hirundo smithii*
Red-rumped Swallow *Hirundo daurica*
Streak-throated Swallow *Hirundo fluvicola*
Northern House Martin *Delichon urbica*

Asian House Martin *Delichon dasypus*
Nepal House Martin *Delichon nipalensis*

Family: *Regulidae*

Goldcrest *Regulus regulus*

Family: *Pycnonotidae*

Black-crested Bulbul *Pycnonotus melanicterus*
Red-whiskered Bulbul *Pycnonotus jocosus*
Himalayan Bulbul *Pycnonotus leucogenys*
Red-vented Bulbul *Pycnonotus cafer*
Ashy Bulbul *Hemixos flavala*
Mountain Bulbul *Hypsipetes mcclellandii*
Black Bulbul *Hypsipetes leucocephalus*

Family: *Cisticolidae*

Zitting Cisticola *Cisticola juncidis*
Bright-headed Cisticola *Cisticola exilis*
Straited Prinia *Prinia criniger*
Grey-crowned Prinia *Prinia cinereocapilla*
Rufous-fronted Prinia *Prinia buchanani*
Grey-breasted Prinia *Prinia hodgsonii*
Jungle Prinia *Prinia sylvatica*
Yellow-bellied Prinia *Prinia flaviventris*
Ashy Prinia *Prinia socialis*
Plain Prinia *Prinia inornata*

Family: *Zosteropidae*

Oriental White-eye *Zosterops palpebrosus*

Family: *Sylviidae*

Chestnut-headed Tesia *Tesia castaneocoronata*
Grey-bellied Tesia *Tesia cyaniventer*
Pale-footed Bush Warbler *Cettia pallidipes*
Brownish-flanked Bush Warbler *Cettia fortipes*
Chestnut-crowned Bush Warbler *Cettia major*
Aberrant Bush Warbler *Cettia flavolivacea*
Grey-sided Bush Warbler *Cettia brunnifrons*
Moustached Warbler *Acrocephalus melanopogon*
Blyth's Reed Warbler *Acrocephalus dumetorum*
Common Tailorbird *Orthotomus sutorius*
Common Chiffchaff *Phylloscopus collybita*
Plain Leaf Warbler *Phylloscopus neglectus*

Dusky Warbler *Phylloscopus fuscatus*
Smoky Warbler *Phylloscopus fuligiventer*
Tickell's Leaf Warbler *Phylloscopus affinis*
Sulphur-bellied Warbler *Phylloscopus griseolus*
Buff-barred Warbler *Phylloscopus pulcher*
Ashy-throated Warbler *Phylloscopus maculipennis*
Lemon-rumped Warbler *Phylloscopus chloronotus*
Hume's Warbler *Phylloscopus humei*
Greenish Warbler *Phylloscopus trochiloides*
Tytler's Leaf Warbler *Phlloscopus tytleri*
Western Crowned Warbler *Phylloscopus occipitalis*
Blyth's Leaf Warbler *Phylloscopus reguloides*
Whistler's Warbler *Seicecrus whistleri*
Golden-Spectacled Warbler *Seicercus burkii*
Grey-hooded Warbler *Seicercus xanthoschistos*
Striated Grassbird *Megalurus palustris*
Bristled Grassbird *Chaetornis striatus*
White-throated Laughingthrush *Garrulax lbogularis*
White-crested Laughingthrush *Garrulax leucolophus*
Striated Laughingthrush *Garrulax striatus*
Rufous-chinned Laughingthrush *Garrulax rufogularis*
Streaked Laughingthrush *Garrulax lineatus*
Variegated Laughingthrush *Garrulax variegatus*
Chestnut-crowned Laughingthrush *Garrulax erythrocephalus*
Puff-throated Babbler *Pellorneum ruficeps*
Rusty-cheeked Scimitar Babbler *Pomatorhinus erythrogenys*
White-browed Scimitar Babbler *Pomatorhinus schisticeps*
Streak-breasted Scimitar Babbler *Pomatorhinus ruficollis*
Scaly-breasted Wren Babbler *Pnoepyga albiventer*
Nepal Wren Babbler *Pnoepyga immaculata*
Black-chinned Babbler *Stachyris phrrhops*
Tawny-bellied Babbler *Dumetia hyperythra*
Chestnut-capped Babbler *Timalia pileata*
Yellow-eyed Babbler *Chrysomma sinense*
Common Babbler *Turdoides caudatus*
Large Grey Babbler *Turdoides malcolmi*
Jungle Babbler *Turdoides striatus*
Silver-eared Mesia *Leiothrix argentauris*
Red-billed Leiothrix *Leiothrix lutea*

White-browed Shrike Babbler *Pteruthius flaviscapis*
Green Shrike Babbler *Pteruthius xanthochlorus*
Blue-winged Minla *Minla Cyanouroptera*
Rufous Sibia *Heterophasia capistrata*
Whiskered Yuhina *Yuhina Flavicollis*
Stripe-throated Yuhina *Yuhina gularis*
Black-chinned Yuhina *Yuhina nigrimenta*
White-bellied Yuhina *Yuhina zantholeuca*
Lesser Whitethroat *Sylvia curruca*
Orphean Warbler *Sylvia hortensis*

Family: *Alaudidae*

Indian Bushlark *Mirafra erythroptera*
Rufous-winged Bushlark *Mirafra assamica*
Ashy-crowned Sparrowlark *Eremopterix grisea*
Greater Short-toed Lark *Calandrella brachydactyla*
Sand Lark *Calandrella raytal*
Crested Lark *Galerida cristata*
Eurasian Skylark *Alauda arvensis*
Oriental Skylark *Alauda gulgula*

Family: *Nectariniidae*

Thick-billed Flowerpecker *Dicaeum agile*
Pale-billed Flowerpecker *Dicaeum erythrorynchos*
Fire-breasted Flowerpecker *Dicaeum ignipectus*
Purple Sunbird *Nectarinia asiatica*
Green-tailed Sunbird *Aethopyga nipalensis*
Black-throated Sunbird *Aethopyga saturata*
Crimson Sunbird *Aethopyga siparaja*
Fire-tailed Sunbird *Aethopyga ignicauda*

Family: *Passeridae*

House Sparrow *Passer domesticus*
Russet Sparrow *Passer rutilans*
Eurasian Tree Sparrow *Passer montanus*
Chestnut-shouldered Petronia *Petronia xanthocollis*
Forest Wagtail *Dendronanthus indicus*
White Wagtail *Montacilla alba*
White-browed Wagtail *Montacilla maderaspatensis*
Citrine Wagtail *Montacilla citreola*
Yellow Wagtail *Montacilla flava*

Grey Wagtail *Montacilla cinerea*
Paddy-field Pipit *Anthus rufulus*
Tawny Pipit *Anthus campestris*
Long-billed Pipit *Anthus similis*
Tree Pipit *Anthus trivialis*
Olive-backed Pipit *Anthus hodgsoni*
Red-throated Pipit *Anthus cervinus*
Rosy Pipit *Anthus roseatus*
Water Pipit *Anthus spinoletta*
Rufous-breasted Accentor *Prunella strophiata*
Black-throated Accentor *Prunella atrogularis*
Black-breasted Weaver *Ploceus benghalensis*
Streaked Weaver *Ploceus manyar*
Baya Weaver *Ploceus philippinus*
Finn's Weaver *Ploceus megarhynchus*
Red Avadavat *Amandava amandava*
Indian Silverbill *Lonchura malabarica*
White-rumped Munia *Lonchura striata*
Scaly-breasted Munia *Lonchura punctulata*
Black-headed Munia *Lonchura mallaca*

Family: *Fringillidae*

Chaffinch *Fringilla coelebs*
Fire-fronted Serin *Serinus pusillus*
Yellow-breasted Greenfinch *Carduelis spinoides*
European Goldfinch *Carduelis carduelis*
Common Rosefinch *Carpodacus erythrinus*
Crested Bunting *Melophus lathami*
Pine Bunting *Emberiza leucocephalos*
Rock Bunting *Emberiza cia*
White-capped Bunting *Emberiza stewarti*
Chestnut-eared Bunting *Emberiza fucata*
Little Bunting *Emberiza pusilla*
Chestnut Bunting *Emberiza rutila*
Black-faced Bunting *Emberiza spodocephala*
Red-headed Bunting *Emberiza bruniceps*
Corn Bunting *Miliaria calandra*

MAMMALS

ORDER: CARNIVORA

Family: *Felidae*

Bengal tiger *Panthera tigris tigris*
Indian leopard *Panthera pardus fusca*
Jungle cat *Felis chaus*
Leopard cat *Prionailurus bengalensis*
Fishing cat *Prionailurus viverrinus*

Family: *Canidae*

Jackal *Canis aureus*
Wild dog (dhole) *Cuon alpinus*
Indian fox *Vulpes bengalensis*
Common red fox *Vulpes vulpes*

Family: *Mustelidae*

Eurasian (common) otter *Lutra lutra*
Smooth-coated otter *Lutrogale perspicillata*
Yellow-throated marten *Martes flavigula*
Honey badger *Mellivora capensis*

Family: *Viverridae*

Small Indian civet *Viverricula indica*
Large Indian civet *Viverra zibetha*
Common palm civet *Paradoxurus hermaphroditus*
Himalayan palm civet *Paguma larvata*

Family: *Herpestidae*

Grey mongoose *Herpestes edwardsii*

Family: *Ursidae*

Sloth bear *Melursus ursinus*
Himalayan black bear *Ursus thibetanus*

ORDER: PRIMATES

Family: *Cercopithecidae*

Rhesus macaque *Macaca mulatta*
Hanuman (common) langur *Semnopithecus entellus*

ORDER: PROBOSCIDEA

Family: *Elephantidae*

Asian elephant *Elephas maximus*

ORDER: ARTIODACTYLA

Family: *Cervidae*

Indian muntjac *Muntiacus muntjak*
Cheetal (spotted) deer *Axis axis*
Sambar *Cervus unicolor*
Hog deer *Axis porcinus*

Family: *Bovidae*

Nilgai *Boselaphus tragocamelus*
Serow *Naemorhedus sumatraensis*
Ghoral *Naemorhedus goral*

Family: *Suidae*

Wild pig *Sus scrofa*

ORDER: LAGOMORPH

Family: *Leporidae*

Indian (black-naped) hare *Lepus nigricollis*

ORDER: RODENTIA

Family: *Hystricidae*

Indian porcupine *Hystrix indica*

Family: *Sciuridae*

Five-striped palm squirrel *Funambulus pennantii*
Red giant flying squirrel *Petaurista petaurista*

Family: *Muridae*

Large bandicoot rat *Bandicota indica*
Lesser bandicoot rat *Bandicota bengalensis*
House rat *Rattus rattus*
Little Indian field mouse *Mus booduga*
Indian Bush rat *Golunda ellioti*
Indian gerbil *Tatera indica*

ORDER: CHIROPTERA

Family: *Pteropodidae*

Indian Flying fox *Pteropus giganteus*
Short-nosed fruit bat *Cynopterus sphinx*

Family: *Rhinopomatidae*

Lesser mouse-tailed bat *Rhinopoma hardwickii*
Little Japanese horseshoe bat *Rhinoplophus cornutus*

Family: *Hipposideridae*

Great Himalayan leaf-nosed bat *Hipposideros armiger*
Least leaf-nosed bat *Hipposideros cineraues*

Family: *Vespertilionidae*

Asiatic greater yellow house bat *Scotophilus heathii*
Lesser Asiatic yellow house bat *Scotophilus kuhlii*
Indian pipistrelle *Pipistrellus coromandra*
Indian pigmy bat *Pipistrellus tenuis*
Brown long-eared bat *Plecotus auritus*
Hodgson's bat *Myotis formosus*
Greater yellow bat *Scotophillus heathi heathi*
Peter's tube-nose bat *Murina grisea*

ORDER: PHOLIDOTA

Family: *Manidae*

Indian pangolin *Manis crassicaudata*

REPTILES

CLASS: REPTILIA

ORDER: CROCODILIA

Family: *Gavialidae*

Gharial *Gavialis gangeticus*

Family: *Crocodylidae*

Mugger crocodile *Crocodylus palustris*

ORDER: SQUAMATA

Family: *Gekkonidae*

Banded bent-toed gecko *Cyrtodactylus fasciolatus*
Brook's house gecko *Hemidactylus brookii*
Yellow-green house gecko *Hemidactylus flaviviridis*

Family: *Agamidae*

Kumaon mountain lizard *Japalura Kumaonensis*
Indian garden Lizard *Calotes versicolor*
Kashmir agama *Laudakia tuberculata*

Family: *Scincidae*

Himalayan ground skink *Scincella himalayanus*

Spotted supple skink *Lygosoma punctatus*

Family: *Varanidae*

Bengal monitor *Varanus bengalensis*

Family: *Typhlopidae*

Slender blind snake *Typhlops porrectus*

Family: *Boidae*

Indian python *Python molurus*
Common sand boa *Eryx conica*
Red sand boa *Eryx johnii*

Family: *Colubridae*

Indian trinket snake *Elaphe helena*
Himalayan trinket snake *Elaphe hodgsonii*
Rat snake *Ptyas mucosus*
Glossy-bellied racer *Coluber ventromaculatus*
Cliff racer *Coluber rhodorachis*
Mackinnon's wolf snake *Lycodon mackinnoni*
Buff-striped keelback *Amphiesma stolata*
Olive oriental slender snake *Trachischium laeve*
Cat snake *Bogia trigonatus*
Many-banded cat snake *Boiga multifasciata*
Cantor's black-headed snake *Sibynophis sagittaria*

Family: *Elapidae*

Banded krait *Bungarus fasciatus*
Common Indian Krait *Bungarus caeruleus*
Spectacled cobra *Naja naja*
King cobra *Ophiophagus hannah*

Family: *Viperidae*

Russell's viper *Daboia russelii*
Saw-scaled viper *Echis carinatus*
White-lipped pit viper *Trimeresurus albolabris*

Checklists were sourced from *The Corbett Inheritance* published in 2007 and compiled by the *Sanctuary Asia* team from the Management Plan of the Corbett Tiger Reserve and other peer-reviewed literature.

BIBLIOGRAPHY

Brijendra Singh, Bittu Sahgal, Bikram Grewal. *The Corbett Inheritance*. New Delhi: Sanctuary Asia, 2007.

Champion, F. W. *With a Camera in Tiger-land*. London: Chatto & Windus, 1927.

Corbett, Jim and Martin Booth. *Jungle Lore*. New Delhi: Oxford University Press, 1999.

Corbett, Jim. *Man-Eaters of Kumaon*. New Delhi: Oxford University Press, 1988.

—. *My India*. New Delhi: Oxford University Press, 1988.

—. *The Temple Tiger and More Man-Eaters of Kumaon*. Bombay: Oxford University Press, 1988.

—. *Tree Tops*. 1st Indian ed. in Oxford India paperbacks. New Delhi: Oxford University Press, 1991.

Datta, Sukanya. *Social Life of Animals*. New Delhi: National Book Trust, India, 2012.

Gadgil, Madhav and Ramachandra Guha. *This Fissured Land: An Ecological History of India*. Perennials ed. New Delhi: Oxford University Press, 2013.

Gouldsbury, C. E. *Tiger Slayer by Order*. London: G. Bell & Sons ltd, 1915.

Grimmett, Richard, Carol Inskipp and Tim Inskipp. *Birds of the Indian Subcontinent*. 2nd ed. New Delhi: Oxford University Press, 2011.

Gupta, Prosenjit Das. *Tracking Jim: A Hunt in Corbett Country*. New Delhi: Penguin, 2005.

Indian Wildlife Insight Guide. 3rd ed. Singapore: APA Publications, 2007.

Kala, D.C. *Jim Corbett of Kumaon*. Revised. New Delhi: Ravi Dayal Publisher, 2009.

Karanth, K. Ullas, ed. *Tiger Tales: Tracking the Big Cat Across Asia*. New Delhi: Penguin Books, 2006.

Krishen, Pradip. *Jungle Trees of Central India: A Field Guide for Tree Spotters*. Premium. New Delhi: Penguin Books, 2013.

Menon, Vivek. *Indian Mammals: A Field Guide*. Gurgaon: Hachette India, 2014.

Mohan, Dhananjai and Sanjay Sondhi. *An Updated Checklist of The Birds of Uttarakhand*. Uttarakhand Forest Department, 2014. Print.

Rangarajan, Mahesh. *India's Wildlife History*. Delhi: Permanent Black, 2005. Print.

Walton, H. G. *Gazetteer of Garhwal Himalaya*. 2nd ed. Vol. 36. Dehradun: Natraj Publishers, 1989. Print.

ACKNOWLEDGEMENTS

A book of this kind is not something that an individual can put together on one's own. It needs a wide range of inputs, help and expertise from various quarters. From the concept to the completion of this book, we were fortunate to have received support of many special individuals and we are grateful to all of them. It may not be possible to recall all of them and mention them individually by name, but in our heart we certainly remain grateful and indebted to each one of them.

However, there are individuals whose names are etched in our memory as friends who deserve a special mention. We would particularly like to thank James Champion for not only sharing valuable nuggets of information about his grandfather F.W. Champion, but also very generously providing us original photographs taken by him.

Prominent among the officers in the forest department who always promptly responded to our requests were Sameer Sinha, the then Field Director of Corbett National Park; Kehkashan Naseem, Neethu Lakshmi M and Koko Rose. We are also thankful to many rangers, forest guards and park guides for their help on various occasions.

Within the friend circle Bikram Grewal, Sumantha Ghosh and Mohit Aggarwal were of great help with anecdotes, suggestions and whatever other demands we placed on them.

We also feel indebted to Gerard David for allowing us the use of his image of the leopard—a sighting far more difficult than seeing a tiger.

We sincerely appreciate the magnanimity of the *Sanctuary Asia* team for permission to use Checklists from *The Corbett Inheritance*.

Manish Srivastav of Corbett River Creek was very helpful in partly supporting this book project. Vivek Pandey and Hem Bahuguna also made our task easier by organising logistics on many occasions.

We appreciate the encouragement and support of Kumar Karun Krant and Sunaina Kashyap. Both of them very liberally shared their collection of books and other invaluable reference material with us.

Dhannasika, Tejas and Tannavi deserve a special mention for their enthusiasm, interest and contribution to the book.

We feel truly honoured that Bittu Sahgal, who is one of the clearest and loudest voices on conservation in the country today, agreed to write the foreword for our book. We sincerely appreciate this gesture.

And last but not the least we feel indebted to all the greats of wildlife conservation who have dedicated their lives for the cause of conservation. We would also like to thank the forest guards—an army of unsung heroes, who risk their lives on a daily basis, patrolling the forests in inclement weather and harsh conditions, so that our wilds remain protected and safe.

Ashima Kumar
Dushyant Parasher

Special thanks to
Corbett River Creek
for partly supporting this book project.